ELYE OF SAINT-GILLES

ELYE OF SAINT-GILLES

A CHANSON DE GESTE

MODERN EDITION AND
FIRST ENGLISH TRANSLATION

BY

A. RICHARD HARTMAN &
SANDRA C. MALICOTE

ITALICA PRESS
NEW YORK
2011

Copyright © 2011 by A. Richard Hartman &
Sandra C. Malicote

ITALICA PRESS, INC.
595 Main Street, Suite 605
New York, New York 10044

All rights reserved. No part of this publication may be reproduced, stored in a retrieval system, or transmitted, in any form or by any means, electronic, mechanical, photocopying, recording, or otherwise, without prior permission of Italica Press. For permission to reproduce selected portions for courses, please contact the Press at inquiries@italicapress.com.

Library of Congress Cataloging-in-Publication Data
Élie de Saint Gille. English & French (Old French)
Elye of Saint-Gilles : a chanson de geste / modern edition and first English translation by A. Richard Hartman & Sandra C. Malicote.
   p. cm.
Includes bibliographical references and index.
Summary: "A dual-language edition, including the first English translation, of the medieval French chanson de geste of Elye de Saint-Gilles, part of the William or Orange cycle. Included is an edition of the original and sole manuscript, which is from the 13th century in the Picard dialect. Illustrations"--Provided by publisher.
   ISBN 978-1-59910-191-0 (hardcover : alk. paper) -- ISBN 978-1-59910-192-7 (pbk. : alk. paper) -- ISBN 978-1-59910-193-4 (e-book)
   1. Chansons de geste--Translations into English. I. Hartman, A. Richard, 1939- II. Malicote, Sandra. III. Title.
   PQ1459.E3E5 2011
   841'.1--dc22
                                                                    2010037037

Cover: "Here begins the true story of Julien of Saint-Gilles who was the father of Elye...." From Paris, BN fr 25516, fol. 76r.

For a Complete List of
Medieval and Renaissance Texts
Visit our Web Site at
www.ItalicaPress.com

About the Editors

Richard Hartman received a B.S. degree from the U.S. Military Academy, a Licence ès lettres from the Université de Nantes, a Maîtrise de lettres modernes from the Université de Bordeaux, and completed a year of course work at the Universidad de Navarra. He holds a Ph.D. in French literature from the University of Colorado. He has published articles on the Old French epic in scholarly journals, such as *Marche Romane, Olifant* and *Revista Hispánica Moderna*. An independent scholar, he currently divides his time between Stillwater, Oklahoma and Steamboat Springs, Colorado.

Sandra Malicote (PhD Indiana University) is the author of *Image and Imagination: Picturing the Old French Epic*. Her articles on the Old French chanson de geste have appeared in *Romania, Romanic Review, Olifant,* and *(Kentucky) Romance Quarterly*. Professor of French at the University of North Carolina at Asheville, she was a *lectrice d'anglais* at the Université de Lille III and formerly chaired UNCA's Humanities Program and its Interdisciplinary Studies Program. Her articles on French literature and civilization have appeared in *The French Review* and in *Contemporary French Civilization*. She is currently at work on a new critical edition of the chanson de geste *Aiol* (with A. Richard Hartman).

CONTENTS

INTRODUCTION	IX
Epic Cycles	IX
The Anti-Islamic Topos and the Epic	X
Elye de Saint-Gilles	XII
Sources and Composition of the Poem	XIII
Summary: Visual and Verbal Presentation in the Manuscript	XIV
Notes on the Edition and the Translation	XVII
ELYE OF SAINT-GILLES	1
Part One	2
Part Two	58
Part Three	74
Part Four	92
Part Five	128
ILLUSTRATIONS	179
NOTES	183
BIBLIOGRAPHY	231
INDEX OF PROPER NAMES	243

INTRODUCTION

The Old French *chansons de geste* or "songs of deeds" mirrored and taught feudal Christian values and provided edifying entertainment for the aristocracy's great communal feasts, such as weddings. Excerpts were sung or chanted to the same tune on the town square after Sunday mass by *jongleurs* or minstrels playing a stringed musical instrument called a *vielle*. Thus the *chansons de geste* appealed to a vast and varied audience and enjoyed widespread popularity from the eleventh to the fourteenth century.

Eighty or so epics come to down us, surviving in written, and sometimes illustrated, form in manuscripts dating mainly from the thirteenth century, many of the poems existing in only one codex or compilation of works. These poems often centered on a historical kernel and were structured in strophes or *laisses* composed of varying numbers of lines. They were assonanced and not rhymed, meaning that the same vowel sound (followed by a different consonant) was repeated in the last syllable of each line. The *chansons de geste* were approved by the church both for their ability to console busy rulers and magnates in their leisure hours and for their usefulness in instructing the uneducated classes.

Epic Cycles

In the late twelfth or early thirteenth century, a minstrel from the Champagne region named Bertrand de Bar-sur-Aube identified three categories of *gestes* or cycles of poems organized around a lineage, or *geste*[1]: the first was the *geste du roi*, or the cycle of the king (usually Charlemagne or Louis

---

1. *"...geste...a désigné...même la famille qui fournissait la matière de ces récits."* Bloch and von Wartburg, *Dictionnaire étymologique de la langue française,* (Paris: Presses Universitaires Françaises, 1975), 293.

the Pious), to which the most famous Old French epic, *La Chanson de Roland* (eleventh century), belongs. This cycle recounts battles against the Saracens or pagans and features distinct Crusade overtones. The second cycle, or *geste de Doon de Mayence*, has been baptised the "rebellious vassal" cycle, featuring nobles who revolt against a sometimes unjust sovereign. This *geste* includes the celebrated poem of *Girart de Vienne*. The third group tells the story of the famous William of Orange, recounting the deeds of the vassal who always remains supportive of and faithful to an often wavering king. A Crusade cycle of songs also developed, including the *Chanson d'Antioche*, which mainly recounts events of the First Crusade and the deeds of Godefroy de Bouillon, ruler of Jerusalem. Parodic epics, such as the *Voyage de Charlemagne à Jerusalem*, and even obscene or scatological parodies, such as *Audigier*, existed alongside their more serious counterparts.

Throughout the medieval period, epics were composed and thrived along with other genres such as the romance, lyric and lay. From the short earlier poems running from 4,000–6,000 verses, the later works sometimes grew to a length of 35,000 lines, testifying to the popularity of the genre. Epics were written, continuously copied and imitated in other countries such as Norway, Germany, Italy and Spain as late as the fifteenth century.

THE ANTI-ISLAMIC TOPOS AND THE EPIC

From the time of the best-known Old French epic, *La Chanson de Roland*, the songs have been characterized by what might be termed the anti-Islamic topos. Originally thought to be either a naïve and incomplete understanding of Islam on the part of the medieval writers or the expression of the remnants of real emotions experienced on the historic battlefields of the Crusades or in political interactions within

Introduction

the Christian kingdoms founded in the Holy Land, this theme has come to be understood more fully.

Scholarship devoted to the so-called postcolonial Middle Ages considers this topos and offers a wide diversity of explanations and perceptions of what was traditionally conceived of as "Pagans are wrong; Christians are right," typifying a banal and clear-cut binary mentality of "good vs. evil" in the context of a psychomachia or epic battle of the conscience within. Scholars have also noted the frequently overall positive image of the "Saracens," both knights and ladies, who are nearly perfect mirror images of their Christian counterparts with the sole glaring difference of their religion separating the two. Critics have long noted the tension between the themes of war and extermination and conversion by love and example or by force present in the epics.

The term "Saracen" itself was broadly applied to a wide variety of ethnic and religious groups, from the Eastern European or Slavic peoples on the eve of Christianization, to the Arabs of the Holy Land. The theme can be viewed as the emblem of an imperialistic, colonial and demonizing impulse on the part of the Western European ruling and intellectual elite, but it can also be studied as an indication of the genuine European interest in alterity, or differing cultures and religions, and as a rich literary vein used in the rhetorical embellishment of the epic during its transition from the classical to the medieval age. This evolution was guided and influenced by medieval historiographers such as Orderic Vitalis, who may have told the original story of the Saracen princess in love with the Christian knight, so frequently recounted in the epics and present in *Elye de Saint Gille*.

Alongside these interpretations stands the genuinely solid philosophical and scientific appreciation of Arab and Islamic learning in the Middle Ages. Influential philosophers and teachers such as William of Conches (active at the court

ELYE OF SAINT-GILLES

of Geoffrey Plantagenet and tutor of the future Henry II of England), avidly sought out and translated the works of great Arabic scientists and teachers, such as Constantine the African, and in so doing modernized and enriched Western medical and scientific knowledge and contributed to the literary development of the epic topos.

ELYE DE SAINT-GILLES

This poem is extant in one thirteenth-century manuscript and is linked to the cycle or *geste* of William of Orange. Along with its much longer companion-poem, *Aiol, Elye* forms the centerpiece of the codex, BNfr 25516, which also contains two completely distinct works, *Beuves de Hanstone* and *Robert le diable*. Some scholars have called the two centerpiece poems the *geste* of Saint Gilles, although they are not referred to as such in the works themselves. Commonly termed "romance epics" and called *romans* or *estoires* in the texts, they tell the story of Count Julien of Saint-Gilles, the last noble defeated by William of Orange in *Le Couronnement de Louis*, who then becomes William's vassal and serves King Louis of France. The poem focuses on the story of Julien's only son Elye, his exploits against the Saracens during his youth and early knighthood, up to his marriage with the sister of the king, whose seneschal he becomes. The cycle's historical kernel is linked to events of the First and Fourth Crusades and the Reconquest of Spain. The sole manuscript containing *Elye* and *Aiol* is found in the 1405 inventory of the library of Margaret of Flanders, duchess of Valois, whose family had been deeply involved as key figures in all three events. In the late twelfth and thirteenth centuries, the court of Flanders became a dynamic center of literary activity unrivalled in production by either Champagne or Paris. From it originated a vast body of works of the noble *trouvères* linked to this court, such as Conon de Béthune, and Philip, count of Flanders was

INTRODUCTION

the sponsor of the celebrated *Perceval* or *le Conte du Graal* of Chrétien de Troyes; its early continuations were similarly sponsored by the court of Jeanne of Flanders.

This *geste*'s relation to the court of Countess Jeanne of Flanders has been shown by references within both *Elye* and *Aiol* themselves, as well as through allusions in close copies and translations in northern Flanders and Norway. Countess Jeanne's father, Baudouin, was the first emperor of the Latin kingdom of Constantinople in 1204, and the poems are connected with the opulent marriage of Jeanne with Count Ferrand, son of the king of Portugal, at the Paris court of King Philip Augustus in early 1212.

Elye contains the earliest appearance in literature of the popular character Galopin, who was imitated in later epics like *Huon de Bordeaux*, evolving and becoming the prototype of Shakespeare's Oberon.

Sources and Composition of the Poem

Elye is replete with literary and visual allusions to other *chansons de geste*. These include poems of the William of Orange cycle, whose highlights *Elye* retells in shortened or abbreviated form. In addition, *Elye* contains references to Arthurian romance, to medieval lyric and to twelfth- and thirteenth-century chronicles, such as that of Ordéric de Vitalis. *Elye* was originally believed by its nineteenth-century editors to have been composed in the twelfth century in central France and reworked by an inferior thirteenth-century Picardian scribe. The extant manuscript version was thought to be the corrupted remains of a *poème primitif*, or original poem, entirely in decasyllables — an opinion forged by the nostalgia for a canonical *Ur-text*. This conjectural *Ur-text* had been reworked to include alexandrines, or verses of twelve syllables. The influential medievalist Gaston Paris similarly concluded that *Elye* represented a reworking of a vigorous, virile original oral epic perhaps featuring a noble of Narbonne, into a pale imitation tinged with romance overtones.

However, upon revisiting the poem, twentieth-century critics such as M. Delbouille and E. Melli discovered its compositional unity and integrity complemented by its extremely sophisticated rhetorical development. Scholars who rely solely on the nineteenth-century point of view have been puzzled by the inclusion of *Elye* in the lavishly executed Old Norse codex, De La Gardie 7, produced at the brilliant court of the king of Norway. The manuscript includes the following other works: first a debate between the body and the soul attributed to William of Conches, the famous Chartrian philosopher and tutor to King Henry II of England; second, a version of *Pamphilus*, a popular work widely used in teaching; and finally the *lais* of Marie de France in a version close to that of the well-known Harley manuscript associated with the Anglo-Norman court. Most of these works were probably taken to Norway by the famous historian and chronicler, Matthew of Paris, where they were skillfully translated and reworked into Old Norse prose versions by Brother or Abbot Robert and others for King Hakon IV shortly after 1226. Such distinguished contemporary reception provides ample proof that in its own time, *Elye* was considered a superior, even exemplary, work.

Summary: Visual and Verbal Presentation in the Manuscript

Sixty-two, two-line undecorated initials in *Elye* signal assonance change, except in the final instance at 2385, which indicates a change in the singer's tone or the *timbre d'intonation*. This comes at the conclusion of a reference to Charles Martel, rare in the epic genre, and to a celebrated proverb. The poem's painter or *pictor* uses illuminations and rubrication to divide the work into five parts. The first

Introduction

illumination (Plate I) is executed to resemble an historiated initial, characteristic of serious material such as history, but the initial at the first line appears in regular size and format. An undecorated three-line initial occurs at 490, which may indicate the end of the poem's prologue, but does not act as a sign of a major division.

The first part of the poem includes the prologue (1–490) modeled after the traditional introduction to the Oxford manuscript's version of the *Chanson de Roland*, giving a sense of the main ideas of the work. It opens with the attention-getting device, or *captatio benevolentiae*, whose aim is to ensure the listener's good will. This Horatian-style invocation to silence uses direct address, the imperative, the interrogative and the apostrophe. It announces that the poem is composed of ".iii. vers de baronie" / "three poems about nobility," indicating the three historical events referred to above. The prologue includes, with the greeting or *salutatio*, the invocation of the blessing of God (*invocatio*) (1–3). The brief exposition of the subject, or *proposito*, immediately follows (4–10). At the prologue's end at 490, Julien announces his intent to dispose of his lands. He challenges and successfully tests his son's courage and aptitude for knighthood, tells a brief but detailed version of his history as a vassal of William of Orange, and then performs the dubbing ceremony, which bestows knighthood upon his son. But Elye takes offense at his father's demeaning remarks and angrily undertakes a self-imposed exile. He quickly encounters a messenger, a relative of Julien, lying mortally wounded, who was on his way from King Louis in Angers, to request Julien's help against a Saracen invasion of Britanny. Elye hears the dying man's confession, administers lay communion with a blade of grass and then single-handedly fights a force of Saracen warriors, releasing William of Orange and his entourage who had been taken prisoner while fighting for the king. In the battles, Elye's mount is killed, and he captured at Arles; William rushes to Julien to ask for help (491–882).

Part II (883–1132) recounts Elye's captivity and sea voyage to the land of Sorbrie, where he refuses to convert to Islam, steals an enemy's steed and daringly escapes from the Saracens to enjoy a meal taken with, unbeknownst to him, a small party of Saracen thieves. The second section of the poem concludes with Elye's wrath at learning the thieves' identity and the battle that ensues in which he defeats them all. Part III (1133–400), tells of Elye's comradeship or *compagnonage* with the Christian dwarf named Galopin, son of Count Tieri of Ardanes, who had become the captive slave of the Saracens. Galopin becomes Elye's vassal, and the two fight the Saracen army against impossible odds. As Elye nears death from multiple wounds, the dwarf valiantly refuses to abandon him and carries him, fully armed, to a nearby tower from which the Saracen emir's daughter, Rosamonde, had been watching.

In Part IV (1401–952), Rosamonde saves the two Christian knights, miraculously cures Elye and supervises their two-week stay hidden in her beautifully painted underground chamber. Rosamonde's father is faced with a challenge from the aged Saracen Lubïen who is seeking both his lands and his daughter in marriage. A debate featuring dialectical argumentation between Elye and the maiden results in Elye's agreement to champion her cause. Her advice to Elye to beware of his opponent's magnificent steed, Prinsaut, causes Galopin promptly to vow to steal the charger for his lord. The fourth part concludes with Galopin's arrival at Lubïen's camp and the beginning of his epic quest to steal Prinsaut.

The fifth part (1953–2761) recounts the successful theft and Elye's rapid victory over Lubïen, followed by the Saracen army's treacherous attack when Elye slays Rosamonde's brother for having struck and defamed her. Galopin and Elye must once more take refuge in the safety of Rosamonde's

INTRODUCTION

tower. Almost immediately, they spot Godefroie, a pilgrim returning from the Holy Land, who is coincidentally the nobleman who had brought up Elye and had trained him in the knightly arts. Godefroie agrees to seek aid from King Louis, Julien and William of Orange. He soon returns from his embassy with all the magnates of Christendom who subdue the Saracens, Christianize and repopulate the land, and baptize Rosamonde. The marriage of Rosamonde and Elye is prevented by consanguinity because Elye stood as godfather at her baptism. Despite their grief, the two accept other suitable marriage partners. Rosamonde's choice falls upon Galopin whom she has always admired; King Louis offers Elye the hand of his sister Avisse. When the Christian army decides to depart, Galopin and Rosamonde agree to stay behind to govern their newly Christianized lands. The French knights fulfill a pilgrimage vow by journeying to Jerusalem, after which they return to Paris for the marriage of Elye and Avisse in festive pomp.

NOTES ON THE EDITION AND THE TRANSLATION

Although extant in only one manuscript, nonetheless the poem presented its original editors in France and Germany with problems and textual considerations based on their comparison of the poem with its later Old Norse translation. These scholars resolved the problem by assuming that both the French and the Old Norse version stemmed from a lost original Old French epic. However, Gerritsen has elegantly lain that hypothesis to rest in a closely related context, and we may accept with confidence that *Elye* was the source for the Old Norse translation and adaptation. The nineteenth-century editors routinely emended to regularize orthography, grammar and syntax, in an attempt to arrive at a conjectural *Ur-text* whose language would conform to that of the earliest epics, especially the *Chanson de Roland* — editorial practices which have been questioned by textual critics such as Fleischman.

Our editorial approach is contemporary, simple and direct. We adhere to the manuscript whenever reasonably possible and avoid corrections of the scribe's language when merely grammatical in nature. We emend to correct obvious errors such as a repeated or omitted word or a misplaced nasal bar, and we modify the orthography of proper names, using the most frequent form. *I* and *J* are distinguished, as are *U* and *V.* Punctuation is modernized; the scribe's word division is generally retained, in keeping with current research by Busby and Clancy showing that scribal word division was frequently a guide to oral presentation. We adhere to Foulet and Speer's guidelines for diacritical marks. All emendations are indicated at the bottom of the Old French text; more lengthy explanations are noted.

Included in the notes is interesting information about the physical state of the manuscript itself (such as damage caused by tears or the presence of holes in the parchment); the notes further indicate instances of scribal expunctuation and cases where words or letters were added by the scribe. When relevant, we also furnish important information such as variant emendations by previous editors (F = Foerster; R = Raynaud) with comments on differences between nineteenth-century and later editorial practices when relevant. Abbreviations are resolved using spellings from the manuscript; a computer-generated reverse concordance was used. Numbers are left as they are written in manuscript; ".c." was read as "cent," but ".m." could be read as either "mil" or "mille," depending on metrical requirements, and the necessary pronunciations are noted. Textual divisions determined by paratextual considerations such as illumination, rubrication or lettering are indicated, and illuminations are reproduced as plates in the appendix.

Introduction

Notes are both textual in nature, as well as interpretative and informational (to elucidate proverb usage and technical terms, for example). Both editors have thoroughly studied the original manuscript at the Bibliothèque Nationale in Paris. In addition, photocopies and microfiche were used, with microfiche transferred to photographic enlargements to enhance reproduction. A diplomatic transcription was made, and the reverse concordance for resolution of abbreviations was used as an editorial aid.

We have translated into modern English, attempting to remain faithful to the meaning, while avoiding archaic usage. In the interest of the modern reader, we have chosen free verse, a form of prose laid out in lines corresponding to the Old French text for ease of reference. We first attempted ten- and twelve-syllable verse with assonance, but it always ended up sounding childish, naïve and repetitive to the modern ear. This decision, however, results in the loss of a rich vein of significant interpretative information concerning versification; we have tried to compensate for this loss through the use of explanatory notes. We have kept some inversions and most repetitions to maintain the poetry's auditory effect. Rather than conserve a vague pronoun usage, we have elucidated it for the modern reader. We also alter verb tense when it might disconcert the reader. Above all, we have tried to retain a certain direct simplicity throughout to allow the audience to experience the poem's original flavor.

ELYE OF SAINT-GILLES

Elye of Saint-Gilles

Ichi conmenche li vraie estoire de Juliens de Saint Gille le ques fu pere Elye duquel Aiols issi ensi con vous orés el livre.

Part One

1.
Or faites pais, Signor, que Dieus vous benëie,   [76r-a]
Li glorïeus del chiel li fieus Sainte Marie!
Plairoit il vous oïr .iii. vers* de baronie?
Certes chou est d'un conte* qui fu nés a Saint Gille.
Signor, il vesqui tant que la barbe ot florie.　　　　　　5
Ains ne fist en sa vie traïson ne boisdie;
Ains ama mout forment le fiex Sainte Marie,
Et mout bien honora mostier et abëie,
Et si fist bons pont faire et grant ostelerie.
Julïens ot a non, mout ot grant signorie.　　　　　　10
.I. jors estoit li quens en se sale perine,
U que il voit ses homes, si lor conmenche a dire:
«Signor baron,» dist il, «li cors Dieu vous garisse!
Il a mout bien .c. ans mes armes portai primes;
Ainc puis ne fis nul jor traïson ne boisdie,　　　　　　15
Dont nus hon crestïens perdist onques la vie.
Sor Sarrasine gent euc je tout jors envie.
Par de desous Biaulande enmi la praïerie,
En ochis je, Signor, en .i. jor plus de quinse.
Jamais n'en ert par moi, je quic, joste furnie,　　　　　　20
Ne nule enpointe faite, ne lance sorbrandie.
Or refaiche autre tel mes gentix fieus Elye!
Desormais me convient reposer et bien vivre,
Bien boire et bien mangier, reposer a delivre.
J'ai encor ma mollier, que je mout aim et prisse;　　　　　　25
Jou ai de lui .i. fil et une bele fille.　　　[76r-b]
Or amenés les moi, ses verai mes enpires.»

10　ms m. grant, creating a hypometric verse, emended by adding «m. ot», for its paratactic effect, as does R; F emends «s'ot m.».
27　ms Amenes. The hypometric verse is emended with the temporal adverb, based on the frequent pattern of «or» with the imperative (cf. 919); F moi cha; R moi tost.

A Chanson de Geste

Here begins the true story of Julien of Saint-Gilles who was the father of Elye from whom Aiol was descended as you will hear now in the book.

Part One

1.
Now be silent lords; may God bless you,
The glorious one of heaven, the son of Saint Mary!
Would it please you to hear three tales of noble knights?
Truly, this one tells of a count who was born in Saint-Gilles;
Lords, he lived so long his beard had grown white. 5
Never in all his life did he commit treason or do wrong.
Rather, he showed great love for Holy Mary's son,
And he generously supported churches and abbeys,
And he had good bridges built and large hospices.
Julien was his name, of high nobility. 10
One day the count was in his great stone hall;
When he beheld his men, he began to address them:
"Noble sirs," said he, "May God protect you!
It has been over a hundred years since I first donned armor,
And never have I committed any treason or wrong 15
From which any Christian man has ever lost his life.
Against the Saracen people I have ever shown hostility.
In the land of Biauland,* upon the fields of strife,
I have slain, lords, in one day more than fifteen of them!
Never was there a joust, I think, nor any brandished lance, 20
Nor any strike of sword turned down by me.
Now may he do likewise, my noble son Elye!
Henceforth I need to rest and live well in repose,
To drink well, and eat well, and relax in comfort.
I still have my wife whom I esteem and love dearly. 25
I have by her a son and a beautiful daughter.
Go bring them to me now. I will see to a meeting of my nobles."

Et il si firent lors, en i corurent quinse;
Les huis ont desfremés et les cambres ovrirent;
Elye i ont trové et sa seror Olive.   30
Droit de devant lor pere les menerent et guient.

2.
Julïens se sëoit ens el palais de marbre,
Tout entor lui sa gent et son barnage.
Il les a apelés conme preudon et sage:
«Signor,» fait il, «li cors Dieu bien vos fache!   35
Bien a .c. ans premier portai mes armes;
Ne puis maïs païne endurer de bataille.
De ma mollier que je mout pris en haste
Ai je .i. fil, Dameldé le me salve,
Et une fille Olive, la bïen faite.   40
Or le me quiert Garin de Piereplate,
Mais mout est jovenes* por avoir marïage.
Veés mon fil qui est en cele sale:
Gent a le cors et leës les espaules.
Mout me mervel confais est ses corages,   45
S'il vaura estre, conme destriers en garde,
Moine reclus a Noël u a Pasques?*
Or deüst estre a Paris u a Chartres,
Ou en Espaigne, u au roi de Navaire,
Et servist tant Loëys, le fïeus Charle,   50
Que de son fief eüst son heritage.
J'en conquis tant quant fui de son ëage,
Dont j'ai encore .iiii. chastieus en garde,
Et .iii.* chités et fretés* juqu'a quatre.
Mais par l'apostle que on requiert en l'arche,*   55
Aler s'en peut et tenir son voiage!»*
Elyës l'ot et tressailli le table;
Aler s'en vaut, quant li vieus le regarde.

---

28   ms i corent; we emend to the *passé simple*, as in the first hemistich, on the basis of the attested verb form in Aiol, 7659. R l. la c
51   ms e. heritage. The hypometric verse is emended with the possessive for parallelism in structure and on the model of 80; F & R e. grant

Part One

And so they obeyed; fifteen of them rushed off,
They unlocked the doors and opened the rooms;
There they found Elye and his sister Olive.   30
Straight before their father they ushered and brought them.

2.
Julien was seated in the marble palace,
All around him gathered his people and his noblemen;
He spoke to them as a worthy and wise man:
"My lords," he said, "may God do good things for you!   35
Over a hundred years ago, I first bore my arms;
I can no longer endure the hardships of battle.
By my wife, whom I wed in great haste,
I have a son, may God save his soul,
And a daughter, the beautiful girl, Olive.   40
Garin of Piereplate* is asking me for her hand,
But she is far too young to wed.*
Behold my son, present in this room:
His demeanor is noble, and his shoulders are broad;
I certainly wonder what is hidden in his heart: 45
If he would like to be, like a carefully guarded warhorse,
A cloistered monk at Christmas or at Easter?
Now he ought to be in Paris or in Chartres,
Or in Spain or with the king of Navarre*;
And he ought to serve Louis, the son of Charles,   50
So that he might earn his fief in his own right.
I conquered so much when I was his age,
That I still have four fortified castles
And three cities and even four fortresses.
But by the apostle of the ark to whom they pray,   55
He can now take leave and make his own way."
Elye heard him and leaped over the table;
He intended to leave, when the old man confronted him:

«Tais toi, lechieres! Li cors Dieu mal te fache!
S'or t'en aloies ensi, sans guïenage,　　　　　　　　　　60
Tost diroit on a Paris u a Chartres,
'Veés le fil Julïen a la barbe! [76v-a]
Par maltalent l'a cachiet de sa marche!'
Ains te donrai mon destrier et mes armes;
S'avra l'espee que je portai de Trapes,*　　　　　　　　65
Quant Aïmers* i fist le vaselage,
Qu'il en ochist Anseïs de Cartage.*
Çaindrai le toi par le resne de paile.
Enmi ces pres sor la riviere large
Une quintaine* metrai sor .ii. estaces,　　　　　　　　　70
Et s'i avra .ii. escus de Navaire,*
Et .i. auberc dont tenant ert la maille,
Et si feras .i. cop par vaselage.
Se tu le perces et tu l'auberc desmailles,
Lonc le proeche le te ferai je auques.　　　　　　　　　75
Et se je voi que tu ensi le faches
Qu'a honte tort n'a moi, n'a mon lignage,
N'en porteras del mien qui .i. seul denier vaille.
Moi et ma fille demorons en mes marces;
Quant je morai, siens ert mes iretages!»*　　　　　　　80

3.
«Pere,» che dist Elye, «puis que vous le volés,
Or me faites les armes et le destrier mostrer,
Et faites le quintaine drechier enmi le pré,
Que par cel saint apostle c'on quiert en Noiron pré,*
Quel que soit que je prenge, soit proëche u bonté,　　　85
Jamais ne girai nuit dedens vostre ireté!»
Li baron en sospirent environ de tout lés;
Meïsme* la contesse en conmence a plorer.
Ele est venue au conte, si conmence a crier:
«Merchi,» dist ele, «Sire, por les saints que fist Dé!　　90
Nous n'avons mais nul oir fors cesti qui est ber!*
Car le laissiés el resne garir et converser,
Car s'or nous sordoit guerre a nesun de no pers,

Part One

"Be quiet, you laggard! May God do you harm!
If you went off like this without an escort, 60
Soon they would say in Paris or in Chartres,
'Look at old Julien's son.
Out of spite he drove him from his lands!'
Instead, I'll give you my warhorse and my arms,
And you'll have the sword that I brought back from Trapes, 65
When Aimer did deeds of knighthood there,
And killed with it Anseis of Carthage.
I will girt it on you with its silken straps.
In the middle of this meadow above the broad river,
A quintain I will put on two wooden stakes, 70
And it will also have two Navarese shields,
And a hauberk whose chainmail will be strong.
And you will strike a knightly blow.
If you pierce through it, and you tear the chainmail,
Long will I pay honor to your prowess. 75
And if I see that you act in such a way
That I or my lineage might have wrongful shame,
You will have nothing of mine worth one denier.*
I and my daughter will remain on my lands:
When I die, hers will be my domains. 80

3.
"Father," Elye said, "since such is your wish,
Now show me the warhorse and the arms
And have the quintain raised in the meadow,
So that, by that holy apostle they pray to in Nero's fields,
Whatever I may do, even if it be prowess or good, 85
Never again will I lie one night in your domains!"
At this the nobles sighed all around;
Even the countess herself started to weep over it.
She came up to the count and began to cry out:
"Have mercy," she said, "my lord, for the saints God made! 90
We have no other heir, except for this one, who is noble.
Please let him protect the lands and remain here,
For if a war were launched against us, by any of our peers,

Qui nous feroit les jostes et les estors campés?»
«Tais, fole!» dist le quens, «trop peut on reposer.   95
Proëche et ardement doit on bien achater.
Par Saint Piere de Rome, ja sera adoubés.
S'il avoit or les armes, par la foi que doi Dé,   [76v-b]
Mar seroit en ma terre ne veüs ne trovés!
Salatré,*» dist li quens, «mes armes m'aportés!»   100
Et chil li respondi, «Volentiers et de grés!»*
Et Elyë s'en arme, li cortois et li ber.
Il a vestu l'auberc, si a l'iaume fremé.
Li viex l'i çaint l'espee a son senestre lés;
Il a hauciet le paume, se li done .i. cop tel,   105
Por .i. poi nel abat et nel fist enverser.
Et quant le voit li enfes, le sens quida derver;
Il dist entre ses dens, coïement a chelé:
«Dan* viex, mout estes faus et gangars et enflés!
Sel eüst fait .i. autre, ja l'eüst conperé!   110
Mais vous estes mes peres, ne m'en doi aïrer.»
On li trait en la place .i. destrier sejorné,
Et Elyë i monte, qui genticx est et ber.
Il geta a son col .i. fort escu bouclé
Et a pris en son poing .i. fort espiel quarré,   115
Et on fait la quintaine tost drechier ens el pré.

4.
Signor, franc chevalier, bien l'avés oï dire,
Quant bachelers s'adoube, jovene a barbe prime,
Por la joie de li, li autre s'esbaudissent.
Si firent il le jor quant montés fu Elye;   120
Tel .vii.c. en i ot qui tout le beneïssent.
Mais onques lor proiere point de bien ne li fissent,
Car ains que soit li vespres, ne sonéë conplie,
Sera pres de la mort et de perdre la vie.
.Xx. chevalier s'atornent maintenant en la vile;   125
Por l'amor del enfant ont tout lor armes prisses,

---

118   ms j. de; the hypermetric verse is emended by the attributive «a»; cf. 265.

Part One

Then who would joust for us and fight the battles?"
"Be quiet, foolish woman!" said the count, "one can be idle
   too long! 95
Prowess and boldness most surely exact their price.
By Saint Peter of Rome, he will be knighted now!
If he already had arms, by the faith that I owe God,
It would be unfortunate for him to be either seen or found
   in my lands!
Salatre," said the count, "bring me my arms!" 100
And Salatre answered him, "Willingly and gladly!"
And Elye, the courtly and the noble, armed himself with them.
He put on the hauberk, and he laced on the helmet.
The old man girded the sword on Elye's left side.
He raised his palm and gave Elye such a blow 105
That he nearly knocked him down and almost bowled him over.
And when the youth felt the blow, he thought he would lose
   his mind.
He muttered between clenched teeth, secretly, not aloud:
"Old knight, you are very false and cruel and proud.
If any other man had done that, he would have paid dearly! 110
But you are my father; I must not get angry."
They brought out to him on the square a fresh warhorse,
And Elye, who was noble and worthy, mounted upon it.
Upon his neck, he hung a sturdy, bossed shield,
And he seized a strong, well-formed spear, 115
And they soon had the quintain raised in the meadow.

4.
Lords, noble knights, it's true what you've heard said
When a young man is knighted, a youth with his first beard,
Sharing in his joy, others are also joyful.
Such was their emotion the day Elye was raised to knighthood. 120
Some seven hundred knights there were, and all blessed him,
But never would their prayers do him any good,
Because before vespers or compline are sung,
He'll be near death and close to losing his life.
Now twenty knights armed themselves in the city; 125
For love of the young man, they all took up their weapons.

Elye of Saint-Gilles

Entr'aus juënt et gabent et behordent et rient,*
Fierent en le quintaine mout grant cop a delivre.
Julïens va avant, si lor conmenche a dire:
«Signor, estés en sus! Li cors Dieu vous garisse!　　　　130
Si laissiés mon enfant trestorner a delivre,
Anqui me mostera de ses chevaleries!»
Il se traient ariere, et li enfes s'aïre,
Et fiert en le quintaine mout grant cop a delivre.　　[77r-a]
Les escus a perciés, et les aubers desclices*;　　　　135
Les estaces abat, et toutes les debrisse.
Quant le voit Julïens, si conmencha a rire;
Il est passés avant, se li conmenche a dire:
«Biaus fiex, mout serés preus! Li cors Dé vous garisse!
Des or vous doins ma terre, se l'arés toute quite!»　　140
«Sire,»* che dist li enfes, «Vous parlés de folie;
Ge ne me remanroie por a perdre la vie!»

5.
Mout fu Juliens lïés por l'amor de son fil,
Quant il voit le quintaine enmi le pré gesir;
Il l'en a apelé, belement li a dit:　　　　　　　　　　145
«Biaus fiex, mout serés preus! Dieus vous puist benëir!
Des or vous doins ma terre et trestout mon païs!»
«Sire,» che dist li enfes, «por noient l'avés dit!
Vous m'avés conjuré et desfendu ausi;
Jamais en votre tere ne soie reverti,　　　　　　　　　150
Ne ja certes par moi ne serés escondit!»
Quant Julïens l'entent, a poi n'esrage vis.
«Por coi dont, maus lecieres, fel quiver de pu lin?
Ançois ai .xx. chastiaus, la Dameldé merci,
Et .xiiii. chités et fretés jusc'a dis　　　　　　　　　　155

139　ms le cors; the article is sometimes given in the oblique case, perhaps on the analogy of the frequently recurring formula, «parmi le cors» (cf. 618, 694, 1225). The scribe uses «li» correctly at 13, 883, 925, and 972, etc.
140　ms d. ore; yields a hypermetric verse; we emend following the identical structure at 147.
145　ms il en; the pronoun is included, on the model of 186.

Part One

Among themselves, they played and joked and jousted
   and laughed.
Many powerful blows they deftly struck upon the quintain.
Julien stepped forward and addressed his court:
"Lords, stand aside, may God protect you,   130
And let my son have room to maneuver freely;
Now he will show me his knightly deeds and prowess."
They all drew back, and the youth summoned his courage
And then skillfully struck on the quintain many great blows.
The shield he pierced through, and he tore the hauberk;   135
He knocked down the posts and broke them to pieces.
When Julien saw that, he began to laugh.
He stepped forward and declared:
"Good son, you will be very worthy. May God protect you!
From this moment on, I'll give you my lands, and they'll be
   yours without reserve."   140
"Sir," thus said the youth, "What a foolish idea.
I would not remain here if it cost me my life!"

5.
Julien was very happy for love of his son
When he saw the quintain lying in the middle of the meadow.
He called him over and gently said,   145
"Good son, you will be very worthy. May God bless you!
From this moment on, I give you my lands and all my domains."
"Sir," thus spoke the youth, "you have spoken in vain.
You banished me, and you forbade me, too,
Ever to come back to your land.   150
I'll certainly never violate this command."
When Julien heard him, he nearly became enraged:
"But why, you scoundrel, you vile coward of a whore's line?
I had twenty castles to offer you, thank the Lord,
And fourteen cities and as many as ten strong forts   155

De coi tu seras sires et feras ton plaisir.»
«Sire,» che dist li enfes, «por noiant l'avés dit;
Je ne m'en remanroie por les menbres tolir!»
Or escoutés, Signor, con al congiet li dist:
«Or va, que ja ne truisses ne terre ne pais   160
Que ne* puisses conquerre vaillant .i. paresis!*
Ja ne truisses tu home qui ja te soit amis;
Certes, ne feras tu, car li ceur le me dist.»
Li danseus en avale les degrés marberins,*
Et li viex le regarde, se li jete .i. souspir;   165
En son ceur le conmande a Dieu qui ne menti.
Il en a apelé Aymer et Thïeri,*
Et Gerardot le rous et Tibaut et Sanghin:
«Alés apres mon fil, Signor, je vous en pri,
Et tant menés des autres des barons del pais,   [77r-b]   170
Que .xx. soiés ensamble de chevalier de pris.
Qui faura l'un de vous, de Dieu soit il honis!»
Des or s'en va Elye, li preus et li gentis;
Dameldieu reclama, qui onques ne menti:
«Or me convient les maus et les paines soffrir,   175
Mais par cel saint apostle que quierent pelerin,*
Mieus voil en autre tere tout jors estre caitis,
Jamais en la mon pere soië jor revertis.»
Toute jor chevalcha que ne s'atarga nis,
Tant qu'il eust mangiet ne beut .i. petit.   180
Si con il chevalcoit, si regarde el chemin,
Si voit .i. messager desous l'onbre d'un pin.
De .iii. lances navrés, malement fu baillis;
La cervele li saut par desous* les sorcis.
Et quant le voit Elye, cele part poignant vint;   185
Il l'en a apelé, belement li a dit:
«Amis, qui t'a che fait? Garde ne me mentir!
Orendroit maintenant en ert venjance* pris!»
Quant l'entent li messages, si respont .i. petit:
«Et toi qu'en caut, biaus frere, chevalier, biaus amis?   190
Tele gent le m'ont fait, qu'esroient orains chi.
Ja t'aroit tous li pires craventé et ochis;

Part One

Of which you will be the lord, and you will do with them
  what you like."
"Sir," said the youth, "you're wasting your breath.
I wouldn't remain if my limbs were torn off!"
Now listen, Lords, to how Julien addressed him when they parted:
"Then leave! May you never find any land or country   160
Where you might conquer anything worth a cent!
May you never find any man who would ever be your friend!
You surely will not, because my heart tells me so!"
The young man ran down the marble steps,
And the old man watched him go and heaved a sigh.   165
In his heart he entrusted him to God who never told a lie.
He called forth from his knights Aymer and Thieri
And Gerard the red-haired and Tibaut and Sanghin:
"Follow my son, Lords, I pray of you,
And take enough of the other nobles of this realm   170
So that altogether you will number twenty worthy knights.
If one of you fails, may God bring him shame!"
Now Elye deparated, the worthy and the noble.
He called upon the Lord, who never told a lie:
"Now I will have to bear hardships and suffering.   175
But by that holy apostle whom pilgrims seek,
I prefer in another land to be forever exiled.
May I never come home again to my father's lands!"
All day he rode without the least delay,
Not even to drink or eat a single bite.   180
And as he was riding along, he looked down the road,
And he saw a messenger in the shade of a pine tree,
Wounded by three lances, he was in sad shape;
His brain was oozing out from under his eyebrows.
And when Elye saw him, he spurred in that direction.   185
He called to him, and he spoke to him gently:
"Friend, who did this to you? Be careful, do not lie to me.
Right away, this will be avenged."
When the messenger heard him, he shot back:
"What does it matter to you, good brother, knight, good friend?   190
Some people did this to me who were riding through here
  just now;
The very worst of them will soon have beaten and killed you,

Elye of Saint-Gilles

Mais prent cel mien ceval, sor millor ne seïs,
Et si t'entorne ariere, si pense del füir.
Par chi passeront ja .iiii.m. Arabi;   195
Se de ceus peus estordre, Dieu aras a ami!
Dont je sui, tu le m'as demandé et enquis:
Je sui nés de Peitiers, fil le conte Amauri;
Julïen de Saint Gille est mes germains cousin.
Mes sire est a la court por son droit maintenir;   200
Je m'en alai en Franche, droit au roi Loëys,*
Lonc les puis de Monmartre, lés le cit de Paris:
La se fist l'enperere coroner et servir.
En apres cele joie, .i. messagier i vint,
Qui li conta noveles et dist qu'en son pais   205
Erent par forche entré paien et Sarrasin.   [77v-a]
Quant l'entendi li rois, mout dolant en devint;
Ne daigna mander ost, ne semonse ne fist;
A che de gent qu'il ot, entra en son pais.
Nous passames le Maine et Auvergne et Berri,*   210
Au costé de Bretaigne, trovames Sarrasin.
A la premiere joste, belement lor* avint;
Plus de .c. en copames et les ciés et les vis.
A l'autre asaut apres, en abatismes vint,
Et quant che vint au tierc, fuissiemes* desconfit,   215
Quant secor nous revient* de Dieu de Paradis,
Et si fort les menames, et fuissent desconfit,
Quant a forche lor salent .iiii.m. Arabi!
Cil encaucent les nos, et atornerent si,
Jusc'a pont desous Loire, lonc la roce declin.   220
Senpre fust l'enperere et detenus et pris,
Quant Guillame d'Orenge .i. gent secor i fist,
Il et Bertran ses niés, li preus et li gentis,
Et Bernart de Brubant et Hernaut li floris.
Cil maintienent le caple as boins brans acerins,   225
Puis furent li baron et retenu et pris.
L'enperere s'entorne, quant il fu desconfis;
Sarrasin l'encauchierent qui l'orent envais;
Ens es ruës d'Angers nous firent ens flatir.

Part One

So take this horse of mine — on a better one you will not sit —
And turn around, and take flight.
Soon 4,000 Arabs will pass this way.   195
If you can escape them, you'll have God for a friend.
Where I'm from, you asked and inquired of me:
I was born at Poitiers, son of the Count Amauri.
Julien of Saint-Gilles is my first cousin.
My lord is at court, seeking to maintain his rights.   200
I was going to France, straight to King Louis,
Up on the hill of Montmartre, near the city of Paris.
There the emperor was being crowned and served.*
After the joy of this occasion, a messenger arrived,
Who told him news and said that into his country   205
Pagans and Saracens had entered by force.
When the king heard this, it caused him much sorrow;
He did not deign to call up an army, nor did he summon
   his nobles;
With what men he had, he entered his lands.
We passed through Maine and Auvergne and Berry,   210
On the coast of Britanny we found Saracens.
In the first joust it all went well for them:
We cut the heads and faces off more than a hundred of them!
During the second assault, we struck down twenty of them;
When it came to the third attack, we would have been defeated, 215
When help came to us from God of paradise,
And we fought them so hard, they would have been defeated,
When, by surprise, there came four thousand Arabs.
They bore down upon us and quickly surrounded us
As far as the Loire's great bridge along the sloping rock.   220
Then the emperor would have been quickly seized and taken,
When William of Orange made a marvellous rescue:
He and Bertrand his nephew, the worthy and the noble,
And Bernart of Brubant and Hernaut the white-bearded.
They fought the battle with good swords of steel.   225
Then the nobles were seized and taken prisoner.
The emperor retreated when he was defeated;
The Saracen invaders pursued him.
Into the streets of Angers they made us flee.

Lors leva par la tere et li bruis et li cris, 230
Si se traient ariere paien et Sarrasin.
Tant me fist l'enperere et dona et promist,
Que l'aloië nonchier Julïen, son ami,
A chou de gent qu'il a .i. secor li fëist.
Quant je parti de l'ost, paiens m'orent coisi, 235
Si m'ont el cors navré, malement m'ont bailli.
Ja ne verai le vespre, ne soleil aconpli.»
Quant Elyë l'entent, a poi n'esrage vis:
«Damoisex, mar i fustes! Tu eres mes cosins!
Par icel saint apostle que quierent pelerin, 240
Por l'amor de ton cors, tel vengance en ert pris*
Que au fer de ma lanche en convient morir .xx.! [77v-b]
Il est passés avant, entre ses bras le prist,
Prist une feulle d'erbe, a le bouce li mist*;
Dieus li fait aconnoistre et ses peciés jehir. 245
L'ame part del mesage, s'est alés a sa fin.*
Et Elyë monta el destrier arabi;
De che fera il ja et que fols et que bris;
Par son cors solement va contre Sarrasins.

6.
Des or s'en va Elye, qui laisse le message, 250
Et Sarrasin esploitent qui par iror cevaucent,
Et sont bien .iiii.m. estre chou des angardes.*
Macabrés les conduist et Jossés qui les garde.*
L'amirax fist venir Rodoé de Calabre
Et le viel Aitropé qui rois fu de Barbastre, 255
Et si fu avoec aus et Ganbons et Orables,
Et li viex Josué, entre lui et Trïacre,
Malpriant fu li dismes, que li cors Dieu mal fache!
«Signor,» dist l'amiral, «entendés mon corage:
Mout nos est Mahomet fierement guïonage. 260
Ces François avons tous desconfis en lor marces!*
Qui tel eskiec enmaine, bien doit estre sor garde;
C'est Guillame d'Orenge qui faissoit les batailles,

---
257 ms et Ciacre; Trïacle is the king later referred to in 364 ff.

Part One

Then there was raised throughout the land the hue and cry 230
So that the pagans and Saracens drew back.
The king had me given and promised much
So that I might go to summon his friend Julien
To bring help with those men he had.
When I left the army, some pagans caught sight of me. 235
They have wounded me and left me in bad shape.
Never will I see vespers nor sundown."
When Elye heard him, he nearly became enraged:
"Fair knight, what a great misfortune! You're my cousin!
By that holy apostle that pilgrims seek, 240
For the love of you, such vengeance will be taken
That by the steel of my lance, twenty of them will have to die!"
Elye came to him and took him in his arms;
He took a blade of grass and placed it in the messenger's mouth.
God inspired him to recognize and regret his sins. 245
The messenger's soul departed and went to its goal;
And Elye mounted upon the messenger's Arabian warhorse,
And by this act he will do something insane and foolish:
All by himself, he'll go up against the Saracens.

6.
Then Elye rode off and left the messenger*; 250
And Saracens hurried onward, who rode on in anger,
And they numbered over four thousand. They were the
  advance guard:
Macabre led them, and there was Joshua, who rode guard.
The admiral sent for Rodoan of Calabria
And old Aitrope, who was king of Barbastre. 255
And also with them were Gambon and Orable
And old Joshua, both him and Triacre.
Malpriant was the tenth, may God do him harm!
"Lords," said the admiral, "Hear my plan:
Mahomet is our most faithful guide! 260
We have defeated all these Frenchmen in their own lands!
Whoever carries off such booty must ever be on guard.
We hold William of Orange, who fought battles:

Elye of Saint-Gilles

Il et Bertran ses niés, li cortois et li sages,
Et Bernart de Breubant et Hernaut a la barbe. 265
Or les trameterons tous sor mer le rivage,*
La troverons nos homes ques auront en lor garde;
Car se Sarrasin sevent Franc se doivent conbatre,
S'en seront plus hardi et tornant et aidable.»
Et respondent paien, «Cis consaus est mout sages; 270
Ensi le feron nous au los de ce barnage.»
Or s'en tornent paien et cis qui les pris gardent,
Et li autre remaignent qui ariere se targent,
Por recerchier le pui et le mont et l'angarde,
Vëoir se troveront nul home qui riens vaille, 275
Cheval ne palefroi ne boin destrier d'Arabe.
Il troverent Elye a l'issir d'un boscage;
Mais ançois qu'il s'en partent, lor fera tel damage, [78r-a]
K'escus i avra frais et armes de cors traites.

7.
Or s'en tornent paien, li .v. en vont devant, 280
Et li autre remaignent qui se vont atargant,
Qui mainent no François tant orgellousement,
As fus et as bastons les vont forment batant.
Et Guillame d'Orenge* s'en va mout dementant:
«Dameldé,» dist il, «pere par ton digne conmant 285
Mar furent notre cors, li preu et li vaillant!
Des or serons sor mer o Sarrasine gent,
Dameldieu penst des armes par son conmandement,
Car li cors sont torné a grant juïsemant!»
Primerains l'entendi .i. paien, Rodoant; 290
Il haucha le baston, ja ferist maintenant,
Quant il a regardé parmi le desrubant,
Et voit venir Elye sor son ceval corant.
Quant le voit li paien, cele part vint poignant,
A sa vois qu'il ot clere, s'escria hautement: 295
«Qui es tu, chevaliers, desor cel auferant?

---

280   ms p. le; the scribal error is analogous to that of 139.

Part One

He and Bertrand his nephew, the courtly and the wise,
And Bernart of Breubant and bearded Hernaut.   265
Now let us transport all of them beyond these shores, overseas.
Our men are there, who will accept them into their custody,
For if Saracens know that they must fight the Franks,
They'll be more bold, well-disposed and more helpful."
And the pagans replied, "This advice is most wise.   270
So we will heed it, because of these nobles' renown."
Then the pagans rode away, and those who guarded the prisoners
Remained with the others who stayed behind
To scout through hills and vales
To search for any man who might be useful to them,   275
Any steed or palfrey or Arabian warhorse.*
They found Elye, as he was leaving the woods,
But before they'll take leave of him, he'll do them such harm
That he will have fresh shields and arms taken from their bodies.

7.
Now the pagans departed. Five went on ahead   280
And the others stayed back, who remained behind,
Leading our French away, so haughtily.
With rods and sticks they harshly beat them as they went.
And as he went along, William of Orange lamented greatly:
"Lord," he said, "Father by your worthy command   285
We noble, worthy knights have met misfortune!
Soon we'll be overseas among the Saracen people.
May God remember our souls, by his command,
Because our bodies are enduring great tortures!"
A pagan, Rodoan, heard him first.   290
He raised his stick; he would have struck him then and there,
When he looked off down the hillside
And saw Elye coming on his swift charger.
When the pagan saw him, he spurred in Elye's direction.
With a loud voice, he called out brashly: 295
"Who are you, knight, mounted on that charger?

Cel destrier reconnois et tout cel garniment!»
«Vasal,» che dist Elye, «en tient a vous noiant?»
«Oïl,» dist li paien, «je les avrai esrant!»
«Tais toi,» che dist Elye, «trop me vas maneçant, 300
Quant tu as si conquis trestous mes garnimens,
Mon auberc et mon elme et mon destrier corant,
Aras tu tel ensoigne, onques n'eüs si grant!

8.
«Sarrasin,» dist Elye, «tu le m'as demandé
Conment jou ai a non et de quel lieu sui né; 305
Vois tu or cel plaiscié lonc cel bos en cel pré?
Iqui est mes repaires, et ichi fu je nés;
Fiex sui a .i. provost qui a avoir assés,
Par sa fiere ricoisse m'a il hui adoubé.
Or m'en vois deportant, mon destrier esprover; 310
Onques Dieus ne fist home qui de mere soit nés,
S'il demande bataille, que n'en soie aprestés.
Or vous voi de vos armes garnis et conraés;
Ces prisons u presistes, que si mal demenés, [78r-b]
Sont che vilain de vile u borgois de chité?» 315
«Nenil,» dist Rodoan, «mais baron naturel;
C'est Guillame d'Orenge, li gentiex et li ber,
Et Bertram ses neveus, li preus et li senés,
Et Bernart de Brubant et Hernaut li menbrés.»
Quant l'entendi Elye, le sens quide derver; 320
A sa vois qu'il ot clere conmencha a crier:
«Paien, mar les cargastes, par les saints que fist Dés!»
Il hurte le destrier par andeus les costés,
Vait ferir Rodoan en son escu listé,
Desor la bende d'or li a fraint et troé, 325
Le blanc auberc del dos desmailliet et fausé;
Enpoin le par vertu, si l'a mort craventé.

---
297   ms t. cil; we emend on the model of 296.
306   ms c. plancie; the noun as given by Godefroy means «a room constructed of wood» and is inappropriate here; we emend with the nearly homonymic noun for «pleasant enclosure».
309   ms m. hui; the hypometric verse is emended by the addition of the subject pronoun.

Part One

That horse I recognize, and all those arms."
"Knight," Elye said, "is it any of your business?"
"Yes," replied the pagan, "I'll take them immediately."
"Be quiet!" Elye said, "Your threats are ridiculous! 300
When you've conquered all of my war arms,
My hauberk and my helmet and my swift warhorse,
You'll have troubles, such have never been seen!"

8.
"Saracen," Elye said, "you asked me
What my name is and in what place I was born.* 305
Do you see that clearing at the edge of the wood in those fields?
That is where I live, here I was born;
I am the son of a magistrate who has great riches.
With his magnificent wealth, he knighted me today,
Now I am out for my amusement, to try out my horse. 310
Never did God make a man who was of mother born,
That if he asked for battle, I wouldn't be ready for it!
Now I see you in full armor and equipped with your weapons.
These prisoners whom you are so mistreating, where did you take them?
Are they townspeople or burghers from the city?" 315
"Neither." said Rodoan, "They are nobles by birth.
This is William of Orange, the worthy and noble,
And Bertram his nephew, the vaillant and wise,
And Bernart of Brubant, and the brave Hernaut."
When Elye heard him, he thought he would lose his mind. 320
In a loud voice, he began to shout:
"Pagan, you'll regret that you beat them, by the saints that God made!"
He spurred his warhorse on both flanks,
He rushed to strike Rodoan on his banded shield;
Upon the band of gold, he broke and pierced it. 325
The white hauberk he rent and tore,
Elye seized him forcefully and dealt him a death blow.

«Cuiver,» che dist Elye, «Dieu doinst toi mal dehé!
Onques li miens lignages ne pot le tien amer!»

9.
Corsus de Tabarie voit Rodoan a tere, 330
U il meurt et angoisse, ne demande confesse;
Il reclaime dïable,* que il l'arme en portaisse.
Il escria Elye .iiii. mos tous a certes:
«Cuiver! mar l'ochesistes, vous en perdrés la teste!»
Quant Elyë l'entent, ne ja prisse une nesple, 335
Ains hurte le destrier, se li lasque le resne,
Vait ferir le paien sor le targe novele,
Desor la boucle a or li fraint et esqartele.
Le blanc hauberc del dos li desmaille et desere,
Si que parmi le cors li mist l'anste novele; 340
Enpoin le par vertu, mort l'abat de la sele.

10.
Quant Elyë ot mort Rodoan de Calabre,
Corsaut de Tabarie jut envers en la place.
Li .iii. paien l'esgardent qui dessendent l'angarde,
Or s'i sont eslaisset, li felon mescreable, 345
Et li ber se desfent, que Dieus ait en sa garde.
Li premiers qu'il encontre n'ot talent d'oïr fable,
Ains l'abati a terre con une raine plate.
Li doi tornent en fuie, et Elyë les cache,
Et Gaidonet l'encauche, qui de mort le manace, [78v-a] 350
Et vait ferir Elye sor le doréë targe;
Desor la boucle a or li a percie et quasse.
Mout fu boin li auberc quant il n'en ronpi maille,
Et li vasal sont preu quant il ne s'entrabatent.
Elië passe avant, se li toli le hanste, 355
Enmi le pré le jete, si a l'espéë traite,
Vait ferir le paien amont desor son elme.
Les pierres et les flors contreval en deserre,*
Tout le va porfendant enfressi qu'es espaules.

Part One

"Traitor!" Elye said, "May God punish you!
Never can my lineage love yours!"

9.
Corsaut of Tabarie saw Rodoan lying on the ground   330
Where he lay dying in anguish; he did not ask for confession,
He called on the devil to carry off his soul.
Corsus cried out to Elye a few harsh words:
"Traitor, you'll rue the day you killed him! You'll lose your
   head for this!"
When Elye heard him, he cared not in the least.   335
Instead, he gave his charger full rein and spurred him on hard,
He rushed to strike the pagan on his new shield;
Above the gold boss, he broke it and tore it apart.
The white hauberk Corsaut was wearing, he rent and tore,
When through his body Elye drove the new lance,   340
He struck him with force, and threw him dead from the saddle.

10.
Elye had slain Rodoan of Calabria,
And Corsaut of Tabarie lay dead, face up on the field;
The three pagans looked on, who were leading the advance guard.
Then they quickly joined the fray, the unbelieving traitors;   345
And the knight defended himself, may God watch over him!
The first one that he met, he wasted no time on idle speech;
Instead, he struck him to the ground like a splayed frog.
The other two turned and fled, Elye in hot pursuit,
And Gaidonet pursued Elye, threatening him with death.   350
He rushed to strike Elye on his gilded shield;
Upon the gold boss, he struck and pierced it.
The hauberk was so stout that its mail did not yield,
And the knights were strong, since they did not unseat each other.
Elye surged forward and tore away the other's lance,   355
In the middle of the meadow he threw it down, then drew
   his sword;
He galloped forward to strike the pagan high on his helmet.
The precious gemstones and flowers went showering to the
   ground.
Elye split his skull clean down to his shoulders;

23

Li ber estort son cop, mort l'abat en la place; 360
Il broche le destrier, si reva ferir l'autre,
Le teste en fist voler devant lui en la place.
Li .v. paien le voient,* qui montoient l'angarde:
«Or esgardés, Signor,» che dist li rois Triacles,
«Veés vous ce vasal qui le tertre en avale? 365
Mout se fait orgellous et hardis par ses armes!
Atendés .i. petit, g'irai a lui conbatre;
Le destrier li taurai, et trestoutes ses armes,
Si les departirons, si serons conmunable.
Ja n'en avra li .i. un denier plus de l'autre!» 370
Dist Josses d'Alixandre, «Grant folië pensastes!
Hui matin, par son l'aube, quant nous nos desevrames,
Conpaignië jurames; faus est qui ne le garde!
Nous l'iromes tout .v. craventer et abatre!»
«Couardisse seroit,» che dist li rois Trïacle, 375
«Se nous aliemes .v. por .i. tou seul abatre*;
Jamais n'en seroit dit proéche ne barnage,
Paien s'en gaberont, et li .i. et li autre!
Mahomet me confonge! N'ait ja qui denier vaille,
Qui de moi et de lui n'esgarde le bataille.» 380
Il hurte le destrier et le resne li lasque.

11.
Il hurte le destrier et li lasque le resne,*
Il escrïa Elye .iiii. mos tout a certes:
«Ies tu, va, crestïens de le malvaise geste,
U se crois Mahomet qui le siecle governe?» 385
«Naië,»* che dist Elye, «mes en Dieu le grant mestre; [78v-b]
Si sui nés de Saint Gille de Provence le bele,
Fiex Julïen, au conte a le chenue teste.
Avant hier m'adouba de ses armes noveles,
Car il me fu bien dit et conté tout a certes, 390
Paien et Sarrasin sont entré en ma terre.
Je les vieng sorvëoir, se trové pevent estre,
Bien les quic estormir, ains que vienge li vespres!»

Part One

The young knight delivered his blow and struck Gaidonet
    dead to the ground.   360
Elye spurred his warhorse on and wheeled to strike the other;
He sent this pagan's head flying before him across the field.
The five pagans saw it, who were mounting the advance guard.
"Now look, my lords," said King Triacle,
"Do you see that knight who is rushing down the hillock?   365
He's shown himself to be quite proud and bold by his arms!
The rest of you wait here; I'll go out to do battle with him;
I'll capture his horse and all his armor,
And we'll divide them up, and we'll share in common:
No one will ever have one denier more than any other."   370
Joshua of Alexandria spoke up: "That's a crazy idea!
This morning at break of day, when we separated,
We all pledged compagnonage; false is he who does not
    keep his oath!
We'll all five go together to slay and strike him down!"
"That would be cowardice," replied King Triacle,   375
"If all five of us combined together to slay one lone knight.
Never would it be called prowess or nobleness;
Our people one and all would soon be making jokes about it.
May Mahomet confound me if there is anyone worth a denier
Who will not watch this battle between him and me!"   380
He spurred his warhorse on, giving it full rein.

11.
He spurred on his warhorse and gave it rein.
He cried out a few sharp words to Elye:
"Are you a Christian of foul lineage
Or do you believe in Mahomet, who rules all?"   385
"Not I!" replied Elye, "But in God, the Master of all!
I was born in Saint Gille, in beautiful Provence,
The son of Count Julien, with the hoary head,
Two days ago he knighted me with his new arms.
I've been told and well informed   390
That into my lands pagans and Saracens have entered.
I've come to seek them out; if I find them,
I'm determined to wage war on them before vespers!"

«Par mon cief,» dist Trïacle, «trop grant deus vous apresse.
Ce destrier vous taurai, si le menrai en destre; 395
A grant honte en serés abatu de la sele,
Les jambes vers le ciel et le cief contre terre!»
Quant Elyë l'entent, ne le prisse une mesple.
Il hurte le destrier, se li lasques le resne,
Vait ferir le paien desor son elme a perles, 400
Qu'il en a abatu et les flors et le cercle.
Le blanc auberc del dos li desmaille et desfere,
Tout la* va porfendant enfresi qu'en l'aissele;
Li ber estort son cop, si l'abat a la terre.

12.
Dist li rois Salatrés, «Esgardés quel damage 405
D'un enfant de .xv. ans qui n'a gaire d'ëage!
Tel vasal nous a mort et conquis par ses armes!
S'il m'atent .i. petit, g'irai a lui conbatre,
Le destrier li taurai et trestoutes ses armes!»
Il hurte le destrier et le resne li lasque, 410
Et Elyë le sien, que il bien point en haste.
Gran cos s'en vont doner sor les vermelles targes;
Sor les bendes a or les peçoient et quassent.
Mout sont boin li auberc quant il n'en ronpent maille,
Et li vasal sont preu, quant il ne s'entrabatent. 415
Li paien trait l'espee qui bien luist et bien taille,
Et vait ferir Elye amont desor son elme.
Les pieres et les flors contre val en dessere,
Le destrïer consui par de derier l'espaule;
.Ii. moitiés en a fait, li ber ciet en la plache. 420
«Par mon cief,» dist Elye, «or m'as tu fait damage!
Mon destrier m'as ochis qui m'estoit guïenage! [79r-a]
Mout est boine t'espee; faus es, se ne le gardes!
Se le tenoie as puins, por le chité de Blaives,
Ne le rendroië mie a mon frere carnable!» 425

---

420 ms b. cief logically should be emended to the verb form «ciet»; F & R emend also.

Part One

"Upon my head," said Triacle, "a great woe awaits you!
That warhorse I'll seize from you, and I'll lead it away;   395
To your great shame you'll be struck down from your saddle,
Your legs towards the heavens, and your head on the ground!"
When Elye heard him, little did he care.
He spurred his warhorse and gave it rein,
He galloped forward to strike the pagan on his pearl-encrusted
   helmet,   400
So that he struck off its flowers and circlets.
The pagan's white hauberk, Elye pierced and rent through,
Splitting it all the way down to the armpits.
The youth then struck his blow and knocked King Triacle
   to the ground.

12.
Said King Salatre, "Now look what great damage   405
Is wrought by a youth who's scarcely fifteen years of age!
What a great peer of ours, he has killed and conquered by his arms!
If he'll just wait for me, I'll go out to fight him.
His warhorse I'll seize from him, and all his weapons!"
He spurred on his charger and gave it full rein.   410
And Elye spurred on his mount as well, riding forward in haste.
Harsh blows they'll deal each other on their vermillon shields!
Upon the bands of gold, they pierced and broke them.
Their hauberks were so strong that their chainmail did not break,
And the knights were so worthy that they did not unseat each
   other.   415
The pagan drew his sharp sword, which gleamed bright,
And he started to strike Elye high upon his helmet;
The gemstones and flower-shaped ornaments showered down
   to the ground.
He struck his warhorse next, just behind its shoulder;
Two halves he made of it; and the young knight fell to the field.   420
"Upon my head," said Elye, "now you've done me harm!
You've killed my horse who was my guide.
Your sword's very good; false is he who can't keep it!
If I had it in my hand, for the city of Blaye,
I'd never give it up, even to my own blood brother!"   425

«Quiver,» dist li paien, «con mar le convoitastes!
Mout est boine m'espee, si est bien a moi salve.
Ja ne consievrai home qui en Dieu soit creable,
Je nen en cop le cief par desor les espaules!»
«Voire,» ce dist Elye, «mais j'en rai chi .i. autre 430
Que mes peres me çainst, Julïen a le barbe,
Qui vous sera privee, se je puis, mout en haste.»
Il l'a saciet del feure, s'il a* feru sor l'iaume;
Les pieres et les flors contreval en avale,
Li brans est trestornés desor le destre espaule, 435
Le brac li a tranchiet, dont se quidoit conbatre,
A tout la boine espee li cai en la plache.
Quant Elyë le voit, si le prent et esgarde:
«Paien,» che dist Elye, «li cors Dieu mal te fache!
Anqui poras veoir ques dieus est plus verables 440
Mahom u Apolin* u Jhesu qui tout salve!
De meïsmes t'espee, t'ira je* honte faire!»
Il le drecha amont, si l'en feri sor l'iaume;
Tout le va porfendant enfressi qu'es espaules.
Li ber estort son cop, mort l'abat en la place. 445
Venus est as prissons qui gisoient soz* l'arbre,
Ses peüst desloier, gente cose eüst faite.

13.
Quant Jossïens voit mort Salatré, son neveu,*
Le cors en .ii. moitiés, ne peut müer ne plor:
«Mahom et Apolin! mal dehet aiés vous! 450
S'or ne faites justiche del quiver dolerous,
Qui m'a mort devant moi le fil de ma seror!
Le fer de ceste lance vous metrai el cors tout!»
Il hurte le destrier des tranchans esperons,
Et a baisié le lanche a tout le confanon, 455
Et vait ferir Elye sor son escu amont;
Desor le bende a or li peçoie et confont.
Le blanc auberc del dos li desmaille et desront, [79r-b]

---

446 ms g. sor; the preposition must be «under», not «on»; we emend, as R does, but see note.

Part One

"Coward," said the pagan, "too bad for you that you covet it!
My sword's very great, and it's my stout protector!
If I ever strike any would-be believer in God,
I'll cut his head right off his shoulders with it!"
"That may be true," Elye said, "but I have another one here   430
That my father girded on me, the bearded Julien,
Which will be your lot right away."
He seized it from its sheath, and he struck him on his helmet.
The gemstones and the flowers showered down to the ground.
The iron sword twisted down into his left shoulder,   435
His arm Elye cut off, with which the pagan intended to do battle;
With that, the good sword fell from him to the field.
When Elye saw it, he picked it up and looked at it:
"Pagan," said Elye, "may God do you harm!"
Now you'll see which god is more true,   440
Mahomet or Apollo, or Jesus who saves all?
With your own sword I'm going to cause you great shame!"
He raised it high and struck the pagan on his helmet;
He split it right down through to his shoulders.
The knight then struck his blow and knocked King Salatre
   to the ground.   445
Elye came to the prisoners who were lying beneath the tree;
If he could have untied them, he would have done a noble deed!

13.
When Joshua saw his nephew Salatre dead,
His body severed in two, he could neither move nor weep:
"Mahomet and Apollo! May you have misfortune   450
If now you don't administer swift justice to that despicable coward
Who's slain, right before my eyes, my sister's son!
This lance's iron tip I'll thrust right through your body!"
He urged on his warhorse with sharpened spurs,
And lowered his lance with its pennant unfurled,   455
And charged to strike Elye high on the shield;
Above the gold band he broke it and destroyed it.
The white hauberk Elye wore, he pierced and tore,

Nu a nu lés le cors le roit espiel li coust.
«Par mon cief,» dist Elye, «tu es vasal mout prous!» 460
Volentiers m'ocesisses, s'en eüsses laissor;
Mais Dieus m'ainme de ceur, qui me gara tous jors!»
Il a traite l'espee dont a or sont li poing,
Vait ferir le paien desor son elme amont.
Les pieres et les flors contreval en deront, 465
Tout le va porfendant enfressi el menton;
Li ber estort son caup, mort l'abat el sablon,
Et dist li rois Salatres, «Enchantere est cis glous!»
«Voir,» dist li rois Priant, «fuions nous ent andous!
Autretel feroit ja et de moi et de vous!» 470

14.
Dist le rois Salatrés, «Dit m'avés vilain mot.
Mahomet me confonge et maldië mon cors
Se je part del François, si savrai son confort.»
Jus de l'angarde avalent, lor escu a lor cos;
Venu sont a Elye desoz* l'onbre d'un lor, 475
Qui estoit as prisons; ce dessiroit il fort
Que fuissent desloiet,* gari fuissent de mort.
Quant cil li escrierent, qui estoient au dos:
«Cuivers, n'i touciés pas, que li François sont no!»
Quant Elyë l'entent, el destrier monte tost*; 480
Sor le targe le fierent,* sor l'escu de son col,
Il li fraint et peçoie desor le boucle a or.
Le blanc auberc del dos li desmaile et desclot,
Nu a nu li conduit son espiel ens el cors.
Dameldieu le garri, por .i. poi ne fu mors! 485
Elyë fiert si l'un, tout li tranche le cors;
Malpriant torne en fuie quant il voit celui mort,
Et Elyë l'encauche et randone mout fort;
Par le mien ensïant, ja l'encauchera trop.

---

475 ms E. desor (see note above).

Part One

The stout sword cut Elye right down to the bare flesh.
"By my head," said Elye, "you're a very brave knight!   460
Willingly you'd have killed me if you'd had the chance!
But God loves me truly and He'll always protect me!"
Elye drew his sword whose hilt was solid gold
And rode to strike the pagan high on his helmet.
The gemstones and flowers rained down to the ground,   465
And Elye split him all the way down to his chin;
The youth dealt his blow; he struck the pagan down dead
 in the sand.
And said King Salatre, "This rogue is an enchanter!"
"True," said King Malpriant, "Let's both get out of here!
He'd do the very same thing to both me and you!"   470

14.
King Salatre replied, "What a dishonorable idea you're
 suggesting to me!
May Mahomet confound me and curse me
If I leave this Frenchman before I take care of him!"
Back from the advance guard they came, their shields hanging
 from their necks;
They came to Elye in the shadow of the laurel tree,   475
Who was with the prisoners; his deepest desire was
That they might be untied and saved from death.
Then the pagans, who were following him, shouted out to him:
"Coward, do not touch them! The Frenchmen are ours!"
When Elye heard this, he sprang to his horse.   480
On the shield they struck him, upon the shield hanging
 from his neck.
They struck it and pierced it upon the gilt boss;
The white hauberk he was wearing, they rent and pierced.
The sword drove into his bare flesh;
God saved him; he very nearly died.   485
Elye struck one of them so hard that he cut through his
 whole body.
Malpriant turned to flee when he saw the other pagan dead,
And Elye took out after him, galloping in hot pursuit:
In my opinion, he'll chase Malpriant very far!

15.

Or m'escoutés, Signor, que Dieus grant bien vous doinst, 490
Li glorïeus del ciel, par son saintisme non.
Si vous dirai d'Elye qui ceur ot de baron,
Con il sieut et encauche par ire le glouton.
Il le vint ataignant, se li dist par iror: [79v-a]
«Sarrasin, c'or retorne, li cors Dieu mal te doinst! 495
Cis destriers que tu maines est isneus et cointos;
Volentiers l'en menaise, que li miens n'en est pros!»
«Vasal,» dist li paien, «trop par es coragous!
Que les roches sont hautes et li gué perillous,
Nus n'i peut trestorner ne destrier prendre cors. 500
Chi devant a .i. pré qui est biaus et herbous;
La poras trestorner et mostrer ta valor.
Se tu me peus abatre, que chië des arçons,
Remener en poras che boin destrier gascon.*
En ta vile en peus prendre .c. livres de mangons.» 505
Quant Elyë l'entent, si grant joie n'ot hon;
Dameldé reclama et son saintisme non:
«Par le vostre amistié, m'en otroiés le don!»
.Ii. liewes le rencauche a force et abandon,
Enmi .i. val l'ataint, se li dist par iror: 510
«Sarrasin, c'or retorne as convent* con avon!»
«Vasal,» dist li paien, «trop par es coragous!
Mes neveus m'as hui mort, .v. u .iiii. en .i. jor;
Or me vas rencauchant; je te tieng por bricon,
Se tu viens plus avant, tu feras grant folor, 515
Car tu troveras ja tex .x.m. conpaignon,
N'i a tel ne port hace en sa main u baston.
S'il vous pevent ataindre, senpre te tuëron!»
Quant Elyë l'entent, ne le prise .i. bouton.

16.

«Chevaliers, tu es fols!» dist li rois Malpriant, 520
«Je avoie .i. eskiec de la terre des Frans,
Que tu m'as hui tolu, par ton fier hardement!
De joster me semons et menu et sovent,

Part One

15.
Now listen, my lords, may God give you highest good,   490
The glorious heavenly One, through His most Holy Name!
I'll tell you about Elye, who had the heart of a noble knight,
How he angrily followed and pursued the scoundrel.
He caught up with him and addressed him wrathfully:
"Saracen, turn around now! May God do you harm!   495
That horse you're leading is swift and graceful;
I'd gladly capture him, since mine is no longer worthy."
"Sir knight," said the pagan, "you're far too presumptuous!
Since these rocks are high and the fords, perilous,
No one can maneuver here, nor can a charger run.   500
Up ahead there is a beautiful grassy meadow;
There you can maneuver your steed and show your valor.
If you can strike me down, so that I fall from between the saddlebows,
You can take this good Gascon warhorse;
Into your city you can take a hundred pounds of gold coins!"   505
When Elye heard him, such joy no one ever had.
He called on God, on His most Holy Name:
"Through your friendship, grant this gift to me!"
Two leagues Elye chased the pagan hard and fast;
Deep in the valley, Elye caught up with him and angrily said to him: 510
"Saracen, turn around now, as we agreed."
"Sir knight," said the pagan, "you are far too foolhardy.
Today you have killed four or five of my nephews, in one day!
And now you're pursuing me: I think you're a fool!
If you come closer now, you'll commit a great folly,   515
For you'll soon find some ten thousand of my comrades!
There's not one of them who doesn't wield a stick or battle axe.
If they can catch you, they'll surely kill you!"
When Elye heard him, he thought nothing of it.

16.
"Sir knight, you're insane!" said King Malpriant.   520
"I had a war prize from the land of the Franks,
That you took from me today through your brazen boldness.
You continually challenge me to do battle,

Ne je n'i puis torner, ne n'en ai aissement.
Tu feras grant folie, se tu vas plus avant, 525
Car tu troveras ja teux .x.m. conbatant;
Se il te pevent prendre, n'aras de mort garant!»
Tant parlerent ensamble, c'a l'ost vinrent poingnant;
Quant le voient paien, si sallent de tous sens,
As armes acorurent plus de .m. et .vii. cens. [79v-b] 530
Dameldé penst hui mais d'Elyë le vaillant!

17.
Quant ore voit Elye que Sarrasin s'aïrent,
Et les os des paiens qui envers li seguient,
Dameldé reclama, le fiex Sainte Marie,
Qu'il garisse son cors d'afoler et d'ochire. 535
Encor voit Malpriant devant lui a delivre;
Souavet va le pas, n'a mes garde d'Elye.
Quant Elyë le voit, a poi n'esrage d'ire;
Ses destriers fu mout boins, s'alaine a recuellie.
Des esperons le hurte, que li sans en defile; 540
Il le vint ataignant, lés .i. gués en .i. ille.
Grant cop li a doné sor le targe florie,
Desor le boucle a or, li desmaille et esmie.
Mout fu fors li haubers quant maille n'en eslice,*
Et la lanche fu roide, ens el gué le sovine. 545
Mout pesoit li auberc, ja noast li traïtres,
Quant Sarrasin i vinrent, la pute gent haïe;
Fors del gué le retraient, sor .i. ceval le misent.
L'enfes prist le destrier que en son ceur dessire;
Isnelement i monte, que ne se targe mie, 550
Et pendi a son col le fort targe florie,
Et prist entre ses poins .i. espiel qui brunie.
Li fers en fu a or, l'alemele acherine;
Puis hurte le destrier aval la praiërie.

---

535   ms q. garissent; the verb is emended to the logical third person singular; cf. 947.
536   ms Encore; yields a hypermetric verse, so we emend, as F & R do.

Part One

And I can neither turn away nor have any peace.
You'll be crazy if you continue any farther,   525
For you'll soon find ten thousand combatants.
If they can seize you, you'll have no protection from death!"
They continued speaking until they approached the Saracen army.
When the pagans saw Elye, they rushed out from all directions,
More than seventeen hundred ran to get their arms.   530
May God now protect Elye the valliant!

17.
Then Elye saw that the Saracens were getting angry,
And saw the army of pagans who were following him.
He called upon God, the Son of Saint Mary,
To protect him from harm and death.   535
Once more he spotted Malpriant right in front of him,
Calmly riding along, as he was no longer mindful of Elye.
When Elye saw him, he nearly lost his mind;
His noble steed had gotten its second wind,
With his spurs he pricked it so hard the blood trickled down.   540
Elye caught up with Malpriant at the ford of a stream.
Heavy blows he dealt upon his painted shield:
Upon the gilt boss; he pierced and broke it;
The hauberk was so sturdy that its mail did not yield,
And the lance was stout; into the ford it knocked him.   545
The hauberk was so heavy that soon the traitor might have drowned,
When Saracens arrived quickly, the vile, hated people!
From the ford they dragged him and placed him on a mount.
The youth seized the horse that he longed for in his heart;
Quickly he mounted it, so that he did not delay,   550
And hung from his neck the strong painted shield,
And took in his hands a gleaming sword:
Its hilt was like gold, its blade steely.
Then he spurred his charger down to the meadow.

18.
Quant Malpriant esgarde son destrier auferant, 555
Et voit sus le vasal que il par haioit tant,
Mout fierement escrie, «Franc Sarrasin vaillant!
Se l'en laissiés aler, tout somes recreant!
Ne savés le damage ne le deul qu'est si grant
Que il nous a hui fait par son grant hardement? 560
Mort nous a Salatré et le preu Rodoan,
Et Brandone* et Triacle de le terre al gaiant,
Et encor .vii. des autres de tous les miex vaillant!»
Quant le voient paien, si saillent en tous sens,
As armes en corurent plus de .m. et .vii.c., 565
Qui encauchent Elye parmi le desrubant.   [80r-a]
Mes li ber les voit bien, si esgarde et atent;
Il repaire as paien, et s'i joste sovent,
Il sist el boin destrier qui plus tost va corant
Que ne fait arbalestre, ne quarel qui destent. 570
Quant il vieut, s'est deriere, quant il vieut, s'est devant.*

19.
Or escoutés, Signor, que Dieus grant bien vous don,
Li glorïeus del ciel, par son saintisme non!
Chi vous lairons d'Elye, si dirons des prisons
Qui gisoient soz l'arbre, dolant et coreçous; 575
De samis* et de cordes orent loiés les puins.
«Dameldex,» dist Guillame, «par ton saintisme non,
Qu'avés fait del vasal qui tant est coragous,
Qu'encaucent li glouton par le pré angoisous?
Hé!* Dieus con fust grant joie, se desloié fuisons! 580
Se l'alison secore, a force et a bandon!»
A iceste parolle,* .i. vilain lor est sors,
Et portoit se cuingnie dont ot ovré le jor.
Quant il voit les paien detranchiés en l'erbous,
En fuïe vaut torner, car mout ot grant paour. 585
Et quant le voit Guillame, si l'a mis a raison*:
«Amis, parolle a moi, bachelier, jovenes hon!

---

575   ms g. sor; cf. 446, 475.

Part One

18.
When Malpriant saw his valliant steed, 555
And saw astride it the knight whom he hated so much,
Fiercely he cried, "Brave, bold Saracens!
If you let him get away, we'll all be shamed!
Don't you realize all the harm and the profound grief
That he's caused us today through his great audacity? 560
From our ranks, he's slain Salatre and the worthy Rodoan,
And Brandon and Triacle, from the land of the giants*
And seven more of the others, the most valliant warriors of all!"
When the pagans saw him, they rushed forth from all sides;
More than seven hundred ran to seize their arms, 565
And they came charging down the slope towards Elye.
But the knight saw them, and he watched and waited;
He turned back towards the pagans, and he jousted often.
He was mounted on the good steed, which galloped faster
Than a bolt shot from a cross-bow or than an arrow that is shot; 570
When he chose, he appeared behind them; when he desired,
   he was in front of them.

19.
Now listen, my lords, and may God provide well for you,
The glorious of heaven, through His most Holy Name!
Here we'll leave Elye, so we can tell you about the prisoners
Who were lying under a tree, grieving and angry. 575
With silk cords and thick wool ropes, their hands were bound.
"Lord God," said William, "by your most holy name,
What have you done with the brave knight in anguish
Whom the scoundrels were chasing through the fields?
Oh, God, what a fine joy it would be, if we were untied! 580
We'd set out to help him in full force!"
As Guillaume was saying this, a villager came towards them,
And he was carrying the hachet he had worked with that day.
When he saw the Saracens cut to pieces in the grass,
He wanted to flee, because he was very much afraid. 585
When William saw him, he called out to him at once:
"Friend, speak to me, worthy youth, young man!

Ja oras tel novele, s'en toi a point d'amor,
Dont tu auras au ceur et pitiet et dolor.
Caitif somes de Franche, et d'amis sosfraitous; 590
Sarrasin nous ont pris, droit a hui .xv. jors.
Onques puis ne fu soir ne matin nes un sous,
Ne livraissent as cors grant paine et grant dolor;
As corgiës noees nous batent cascon jor.
Or nous vient* desloier, si feras que preudon, 595
Et prent tous ces destriés qui tout sont devant nous!»
«Sire,» dist li vilains, «qu'en feroië ge dont?
N'ei tant de tous avoirs dont les peusse .i. jor;
.Vii. enfans ai a paistre, par le foi que doi vous,
Que je n'ai que je meche en la main al menor, 600
Car tous jors ai ovré a .i. maistre orgellous,
Qui me taut me deserte et delaië* tous iors!   [80r-b]
A Dameldé m'en plaing, le verai glorïous,
Qu'il me fache justice, par la soië douçour!»
Et quant l'entent Guillame, au ceur l'en prist tenror, 605
Le vilain apela, se li dist par amor:
«Or pren tous ces blïaus, ces hermins pelichon,
Si les vens* a deniers, et si soïes preudom,
Et proië Dameldé, le verai glorious,
C'ait merchi dou vassal* ques a mort hui cest jor!» 610
Quant li vilains entent le consel del baron,
Il a trait son coutel, si les delië tous.

20.
Quant Guillame d'Orenge se senti desloiés,
Por nule riens en terre ne se fesist si liés.*
Il est passés avant, si saissi .i. espiel, 615
Et jure Dameldé, le glorïeus del ciel,
«Mieus vauroit estre mors, ocis, et detranchiés,
Parmi le cors feru de .vii. tranchans espiés,
De .xxx. u de .xl., et devant et derier,

---

600   ms c. tout; we emend, following the model of 602.
602   ms e. delai; the verb form is emended to correct the hypometric verse.
604   ms l. soi d.; we emend to correct the hypometric verse, as in 602.

Part One

If there's any love in your heart, the story you will now hear
Will fill your heart with grief and pity!
We're friendless captives from France;   590
Saracens seized us two weeks ago from today.*
There's not been a single night or day
That they haven't inflicted upon us harsh grief and pain;
With knotted scourges they've beaten us every day.
Come on and untie us, and you'll be a worthy man,   595
And take all of these horses that are right there before us."
"Sir," said the peasant, "what would I do with them?
I don't have enough money to feed them for one day;
I've got seven children to feed, by the faith I owe you,
And I don't have anything to put in my youngest's hands,   600
Because I've always worked for a haughty master
Who constantly takes from me and delays my just wages.
To God I plead, the true glorious one,
To grant me justice through His mercy!"
When William heard him, tenderness flooded his heart;   605
He called out to the peasant, and he said to him out of love:
"Then take these tunics, these furs and fur-lined cloaks,
Sell them for money, and you'll be a worthy man,
And pray to God the true glorious One,
That He show mercy on the knight who died this day."   610
When the peasant heard the baron's advice,
He drew his knife and untied them all.

20.
When William of Orange felt himself unbound,
Nothing else on earth could have made him happier.
He went and quickly seized a sword,   615
And swore to God, the glorious King of heaven,
"I would rather be slain, dead and dismembered,
Stabbed through my body with seven sharp swords,
By thirty or forty, in front and behind,

Jamais par Sarrasin fuisse pris ne loiés!»　　　　　　　　620
Dist Bernart de Brubant, li kenus et li viés:
«Se je n'avoië d'armes mes c'un pel aguisiés,
S'en abatrai je .c. devant el premier cief!»
«Signor,» che dist Hernaus, «n'ai soing de manecier!
Secorons le preudome, le vaillant chevalier　　　　　　　625
Qu'encachent li gloton parmi le pui plenier!»
Et respondi Bertram, «Or oi plait qui bien siet!
Courés vous adouber, nobile chevalier!
Alés prendre les armes de ces felons paiens
Qui gisent a la tere, ochis et detrenchiés!»　　　　　　　630
Et cil ont respondu, «De gré et volentiers!»
Il sont venu as mors, si les ont despoilliés,
Et vestent les aubers, s'ont les elmes laciés,
Et çaingent les espees a lor flans senestriers,
Et monterent es seles des boins corans destriers,　　　　635
Et jetent a lor caus les escus de quartiers,
Et prissent en lor poins les rois tranchans espiés.
Parmi .i. val s'en vont poingnant tous eslaisiet.　[80v-a]

21.
Or chevalcent tout .iiii. ensanble li baron;
C'est de la flor de Franche, des millors qui i sont.　　　640
Il encontrent paien lés le costé d'un mont,
Qui encachent Elye a coite d'esperon.
A .i. gué l'ont atroint, se li toillent le cour;
Ja l'eüssent ochis, li Sarrasin fellon,
Quant Guillame d'Orenge tout .i. val lor est sours,　　　645
Il et Bertran ses niés, li vasal et li prous,
Et Bernart de Brubant, et Hernaut l'aïrous.
En la presse se fierent ensement conme lous;
La veïssiés bataille et mervellos estour,
Voler sanc et cervelle conme pleve qui court!　　　　　650
Qui Bernart de Brubant esgardast en l'estour,
Con il croille la barbe et fronce le gernon!*

642　ms a cointe; the scribe has written the word for «wise, clever» in place of «coite», or «pricks», more appropriate here.

Part One

Than ever be taken prisoner or bound by Saracens!" 620
Said Bernart of Brubant, old and white-haired,
"If I had no arms except for a sharpened stake,
I'd slay a hundred of them with my first blow!"
"My lords," said Hernaut, "I'm not one for idle threats;
Let's help the brave knight, the valiant warrior, 625
Whom the enemy are chasing over the hills."
And Bertram answered, "That's what I like to hear!
Run to put on your armor, noble knights!
Go get the arms off those foul Saracens
Who're lying on the ground, slain and cut to pieces!" 630
And they answered, "Gladly and willingly!"
They came up to the dead, and they stripped off their armor,
And put on the hauberks, and laced on the helmets,
And they girt the swords on their left sides,
And mounted on the saddles of the good, fast horses, 635
And they threw around their necks the quartered shields,
And took in their hands the sharp, stout swords.
Through the valley they went galloping off.

21.
Now all four noble knights rode off together;
They were the best there was, the flower of French knighthood! 640
They encountered pagans near a mountain side,
Who were pursuing Elye with sharp pricks of spurs.
At a ford the enemy caught up with him, and they blocked
   his way.
There they would have killed him, the evil Saracens,
When William of Orange charged out of the valley, 645
He and Bertran, his nephew, the good, bold knight,
And Bernart of Brubant and Hernaut, the fierce,
Into the press they all rushed together, like wolves.
There you'd have seen a battle and wondrous combat;
The blood flying and brains falling like rain! 650
You could see Bernart of Brubant in combat,
How he'd frown with his moustaches and thrust his beard!

Dist Jossés d'Alixandre, «Cis viex est mervellous!
C'est Artus de Bretaigne u Gavain ses nevos,
U Pilate d'enfer u Mordrant l'airous, 655
Qui mangüent les homes .v. u .iiii. en .i. jor!
Par le foi que vous doi, si fera il nous tous!
Car poignomes a l'ost, qu'il nous facent secor!»

22.
Ausi con li faucons fait les oiseus füir,
Fait Guillame d'Orenge paien et Sarrasin. 660
Elyës sist el vair que Malpriant toli,
S'il s'en vausist aller, ne doutast Sarrasin,
Mais il ne vaut François ne fauser ne güerpir;
Ains retorne sovent avoec aus por ferir,
Elyë li gentix, qui Dieus puisse garrir! 665
Sor l'escu de son col, vait ferir Salatrin,
Et Trüant de Baudas, et le preu Menalis.
.Vii. en a craventés devant lui el chemin.
Franc ne porent lor cos endurer ne sofrir,
Que lor donent entr'ax paien et Sarrasin; 670
Ains s'en tornent en fuie tout .i. feré cemin,*
Desor l'aige del lac, sor .i. antis sentir,*
La corurent François, qui la sont defüi.
Mais paien les ont si souspris et envais, [80v-b]
Il lor lancent fauçars* et boins espiels forbis. 675
Ja fuissent no François et retenu et pris,
Quant Elyë esgarde tout .i. feré chemin,*
Et voit .xx. chevalier qu'avalent .i. lairis,
Qui querroient Elye; ses peres les tramist.
Mais trop ont demoré et targié de venir; 680
Li messagier les ot deslaiés el chemin,
Que il troverent mort, si l'ont en terre mis.
Et quant les voit Elye, mout joians en devint;
De la joië qu'il ot, fait le ceval saillir,
Li destrier s'en repaire contreval le lairis, 685

---

671 ms .i. cemin; we emend the hypometric verse on the analogy of 677; and see note.

Part One

Joshua of Alexandria said, "That old man's a wonder!
He's like Arthur of Brittany, or Gawain his nephew,
Or like Pilate of hell, or the angry Mordrant,   655
Who in one day ate up four or five men!
By the faith I owe you, he'll do the same to us all!
Let's ride quickly to the army, so they can help us!"

22.
Just as the falcon sends the other birds fleeing,
So did William of Orange pursue the pagans.   660
Elye was mounted on the charger that he had taken
    from Malpriant;
How he would have liked to go on; he would not have
    feared the Saracens!
But he did not want to leave the French nor let them down.
Instead, he turned back often with them to deal blows.
Elye the noble, may God protect him,   665
Went to strike Salatrin on the shield upon his neck,
And Truant of Baudas, and the brave Menalis;
Seven of them he killed before him along the path.
The French could no longer withstand nor endure the blows
That all the pagans and Saracens were dealing them;   670
Instead, they turned in flight down the paved road.
Across the waters of a lake, down an ancient road,
There ran the French, fleeing in defeat.
But the pagans overtook them and invaded their ranks;
They hurled at them falsarts and good sharp lances.   675
Now our French would have been taken and seized,
When Elye looked all the way down the road
And saw twenty knights coming down a hillside,
Who were looking for Elye; his father had sent them.
But they had delayed too long and were late in coming.   680
The messenger had slowed them down,
When they had found him dead, they had buried him.
And when Elye saw them, he was filled with joy;
In his elation, he made his charger leap.
The horse took off again through the valley.   685

Onques Dieus ne fist beste qui si peüst tenir,
Cers ne dains ne aloe, faucon ne esmeril,
Et revient Ataignant,* .i. felon Sarrasin;
Cil fu fiex l'amiral qui le guerre maintient,
Et frere Rosamonde, c'ainc si bele ne vi. 690
Elyës laisse corre le destrier u il sist;
Vait ferir le paien devant, en l'escu bis.
Le blanc auberc del dos desront et dessarti,
Trestout parmi le cors son boin espiel li mist;
Enpoin le par vertu; mort l'abati sovin. 695
A tant e vous poignant tout .i. sentier anti
Bertram le preu, le sage, le chevalier hardi;
Sor l'escu de son col va .i. paien ferir,
Que il li a percié, et l'auberc desarti.
Le ceur qu'il ot el ventre li a en deus parti. 700
Enpoin le par vertu, mort l'abati enqui;
Et Bernars le regarde, li vieus quenu flori,
Envïeus fu del cop qu'il vit faire son fil.
Ja sera mout dolans se .i. paien n'ochist!
Sor les las de son elme va .i. paien ferir, 705
La teste en fait voler, a tout l'elme bruni.
Guillame fiert le quart, Hernaut feri le quint;
Et li .xx. chevalier ne sont pas alenti:
Cascons des .ii. barons re* .ii. paien ochis.

23.
Mout fu grant la bataille et li estor campés; [81r-a] 710
Dieus! Con i fiert Guillame, li marcis au cort nés!
Les .iiii.m. escus ont si mal atornés,
N'en fust ia nes uns seus estors ne escapés,
Quant i vint le grant force que conduist Macabrés.
Cil ont si nos François ferus et ramenés, 715

---

686 ms Onques ne; we, like F, emend the hypometric verse with the addition of «Dieus»; 686-7 are identical to 2160-1. R. likewise emends, but with the form «Dé».
706 ms f. valer; «valer» («to cause to fall») is an attested form according to Greimas, but not until the early 14th century. The scribe usually uses «voler» in this context, so we emend accordingly, as did F & R.

Part One

There never was an animal who could run so fast,
Neither deer, nor stag, nor lark, nor falcon, nor merlin.*
Elye rode back and caught up with Ataignant, a foul Saracen;
This was the son of the admiral, who was waging the war,
And the brother of Rosamonde, never was there such a
    beautiful maiden!   690
Elye let his steed run ahead at full speed;
He rushed to strike the pagan on his painted shield;
The pagan's white hauberk, Elye pierced and tore,
Through the Saracen's entire body, the youth plunged his
    good lance.
Elye thrust it vigorously, and quickly struck the pagan dead.   695
Then here came riding down an ancient path
Bertram, the bold, the wise, the brave knight.
He rushed to strike a pagan on the shield on his neck,
And he pierced it and rent the hauberk.
The heart in the pagan's chest, Bertram split in two;   700
Bertram thrust it vigorously, then struck him dead.
And Bernard watched him, the old white-bearded man;
He envied the blow that he saw his son dealing;
He would be very sorry if he didn't kill a pagan too.
Bernard rushed to strike a pagan upon his helmet's straps;   705
Bernard sent his head with its shining helmet flying.
William struck down the fourth man; Hernaut slayed the fifth,
And the twenty knights did not slow down:
Each of two knights killed two more pagans.

23.
The fighting was very heavy, and the battle raged.   710
God! How William struck blows, the short-nosed marquis!
The four thousand shields were in such desperate straits,
That not a one of them would have escaped the battle,
When there arrived the great force that Macabre led.
These struck and forced back our French so far   715

Que des .xx. chevaliers, n'en sont que .x. remés;
Les .x. autres ont pris, loiés, et atrapés.
Nostre François sont trait a .i. regort de mer;
Il escrient, «Elye, chevalier naturés!
Traiés vous envers nos, si serons plus doutés!» 720
Et il si feïst senpre, bien s'en fu apensés,
Quant i vint .i. paien quil semont de joster.
Et quant l'entent Elye, le sens quide derver;
Miex vauroit estre mors, que coars apelés.
Il hurte le destrier par andeus les costés, 725
Et a brandië l'anste de l'espiel noëlé*;
Vait ferir le paien sor son escu bouclé.
Desor la boucle a or li a fraint et quassé;
Enpoin le par vertu, si l'a mort craventé.
«Outre, quiver,» dist il, «Dieus te puist mal doner! 730
Onques li miens lignages ne pot le tien amer!»

24.
Elyës vit ses homes et pris et retenus;
Dieus, con or se demente desous son elme agu:
«Baron,» che dist Elye, «Con mar m'avés seü!
Se ne vous puis vengier, ainc si dolant ne fui!» 735
Guillame est en la presse, et Bertram avoec lui,
Et Bernart de Brubant, et Hernaut li kenu.
Il escrient, «Elye a la fiere vertu!
Ber, car te trai vers nous, si serons plus cremu!
Jamais n'en penras mort tant con en dura uns!» 740
Et il si feïst senpre, bien s'en est percheüs,
Quant i vint .i. paien qui .vii. piés ot de bu:
«Par Mahomet, François, mout es hui maintenu,
Que par nul Sarrasin ne fus hui abatu!
Va, si guerpi ta loi et ton Dieu mescreü; 745
Si croi en Mahomet qui nous fait les vertus, [81r-b]

---
718 ms n. francoit; we emend to the usual form in agreement with R. While F emends, he is unsure whether the ms reading is «t» or «c».
742 ms de u; we emend to «bu», since the context clearly means that the opponent is 7 feet tall.

Part One

That of the twenty knights, there remained only ten.
The ten others the Saracens captured, tied up and took prisoner.
Our Frenchmen all drew back to a small inlet.
They shouted, "Elye, true knight,
Draw near to us, and we'll be more formidable!"   720
And he would have done so quickly, he'd already thought of it,
When up rode a pagan who challenged him to combat.
And when Elie heard him, he nearly went mad with rage:
He'd rather be dead than called a coward.
He spurred his horse on both flanks,   725
He brandished the newelled hilt of his lance.
He rushed to strike the pagan on his bossed shield;
Upon the gilded boss, he struck and smashed it.
Then Elye thrust deep and struck him dead.
"You're finished, coward!" said he, "May God give you harm!   730
Never can my lineage love yours!"

24.
Elye saw his men captured and seized.
God, how furious was his grief, beneath his pointed helmet.
"Noble knights," said Elye, "woe to you who followed me!
Never will I grieve so, if I can't avenge you!"   735
William was in the middle of the fray, and Bertrand with him,
And Bernart of Brubant, and Hernaut the white-haired.
They shouted, "Elye, mighty knight!
Noble youth, draw closer to us, and we'll be more formidable!
You'll never meet death so long as one of us remains!"   740
And he'd have done it immediately, he'd perceived as much himself,
When a pagan arrived, who stood seven feet tall:
"By Mahomet, Frenchman, you've fought well today,
Since no Saracen has so far struck you down!
Now give up your faith and your absurd God,   745
And believe in Mahomet, who gives us strength,

Qui fait issir del fust et le flor et le fruit!»
«Va, glous!» che dist Elye, «tu es fols esperdus!
Mahon ne Apolin ne font joië ne bruit;
Ne vaut .iiii. deniers fors l'argent qui est sus, 750
Dont vous les avés tous aornés et vestus!»
Quant li paien l'entent, ainc si dolant ne fu;
Onques puis ni ot resne ne saciet, ne tenu.
Gran cos s'en vont doner es conbles des escus!
Toutes plaines lor lances se sont entr'abatu; 755
Elyë trait l'espee, qui roi Salatré fu;
Vait ferir le paien desor son elme agu.
Enfressi qu'es espaules l'a trestout porfendu;
Puis l'a mort abatu en mi le pré herbu.
Malpriant i sorvient, qui son ceval connut; 760
Il a traite l'espee, s'est a Elye* venu.
Ja li caupast le cief senpre desor le bu,
Quant Gerart li escrie, ausi pres con il fu:
«Tais, paien, nel ochie, maleois soies tu!
C'est li fieus Julïen, le hardi conneu! 765
Grant avoir en auras, s'en prison l'as tenu!»
Quant l'entent li paien, ainc si joiant ne fu;
A plus de .m. paien a il l'enfant rendu;
Se li loient les mains, que li sans en ciet jus.
Guillame est en la presse, et Bertram avoec lui; 770
Elyës lor escrie, ensi pris con il fu:
«Ber, laissiés le bataille, puis que sui retenu!
Miex aim que je seus soie et pris et retenu,
Que vous autre fuissiés ne jugié ne pendu!»
Quant Guillame l'entent, ainc si dolant ne fu; 775
A haute vois escrie, «Chevalier, qui es tu?
Encor ne te connois, mout es hui maintenu!»
«Certes,» che dist Elye, «ne me celerai plus;
Je sui fiex Julïen de Saint Gille, le duc!»
Quant Guillame l'entent, ainc si dolant ne fu; 780

---

750 ms e. sous; the expensive ornamentation of gold and silver-plate and precious gems is «on» rather than «under» the statue.
767 ms Q. lentens; obviously a scribal error for the intended «t».

Part One

Who causes the flower and the fruit to bloom upon the branch!"
"Worthless scum," said Elye, "you are a hopeless fool!
Neither Mahomet nor Apollo creates joy, nor sound,
Neither is worth four deniers, except for the silver plating   750
With which you have decorated and clothed all your idols!"
When the pagan heard him, he never had been so grieved.
After that, he'd never hold in or pull on his rein.
They'll deal each other heavy blows upon their shields!
With full force, their lances clashed together.   755
Elye drew the sword that had belonged to King Salatre;
He rushed to strike the pagan hard on his pointed helmet;
Straight down through to the shoulders Elye split him,
Then he struck the pagan dead onto the grassy field.
Malpriant rode up and recognized his mount;   760
He drew his sword and approached Elye;
Malpriant would have cut his head off above the shoulders,
When Gerart, who was nearby, cried out to him,
"Stop, pagan! Don't kill him! Damn your soul!
This is the son of Julien the famed bold knight!   765
You'll get great wealth from him, after you have taken him prisoner!"
When the pagan heard him, he had never been so joyful.
To more than a thousand pagans, he gave the youth;
They bound his hands so tightly that the blood spurted forth.
William was in the heart of the battle, and Bertram with him,   770
From his captivity, Elye shouted to them,
"Noble knights! Leave off the fight, since I've been taken prisoner!
I'd rather be taken and held captive alone,
Than see you others judged or hanged!"
When William heard him, he had never been so grieved!   775
Loudly he cried, "Bold knight, who are you?
I still don't know you; you've fought well today!"
"Truly," said Elye, "I'll no longer hide my identity:
I'm the son of Julien, the duke of Saint Gilles."
When William heard him, never had he been so grieved;   780

Elye of Saint-Gilles

A haute vois escrie, «Bertram, niés, que fais tu?
Ja est pris li vasaus qui tant a de vertu;   [81v-a]
Se l'en laisons aler, mors sons et confondu!»
Il hurte le destrier des esperons agus,
Et Bernart de Brubant, et Hernaut li chenus;   785
En le presse se fierent tout ensanble, a .i. hu.
La veïssiés bataille et estor maintenu!
Onques mais par .i. home ne fu si fier veü,
Mais ne lor vaut lor forche valissant .i. festu,
C'Elyës li vasaus est pris et retenus.   790
Et Guillame s'en torne, et Bertram avoec lui,
Et Bernart de Brubant, et Hernaut li chenus.
Sarrasin les encauchent, a force et a vertu;
Ariere s'en retornent, n'en pevent baillier un.
Et Guillame chevalce, a la fiere vertu,   795
Enfressi a Saint Gille, n'i ot resne tenu.
A la porte ont trové .i. quiver mescreü;
Prismes* parla Guillame au cor nés de Leün:
«Amis, evre la porte, que Dameldé t'aihut!
Au conte Julïen voil je mander salu!»   800

25.
Li portier fu mout fel, glous, et desmesurés;
Il ovri le guicet quant il les ot parler,
Et a coisi Guillame, le cief ot desarmés.*
Lors a parlé li glous, que Dieus puist mal doner:
«Por auteus recouvrir, ne por messe canter,   805
Ne vous fu mië faite la bouche soz le nés!*

---

785 ms l. floris. We emend on the model of 792, to maintain the assonance; R & F emend with «kenus» and «quenus», respectively.
791 ms et avoec lui Bertram, but the scribe indicated by parallel lines before «lui» and «Bertram» that the latter is to be inserted before the former, to maintain the assonance. «Avoec Bertram lui» is syntactically incorrect, and the word order must be emended.
792 ms Bernart et de; the additional abbreviation for «et» should have been expunctuated and is a scribal oversight.
800 ms c. Julie vail; the scribe omitted the nasal bar of «Julien» and, as in 706, miscopied «a» for «o» in «voil».
805 ms a reconurir, from misuse of the abbreviation «con», causing a hypermetric verse.
806 ms b. sor; cf. 446.

Part One

Loudly he shouted, "Bertram, nephew, what are you doing?
This courageous knight has just been taken;
If we let him go now, we're shamed and dead!"
He spurred his horse with sharp spurs,
And Bernart of Brubant, and Hernaut, the white-haired,   785
Into the press they struck, all together in one great hue.
There you'd have seen a battle and a combat fought!
Such ferocious fighting has never been seen since!
But all their might was worth nothing to them;
For Elye the brave knight was taken and held.   790
And William turned back, and Bertram with him,
And Bernart of Brubant, and Hernaut, the white-haired.
Saracens pursued them with might and strength.
They retreated, they could not save one man.
And William rode away, with steadfast strength,   795
All the way to Saint-Gilles, he did not hold in the reins.
At the city gate, they found an evil, miscreant gatekeeper.
First spoke William the short-nosed one from Laon:
"Friend, open the gate, may God help you!
I intend to ask for help from Count Julien!"   800

25.
The porter was evil, base and arrogant*;
He opened the spy hole when he heard them speaking.
And he spotted William, who had removed his helmet;
Then the porter spoke, the miscreant, may God give him harm:
"Not to cover altars, nor to sing mass   805
Was your mouth below your nose ever made!

Bien me samblés espie de cel autre resné,
U vous estes Guillame, li marcis au cor nés!
Or vous alés hui mais en cel bourc osteler,
Enfressi a demain, que li jor parra cler,   810
C'au conte Julïen venrés lasus parler.»
Quant Guillame l'entent, le sens quide derver;
Il hurte le destrier, qu'il vaut laiens entrer.
Li portiers saut en piés, s'a .i. baston conbré,
Ferir en vaut Guilllame, le marcis au cor nés.   815
Quant li quens l'a veü, l'escu li a torné,
Et li glous i feri, qui fu fel et irés;
.I. grant piet li fendi de l'escu noëlé.* [81v-b]
«Oncle,» che dist Bertram, «vous a il adessé?»
«Nenil,» dist il, «biaus niés, la merchi Dameldé!   820
Et Bertram passe avant, a loi de bacheler,
Le poin senestre li a el cïef mellé,
Enpoin le bien de lui, el fossé l'a jeté:
L'aigue fu grant et rade, aval l'en a mené.
Quant li fiex au portier vit son pere tüer,   825
Enfressi el palais ne se vaut arester;
A sa vois qu'il ot clere, s'est pris a escrier.

26.
Es le fil al portier ens el palais venu;
A sa vois qu'il ot haute, s'escrië par vertu:
«Julïen de Saint Gille, mout t'est mal avenu!   830
Mes peres t'a servi .xiiii. ans, voire plus,
C'onques ne li donas palefroi,* ne boin mul.
Mout malvais gueredon l'en as tu hui rendu;
C'a ta porte a trové .i. glouton mescreü!
En l'aige l'a jeté, desor le pont la jus!»   835
Quant Julïens l'entent, ainc si dolant ne fu;

---

809 ms b. oster; the context demands «osteler» which corrects the hypometric verse.
816 ms v. lesca; we emend to «escu» for the context.
833 ms a. hui The hypometric verse is emended by the addition of the pronoun; R emends similarly, while F changes the person to emend «a on», creating an unnecessary hiatus.

Part One

It looks to me like you're either a spy from that other realm,
Or else you're William, the marquis with the short nose!
Now, go ahead today and find lodging in this town,
Until tomorrow, when the dawn breaks brightly,   810
Then you can enter here to talk to Count Julien."
When William heard him, he thought that he would go mad.
He spurred his horse, for he intended to enter.
The porter jumped up and seized a staff;
He meant to strike William, the marquis with the short nose.   815
When the count saw him, he turned his shield towards him,
And the evil porter, who was cruel and angry, struck him,
A good foot down into it, he split William's newelled shield.
"Uncle," said Bertram, "did he he touch you?"
"Not at all," he said, "good nephew, by the grace of God!"   820
And Bertram sprang forward, as a young knight should,
With his left hand he grasped the porter's head,
Bertram thrust his sword into him, then threw him into
   the moat.
The water was deep and swift; it carried him downstream.
When the porter's son saw his father killed,   825
He did not stop until he got to the palace;
In a loud voice, he began shouting.

26.
The porter's son then entered the palace;
In a loud voice he shouted angrily:
"Julien of Saint-Gilles, much harm has befallen you!   830
My father served you for fourteen years or more,
Never did you give him a good mule or a saddle horse;
A very poor reward you've given him today,
For at your gate, he found a foul enemy.
Into the water he threw him, from the bridge down there!"   835
When Julien heard him, never had he been so grieved;

Il jure Dameldé qui el ciel fait vertu,
Ja n'istront de cel resne, si esteront pendu.
A tant e vous Guillame au cor nés de Leun,
Et Bernart de Breubant, et Hernaut li* kenus,　　　　840
Et montent el palais tout a .i. bruïe.*
Premiers parla Guillame au cor nés, li menbrus:
«Cil Dameldé de gloire, qui el ciel fait vertu,
Si garde Julïen, ses amis et ses drus!
Amis, je sui Guillame, ne me celerai plus,　　　　　845
Cist autre sont mi frere* qui tant sont parcreü;
C'est Bertram et Hernaus et Bernart li kenus;
Fil somes Aymeri de Nerbone au chenu.
A ta porte ai trové* .i. glouton mescreü,
Qui ne nous vaut ens metre; mout en sui irascu;　　850
En l'aigue l'avons geté,* desor le pont la jus.
Certes, car d'une cosse m'ere mout irascus:
Qu'Elyës li vasaus est pris et retenus!
Mais selonc l'aventure, nous est bien avenu.»　[82r-a]
Quant Julïen l'entent, ainc si dolant ne fu;　　　　855
La dame chiet pasmée, qui tenüe ne fu.
Julïen l'en redreche, li vieus et li kenu.
«Dame,» che dist li dus, «mal nous est avenu,
C'Elyes nos chiers fieus est pris et retenus!
Mais selonc l'aventure, nous est bien avenu,　　　860
Quant cil sont escapé, qui tant ont de vertu:
Par ceus aurai Elye, ja si bien n'ert tenu.»
Il a dit a ses homes, «Car levés sus!*
Che sont mi droit signor, a Dieu ren ge salu!»
Guillamë* ai mandé a Rains u a Leun,　　　　　　865
Au riche roi Loeys, que secor li aiüt,
Et cil li amena .xl.m. escus.
Aymeri de Nerbone est au secor venus,
Tant en a asamblé, .c.m. sont et plus.
Chi lairons de Guillame au cor nés, le menbru,　　870

---

841   ms .i. bruis. See note.

Part One

He swore to God who rules in heaven,
That the slayers would never leave this realm, but would
   be hanged.
Just then William appeared, the short-nosed one from Laon,
And Bernart of Breubant, and Hernaut the white-haired.   840
And they entered the palace together, all at once.
First spoke William the short-nosed, the valiant:
"May God of glory, the just Ruler of heaven,
Protect Julien, his friends and his loved ones!
My friend, I am William; I'll not hide my identity.   845
These other stalwart lads are my brothers:
This is Bertram, and Hernaut, and Bernart the white-haired.
We are the sons of Aymeri of Narbonne, with the hoary mane.
At your gate I found a foul vermin,
Who refused to let us in; I was furious about it!   850
Into the water I hurled him, from the bridge down there,
Truly, for I was outraged about one thing:
That the valiant Elye is captured and held prisoner;
But, as things happened to turn out, they went better for us."
When Julien heard him, he had never felt such grief.   855
The lady, who wasn't able to stay standing, collapsed in a faint;
Julien lifted her up, the old white-haired man:
"My lady," said he, "misfortune has befallen us,
Since Elye, our beloved son, has been captured and held
   prisoner;
But fortunately, things have turned out well for us,   860
Since these valliant men have escaped,
Thanks to these men, I'll get Elye back, no matter how closely
   he's guarded!"
He said to his men, "On your feet!
These are my rightful lords; to God, I give thanks!"
William sent to Reims or to Laon   865
To mighty King Louis to seek his help;
And the king sent forty thousand shields.
Aymeri of Narbonne came to their aid,
So many did he assemble that there were a hundred thousand
   and more.
Here we'll leave the short-nosed brave William,   870

Si diromes d'Elye a la fiere vertu,
Que Sarrasin enmainent, li quiver mescreü!
Dist Jossés d'Alixandre, «Mal nous est avenu,
Quant cil sont escapé, qui tant ont de vertu!
Or vauront repairier, dusc'a .vii. jors au plus, 875
S'auront* en lor conpaigne plus de .xx.m. escus.
Nus ne dura vers aus, car trop ont de vertu.
Car issons de lor terre, ains que soions veü!»
Et cil ont respondu, «Cis consaus ert creü.»
Il vinrent a la nef,* u la navië fu, 880
Ens el font d'une barge getent Elye jus;
Se li loient les mains, que li sans en ciet jus.*

---

871 ms s. dirons, yielding a hypometric verse, correctible with the characteristic Picard form of the future, as attested in *Aiol* and commented upon by Gossen (p. 136). Both forms exist in the Picard scripta.
876 ms saveront; we emend to the more often found «s'auront» to correct the hypermetric verse; v. note.

Part One

And we will tell of the steadfast, valorous Elye,
Whom Saracens were taking away, the faithless scum!
Said Joshua of Alexandria, "Misfortune has befallen us,
Since those men escaped, who have such great valor!
Now they'll try to come back in a week at the most, 875
And they will have at their sides more than twenty thousand shields!
Nobody can withstand them, for they're far too mighty warriors!
Let's get out of their land before we're spotted!"
And the pagans replied, "That's a good idea!"
They reached the ship, where the fleet was waiting. 880
Into the hold of a ship, the pagans threw Elye down,
And they tied his hands, so that the blood ran down.

Elye of Saint-Gilles

Part Two

27.
Or s'en tornent paien, que li cors Dieu maldie,   [82r-b]
Qui les .vi. chevaliers enmainent, et Elye;
Il se poignent* en mer, si se boutent de rive,   885
Et trespassent Baudas et le terre d'Ongrie.
A senestre, laissierent Romaigne et Femenie,*
Et a destre, laissierent la chité de Rousie,
Et virent les palais et les herbergeries,
Les tors vielles et droites, qui vers le ciel baulient.*   890
Macabré, l'amiral, ne s'aseüra mie;
Devant lui fait venir no François a delivre.
Il a traite l'espee, qu'il les voloit ochire,
Quant i vint Josïas, qui d'Irlande estoit sire:
«Por Mahon, Amirals, ne les ochiés mie!   895
Ja ai ge fait por vous mainte chevalerie,
Tante lanche brisie, tante espee croissie;
Onques n'en euc del vostre vaillant une angevine!
Donés moi les François en la moië baillie,
Je les ferai mener en Irlande, ma vile;   900
Ferai lor aourer Mahomet et ses idles,...»*
«A mollier li donrai Rosamonde ma fille,
La plus bele pucele de toute paienie,*
Et si nel voillent faire, livré sont a martire!»
Macabré, l'amiral, ne s'aseüra mie;   905
Devant lui fait venir Mahomet et ses idles.
Covert fu d'un brun paile, por le caut qui l'aigrie;
Derier* fu apoiés, d'un arbre de Surie,
Que de devant ne versse, ne de derier, ne plie,
Ensi encortiné conme feme en gesine.   910

---

894 ms d. lande, emended following 900.
898 ms v. une. The decasyllable is emended to a dodecasyllable, on the model of 937.
901 ms s. indeles, yielding a false assonance and a hypermetric verse.
906 ms s. ideles; cf. 901.
909 ms d. deriere, which makes the verse hypermetric. We emend on the model of 908.
910 ms feme gesine. The scribe inadvertently omitted the preposition.

A Chanson de Geste

Part Two

27.
Now the pagans turned back, may God curse them,
Who were leading away the six knights and Elye.
They quickly set out to sea and rushed away from the shore, 885
And they passed Baux and the land of Hungary*;
On their left, they passed Romania and Femenie,
On the right, they passed the city of Rusa,
And saw the palaces and the great lodgings,
The upright, old towers that reached up towards heaven. 890
Macabre, the ruler, felt uneasy;
He quickly had our Frenchmen brought before him.
He drew his sword, intending to kill them,
When Josias stepped forward, who was lord of Ireland:
"By Mahomet, admiral, don't you dare kill them! 895
For you, I've done so many deeds of chivalry,
Broken so many lances, crossed so many swords;
Never have I taken one angevine of yours!
Hand the Frenchmen over to me;
I'll have them brought to Ireland, my city, 900
I'll have them worship Mahomet and his idols...."
"I'll give him Rosamonde, my daughter, in marriage,
The most beautiful maiden in all the pagan lands!
And if they refuse, they'll be martyrs!"
Macabre the emir felt uneasy; 905
He quickly had Mahomet and his idols brought before him.
The statue was covered with a brown cloth, because of the heat that bothered it;
It was propped up from behind by a Syrian tree,
So that it would not tip forward nor fall backward,
Thus it was cloaked like a pregnant woman! 910

Plus de .m. Sarrasin l'aourent et aclinent;
Macabré, l'amiral, l'aouroit il meïsmes.
Il garde devant lui, si a coisit Elye
Qui avoit en son dos une bronge trellie*;
Il n'ot point en son cief de hiaume de Pavie,   915
Sarrasin li tolirent tantost, con il le prissent.
Il est passés avant, les .ii. poins li delie,
Et le prist par le main, a Mahomet le guie:
«Or me di, Crestïens, par le toi baptestire,* [82v-a]
Veïs mes, chevaliers, si biaus dieu, ne si riche?*   920
Il me done trestout quanque voil et desire.
Quant je voil, il me guie el resne de Surie,
U en cel de Baudas, u en cel d'Aumarie.»
Quant Elyë l'entent, ne peut müer, n'en rie:
«Caitis rois orgellous! Li cors Dé te maldie!   925
Por coi tiens tu a dieu une cose falie?*
Il n'en a ame el cors, ne parolle, ne vie!
Quil feroit .xv. cos d'un baston lés l'oïe,
Il ne l'en feroit ja, ne maltalent, ne ire,
Ne n'en grongeroit ja, ne plus que une bisse!   930
Car pleüst ore a Dieu, le fieus Sainte Marie,
Que l'eüsse en Provenche, ens el mostier Saint Gille;
Il auroit ja brisiet le nés et les orilles;
J'en osteroië l'or et les pieres plus riches,
Sodoier les donroie, ses en feroië riche,   935
Puis, vous venroie seüre, o mout grant ost banie;
Je ne vous laisseroie vaillant une angevine!»
Quant l'amiraus l'entent, a poi n'esrage d'ire;
Il vint a Mahomet, se li a pris a dire:
«Gentiex dieus de boin aire, ne vous en poist il mie,   940
D'ou François orgellous, qui si vous contralie?*
Tenés la moië foi, vous sera ja plevie;
J'en prendra la venganche, mes que je vienge a vile!

---

920 ms m. si. The hypometric verse can be emended with the addition of a form of address previously used by a Saracen to a Christian, i.e. 296. See note.
925 ms d. de; we emend to the logical pronoun, «te».
933 ms l. orelles, emended here for the -i assonance, on the model of 1002.

Part Two

More than one thousand Saracens bowed down to it and worshiped.
Macabre the emir worshiped it himself.
He looked out and saw Elye,
Who had on his back a decorated shield;
On his head he was not wearing his helmet from Pavia. 915
The Saracens had taken it from him as soon as they captured him.
Macabre rushed forward; he untied Elye's two hands,
Took him by the hand and led him to Mahomet:
"Now swear to me, Christian, by your baptism,
Did you ever before see such a handsome or powerful god? 920
He gives me whatever I want and desire.
When I want it, he helps me rule the kingdom of Syria
Or the realms of Bagdad or Aumarie."
When Elye heard him, he could neither move nor laugh:
"Wretched, arrogant king, may God curse you! 925
Why do you hold as a god this empty thing?
It has no soul in its body, nor words, nor life.
If someone dealt it fifteen blows with a stick against the side of its head,
It wouldn't show any anger or ill-will,
It wouldn't even growl as much as a bitch! 930
Now, if it were to please God, Son of Holy Mary,
That I might have it in Provence, in the Church of Saint Gilles,
It would already have its nose and ears smashed.
I'd take off the gold and its most costly gems.
I'd give them to mercenaries and make them rich. 935
Then I'd come against you, having assembled an enormous army.
I'd leave you nothing worth one angevine."
When the emir heard him, he nearly went mad with rage.
He went to Mahomet and began to pray,
"Good, noble god, may it not offend you at all, 940
That this arrogant Frenchman is taunting you so!
You have my allegiance; it will be always pledged to you!
I'll take vengeance for this outrage before I reach the city!

Paien, drechiés les forces! Mahomet vous maldie!
Ja mora li François, n'ert consaus de sa vie!»   945
Quant l'entendi Elye, n'a talent qu'il en rie;
Dameldé reclama, le fiex Sainte Marie,
Qu'il garisse son cors d'afoler et d'ochire.
Ançois que il soit vespre, ne soneë conpliee,
Ara paör de mort, d'afoler, et d'ochire.   950
Encor voit Malpriant devant lui a delivre,
Qui tenoit le destrier que il toli el ile*;
Bien estoit enfrenés, et la sele estoit mise;
Il le tient par le resne, .i. paien le delivre.
Quant Elyë le voit, a poi n'esrage d'ire;   [82v-b]   955
Dameldé reclama, le fieus Sainte Marie:
«Dameldieus, Sire pere, con hui main estoi riches,
Quant je che boin destrier avoie en ma baillie!
Car le me rendés ore, Dame Sainte Marie!
Certes, miex voil morir a espeë forbie,   960
Que je nel aie* anqui en la moië baillie!»
Par mi lieu* de la nef, a sa voie aquellie;
Il fiert si le paien, qui le tient lés l'oïe,
Que la char li blecha, et les os li debrisse.
Devant lui l'abat mort, en le nef le sovine.   965
Lors a pris le destrier, que en son ceur desire,
Isnelement s'en torne, que ne se targe mie;
Il s'est ferus en l'aigue* qui cort de grant ravine.
Li destriers fu mout boins, qui se noe a delivre;
Il est venus a* terre en une praïërie.   970
A sa vois qu'il ot clere, hautement li escrie:
«Paien, or m'en vois je, li cors Dieu te maldie!
Et vous drechiés les forces enmi le praïërie,
Si pendés li un l'autre, malvaise gent aïe!»
Quant l'amiraus l'entent, a poi n'esrage d'ire;   975
Il vient a Mahomet, se li a pris a dire:
«Gentiex dieus deboinaires, entent que je voil dire;

---

952   ms el lile. See note.
967   ms n. targe. The hypometric verse is emended by adding the reflexive pronoun for its parallelism with the first hemistich of 967, and what follows in 968. R uses the subject pronoun «que il».

Part Two

Pagans, prepare your arms! Elye, may Mahomet curse you!
Now the Frenchman will die; there's no saving his life!" 945
When Elye heard this, it did not make him feel like laughing.
He called on the Lord God, the Son of Saint Mary,
That he might protect him from harm and death.
Before it is vespers, or compline sounds,
He'll fear dying, being wounded and being killed. 950
He spotted Malpriant standing free before him,
Holding the steed Elye had taken from him on the island.
It was well-bridled and saddled.
Malpriant was holding it by the reins; a pagan was giving it to him.
When Elye saw that, he was nearly enraged; 955
He called on the Lord God, the Son of Saint Mary:
"Lord God, Father, this morning I was rich,
When I had in my possession that good horse.
Please give it back to me now, lady, Saint Mary;
Truly, I would rather die by a sharp sword 960
Than not have it this day in my possession."
Through the middle of the ship, he made his way;
He struck the pagan, who held it, so hard on the
   side of his head
That he slashed his flesh and shattered his bones.
Elye struck him down before him, dead in the ship, 965
Then he seized the warhorse, his heart's desire.
Quickly he departed, he did not hesitate an instant.
He plunged into the swiftly flowing water.
The warhorse was very good, for it swam with ease.
He came ashore at a field. 970
In his strong voice, he shouted loudly:
"Pagan, now I'm leaving, may God curse you!
Now draw up your armies amid the field,
And go hang yourselves, evil, hated people!"
When the emir heard him, he nearly roiled with anger. 975
He came to Mahomet and began to pray to him,
"Good, noble god, listen to what I'm going to say

D'ou François orgellous, qui tant te contralie,
Fai le moi arester la devant, a cel rive!
Se nel fais arester, n'as consel de ta vie; 980
Je t'arai ja brisiet le nés et les narines!»*
Quant che voit Macabré,* c'ades s'en vait Elye,
Il vient a Mahomet, se li a pris a dire:
«Gentiex dieus deboinaire, or ai ma foi mentie;
Car li François s'en va; je nel ataindrai* mie!» 985
Il hauce le poing destre, si le fiert lés l'oïe,
Qui la mout mal mené, et trestout le debrise;
Devant lui l'abati, en la nef le sovine,
Que tuit le escarboncle fors del cief li saillierent.
Quant Sarrasin le voient, a poi n'esragent d'ire; 990
Vienent a Macabré, se li ont pris a dire: [83r-a]
«Caitis rois orgellous! por coi nous contralie,
Qui si bas nostre dieu et confons et justiche?
Se tu ne l'en fais droit, n'ert consaus de ta vie:
Tu t'en veras contrais, ains l'eure de conplie!» 995
Quant l'amiraus l'entent, durement s'umelie;
Il vient a Mahomet, .c. fois merchi li crie:
«Gentiex dieus deboinaire, ne vous en poist il mie!
Certes que j'ere plains et de corous et d'ire!
Tenés, je vous frai droit a la vostre devise; 1000
Je vous donrai .m. mars, mes que je vieng a vile,
Dont je vous referai le nés et les orilles!»*
Il a pris son gant destre, ens el puin li afice.

28.
«Signor,» dist l'amiraus, «malement sui bailliés!
Chou que tieng a mes poins, ai geté a mes piés! 1005
J'eusse encor le Franc, se ne fust desloiés!»
Il en a apelé Baligant et Gontier:
«Vous serés .iiii.xx. sor les corans destriers,
Si m'en irés de cha nobile chevalier;

---
982   ms v. Malpriant. See note.
989   The copyist misplaces the nasal bar on the wrong side of the «b»; the word is clearly meant to be «escarboncle.»

Part Two

About the arrogant Frenchman, who mocks you so:
Make him stop for me, right here before this shore!
If you don't make him stop, there'll be no saving your life!   980
I'll have your nose and your nostrils broken!"
When Macabre saw that Elye was getting away,
He came up to Mahomet, and he began to address him:
"Good, noble god, now I have belied my faith,
Because the Frenchman is getting away; I'll never catch him!"   985
He raised his right fist and struck the side of its head,
So that he caused it much damage and shattered it everywhere;
He knocked it away from in front of him, down into the ship,
So that all the carbuncles* went flying from its head.
When the Saracens saw this act, they nearly went mad
   with rage: 990
They came to Macabre, and they began to address him:
"Wretched, vain king, why are you mocking us,
By defiling and bringing our god so low?
If you don't set things right, there'll be no saving your life!
You'll be avenged before the hour of compline."   995
When the emir heard this, he was deeply humbled.
He came to Mahomet; he begged him for mercy a hundred
   times:
"Good, noble god, don't take offense!
Truly, I was full of anger and rage.
Listen, I'll make things right for you any way you want.   1000
I'll give you a thousand marks before I get to the city,
Which I'll use to redo your nose and your ears."
He took his right glove; in Mahomet's hand he affixed it.*

28.
"My lords," said Macabre, "I've been robbed.
What I held in my hands, I've dashed at my feet.*   1005
I'd still have the Frenchman, if he hadn't been untied!"
He called forth from his knights Baligant and Gontier:
"You'll get eighty men on most swift warhorses,
And you'll set forth for me, noble knights,

Elye of Saint-Gilles

Se trovés le François, mors soit et detranciés,   1010
Il n'a port en ma terre u il soit herbergiés,
Qu'il ne soit senpre mors, u tués, u noiés!»
Et cil li respondirent, «De gré et volentiers!»
Isnelement et tost s'en vont aparellier;
Il vestent les aubers, lacent elme d'achier,   1015
Et çaingent les espees, et montent es destriers,
Et pendent a lor caus les escus de quartiers,
Et prendent en lor poins les rois trancans espiés.
Tout droit apres Elye s'en sont tout eslaissié.

29.
Signor, desous Sobrie sont paien arivé;   1020
Et Elyë s'en vait, qui lor est escapé.
Toute nuit chevalça, parmi le gaut ramé.*
A iceste parolle,* a son vis trestorné,
Contre la lune garde, qui jetoit grant clarté,
Et vit les Sarrasin sor les destriers armés,   1025
Devant trestout* les autres, vint le rois Codroés.
A sa vois qu'il ot haute, se prist a escrier: [83r-b]
«Par Mahomet, François, or avés mal alé!
Je vous renderai pris mon signor Macabré,
Et si fera de vous toutes ses volentés!   1030
Il vous pendra a forques, u noiëra en mer!»
Et respondi Elye, «Dan glous, vous i mentés!
Venistes vous me quere por tel cose trover?
Par selonc le merite, le loier en aurés!»
Il hurte le destrier des esperons dorés,   1035
Vait ferir sor l'escu le fort roi Codroé;
Desor la boucle d'or, li a fraint et quassé,
Et le hauberc del dos desront et desclavé.*
Tant con anste li dure, l'abati mort el pré.
A tant e vous poignant Sarrasin et Escler,   1040
Et trevent chelui mort; n'osent avant aler.
Cele nuit gut Elye dedens le gaut ramé;

1023 ms v. trestone; we emend to correct the scribal error. R believed that the scribal orthographic confusion is partly due to the fact that the «r» was not pronounced in Picard.

Part Two

And find the Frenchman. I want him killed and cut to pieces! 1010
There's no port in my land where he'll be given shelter,
Where he won't instantly be put to death, killed or drowned!"
And these knights replied, "With pleasure and gladly!"
Immediately and quickly they began to arm themselves.
They put on their hauberks, laced on their steel helmets, 1015
Girded on their swords and mounted their war horses,
And hung their quartered shields on their necks,
And took in their hands their stout, sharp swords.
Straight after Elye they all raced.

29.
My lords, the pagans arrived below the walls of Sobrie,* 1020
And Elye rode on, who had escaped them.
All night he rode through the dense forest.
At this point, he turned his head quickly,
Towards the moon he peered, which was casting bright light,
And he spotted the Saracens, armed on their warhorses. 1025
Ahead of all the other pagans came King Codroe.
In his loud voice, he began to shout:
"By Mahomet, Frenchman, this time you've made a mistake!
I'll give you back to my lord Macabre,
And he'll do whatever he wants with you 1030
He'll hang you from the gallows, or drown you in the sea!"
And Elye answered, "Sir worthless, you're lying!
Did you come looking for me just to tell me that?
According to your merit, you'll have your reward!"
He spurred on his steed with gilded spurs. 1035
He struck upon his shield the mighty King Codroe;
Upon the boss of gold, he struck and smashed it,
And the hauberk he was wearing, Elye pierced and tore.
He thrust his lance to its breaking point and struck him
   dead in the field.
Just then came riding up Saracens and Slavs. 1040
When they found King Codroe dead, they did not dare go ahead!
That night Elye slept in the dense wood.

Ne but ne ne manga, ne li fu apresté;
Ses chevals ne gousta de feure ne de blé.
Jusques a le matin, que li jor parut cler,*   1045
Qu'Elyes se leva, quant il vit le clarté;
Il est issus del bos, s'est entrés en .i. pré,*
Dameldé reclama, et la soie bonté:
«Dameldieu,» fist il, «pere qui me fesistes né,
Je ne mangai de pain, bien a .iii. jors passé.   1050
Puis a je tant maint cop recheü et doné;
Vous me donés hui hon qui me doinst a disner.»
A iceste parolle, a gardé en .i. pré,
Et vit .iiii. larons sous un arbre aresté;
Si partoient avoir qu'il avoient enblé: 1055
Murgale de Turnie l'ont tolu et robé.
Cil orent .i. mangier mervelleus a presté:
De .ii. paons rostis, et d'un cisne enpevré,
Et .ii. gastieus tous blans de forment buleté,
Et .ii. boucieus tous plains de vin et de claré.   1060
Quant Elyë les voit, cele part est alés,
Sor le corant destrier est cele part tornés;
Et avoit en son dos .i. blanc auberc safré,   [83v-a]
Et ot çainte l'espee qui fu roi Salatré.
N'ot point ens en son cief de vert elme gesmé: 1065
Sarrasin li tolirent, quant fu enprisonés.
Quant li laron le voient, mout en sont esfraé;
Espïé quident estre; si sont en piés levé,
Por lor cors a desfendre, sont mout bien apresté.
«Signor,» che dist Elye, «mië ne vous doutés!   1070
De moi n'aves vous garde, si me garrisse Dés!»
Il a geté sor l'erbe son fort escu bendé,
Son boin destrier corant, atacha a .i. pel;
Venus est as larons, si les a salués:
«Cil Dameldé de gloire, qui en crois fu penés,   1075
Cil vous gart, biaus Signor, se vous en lui creés!
Et se vous ne creés Jhesu de majesté,
Cil Sires vous confonge, qui en crois fu penés!»
Et li laron se taissent, que n'i ont mot soné*;

Part Two

No food or drink was prepared for him.
His horse did not taste hay or wheat,
Until the morning, when the day dawned brightly. 1045
Then Elye arose when he saw the daylight.
He rode out of the woods, and he entered a field.
He called on the Lord God and on his goodness:
"Lord God," he prayed, "Father, who caused me to be born,
I haven't eaten bread for at least three days now. 1050
Since then I've given and received many blows.
Send me today someone who'll give me food to eat."
After saying this, he looked into a field,*
And saw four thieves who had stopped beneath a tree
And were dividing up the wealth that they had stolen. 1055
Murgale of Turnie they'd robbed and pillaged.
These men had prepared a marvelous meal
Of two roasted peacocks and peppered swan
And two plump white cakes made of sifted wheat
And two goatskins bulging with wine and claret. 1060
When Elye saw them, he rode in their direction.
On his swift steed, he turned towards them quickly.
He was wearing a white, fur-lined hauberk,
And he'd girded on the sword that had been King Salatre's,
But he wasn't wearing his green, gemmed helmet. 1065
The Saracens had taken it from him when he was taken prisoner.
When the thieves saw him, they became very much afraid.
They thought he was a spy, and they sprang to their feet;
They were well-prepared to defend themselves.
"My lords," said Elye, "don't be at all afraid! 1070
Don't let me worry you, so help me God!"
He threw down onto the grass his strong painted shield;
His good, swift warhorse he attached to a post.
He approached the thieves and greeted them:
"May Lord God of glory who suffered on the cross 1075
Protect you, good lords, if you believe in him!
And if you don't believe in Jesus of majesty,
May the Lord who suffered on the cross confound you!"
And the thieves kept so quiet they didn't say a word.

Li maistre des larons s'en est en piés levés; 1080
Il a dit a Elye, «Vasal, vous que querrés,
Quant n'avés avoec vous sergant ne bacheler?»
«Sire,» che dist Elye, «je nel puis amender;
Nés sui de douche Franche, de mout grant parenté.
Guillames est mes oncles, li marcis au cor nés, 1085
Mes grans sire Aymeri de Nerbone sor mer,
Et sui fieus Julïen de Saint Gille, le ber.
Paien et Sarrasin m'orent enprissoné;
Par ma fiere proeche, lor suië* escapés.
Or ne mangai de pain, bien a tier jor passés; 1090
Or voi chi le mangier garni et apresté,
Certes, g'en mangerai, qui qu'en doië pesser!»
Ains ne demanda aige por ses mains a laver;
Au mangier s'est assis, sans congiet demander.
Tant ne sorent li dui ne taillier ne haster, 1095
Con Elyë manga, qu'il l'avoit dessiré.
Quant li maistres le voit, se li a escrié:
«Par icel saint apostle c'on quiert en Norron pré,
Por widier escuële, ne por anap torner,* [83v-b]
Millor mains que les vostres, ne poi onques trover! 1100
Chevalier, tu es fols, che sache de verté,
Qui mangus no vitaille, si ne nous en sés gré!
Mes par* le foi que doi mes conpaignons porter,
N'avés mangiet morsel, qui le col ait passé,
Ne vous caust anque nuit .i. marc d'or, cuit pessé*!» 1105
«Sire,» che dist Elye, «merchi, por l'amor Dé!
Encore est cis mangiers, s'il vous plaist, a conter!
Certes, je sui tous prest de mon escot livrer,
U je païerai tout, se vous le conmandés!»
Et dist a l'autre mot, li gentiex baceler, 1110
«Con est ciers chis pais, envers cel u fui nés!
L'autre jor,* fui en Franche, a Paris la chité,

1095 ms d.taillier; the emendation restores the negative accidentally omitted by the scribe and corrects the hypometric verse.
1103 ms M. pa; we use same spelling used throughout the manuscript for this formulaic expression, so often encountered. However, see the note.

Part Two

The master of the thieves stood up; 1080
He said to Elye, "Knight, what do you want,
Since you have no servant nor squire with you?"
"My lord," said Elye, "I can't help it.
I was born in sweet France of a very great family:
William is my uncle, the short-nosed marquis*; 1085
My grandfather's Aymeri of Narbonne by the sea*;
And I'm the son of Julien of Saint Gilles, the nobleman.
Pagans and Saracens had taken me prisoner.
Through my knightly prowess, I escaped them.
For three full days now, I haven't eaten bread 1090
And before me I see this meal, all prepared and readied.
I'm determined to have some, no matter whom it offends."
Without asking for water to wash his hands,
He sat down to the meal without asking leave.
The two thieves couldn't get him to stop or hurry him along, 1095
Until Elye had eaten as much as he wanted.
When the master saw this, he cried out to him:
"By that holy saint pilgrims pray to in Nero's fields,
For emptying a bowl, or for draining a cup,
Better hands than yours could never be found! 1100
Sir knight, you're foolish. Know this for a fact:
That you're so hungry for our food that you don't thank us
  for it.
But by the loyalty that I owe to my companions,
You have not swallowed a morsel that has gone down your
  throat
That will not cost you tonight a mark of solid gold." 1105
"Sir," said Elye, "mercy, for the love of God!
This meal hasn't been tallied up yet, if you please!
Of course, I'm fully prepared to pay my share,
Or I'll pay for it all, if you command me."
And the noble young knight added something else: 1110
"How expensive this country is, compared to where I was born!
Recently, I was in France, in the city of Paris;

Por .c. saus de deniers, en eüsse autretel!
Or, prendés de mon dos mon hermin engolé,
Qui bien cousta .c. mars, quant je fui adoubés, 1115
Il n'a que .iiii. jors, par le foi que doi Dé,
C'on* me fist chevalier, mout l'oc en grant chierté,
Julïen de Saint Gille, mes peres, li senés.
.C. saus valent les gones,* de deniers monaés;
Et se me clamés quite; grant aumoisne ferés.» 1120
Et dist li maistre leres, «De folïe parlés!
Ne vous coutera gaires, se vous* i l'oist parler;
Cel destrier coureor, que voi la aresné,
Cel auberc de cel dos, et cel branc del costé,
Cel hermin peliçon, cel bliaut engoulé; 1125
Tous nus piés et en langes, a ton col .i. grant pel,
Trestous seus en irés, tout le chemin feré!
Et se tu chou n'otroies volentiers et de gré,
Ja seras tant batu, jel te di par verté,
Dont li caup te vauront .i. destrier sejorné!» 1130
Quant Elyë l'entent, le sens quide derver;
Maintenant respondi, car le ceur ot iré.

Part Two

For a hundred sous I'd have had a meal like this!
So, take off my back my fur-collared ermine,
Which cost fully a hundred marks when I was knighted.* 1115
It was only four days ago, by the allegiance that I owe God,
That I was knighted by someone who meant so much to me,
Julien of Saint-Gilles, my father, the wise old man.
Its skirts are worth a hundred sous of minted deniers,
And if you say we're even, you'll do a generous act of charity." 1120
And the master thief said, "What you're saying is absurd!
It won't cost you much at all, if you can stand to hear it:
That swift steed there, which I see bridled up,
That hauberk you're wearing and that steel blade at your side,
That ermine cloak and that long fur-lined tunic. 1125
Barefoot and in rags, with a great staff hanging from
   your neck,*
All alone you'll go down the paved road.
And if you don't grant this gladly and willingly,
You'll be beaten so much — I'm telling you the truth —
You'll think these blows were worth a fresh warhorse." 1130
When Elye heard him, he thought he'd go mad.
Now came his answer, from a heart seething with anger.

Elye of Saint-Gilles

Part Three

30.
Elyës li vasal, qui tant fait a prissier, [84r-a]
Respondi as larons, que Dieu doinst enconbrier!
«Fil a putain! glouton!» dist Elyë li fier, 1135
«Quant je vous trovai ore chi illeuc a mangier,
Quidai que vous fuissiés sergant u chevalier,
Ou marcheant prodome, et d'avoir enforcié,
Qui seüssent prodome servir et a aisier.
Or voi que laron estes, leceor pautonier, 1140
Si me volés tolir iert auferant destrier.
Se j'en eüsse .i. autre, quite vous fust laissiés,
Mais je sui fiex a conte, ne sai aler a piet,
Julïen de Saint Gille, le nobile guerrier.
Seés vous or tout coi, que ne s'en meüe piet; 1145
Par le foi que je doi al Glorïeus del ciel,
Il n'i a cel de vous si hardi, ne si fier,
S'il se dreçoit amont, por mes resnes baillier,
Quant li partroit de moi, ja mes ne seroit liés!
Autre force i convient, por mon cors justichier.» 1150
Li mestres des larons s'en est mout corecié;
Il tenoit en sa main .i. baston de pumier*;
Ferir en vaut Elye, parmi le crois del cief.
Li enfes fu mout sages, qui bien se sot gaitier;
Il haucha le poing destre, qu'il ot gro et plenier, 1155
Venus est au laron, .i. ruiste cop le fiert:
Le maistre os de la geule li a parmi brisiet,
Que mort l'a abatu, devant lui a ses piés.
Puis a pris en son poing le baston de pumier, [84r-b]
Si fort en feri l'autre, mort l'abat a ses piés. 1160
Et li tiers torne en fuie, enmi le bos se fiert.
Galopin fu li mieudres,* se li cheï as piés,

1145   ms v. ore, gives a hypermetric verse.

A Chanson de Geste

Part Three

30.
Elye, the knight, who'd displayed such prowess,
Answered the thieves, whom God ought to punish:
"Whore's son, worthless good-for-nothing!" said Elye
   the proud,   1135
"When I found you here eating a while ago,
I mistook you for foot-soldiers or knights,
Or worthy merchants of great wealth,
Who'd be able to serve and comfort a worthy man.
Now I see that you're thieves, cowardly gluttons,   1140
And you want to steal my fine warhorse.
If I had another one, I'd freely leave it with you;
But I'm the son of a count, Julien of Saint-Gilles,
The noble warrior, and it's unthinkable that I would
   travel on foot.
Now sit there quietly; no one move a muscle.   1145
I swear to the glorious King of Heaven,
There's not one of you so brave or so bold
That, if he stands up to seize my reins,
Once I'd finished with him, he'd never be happy again!
It'll take more force than you've got to handle me!"   1150
These words made the master of the thieves very angry.
He was holding in his hand an apple-wood club;
He attempted to bash Elye over the head with it.
The youth was very intelligent and knew how to look
   after himself.
He raised the great mass of his right fist,*   1155
He came up to the thief, struck him with a fierce blow,
And the main bone of his throat he cracked in two.
Elye struck him so hard that he fell dead at his feet.
Then he picked up the apple-wood club,
And he violently smashed the other thief; he struck him
   dead at his feet,   1160
And the third one turned in flight; into the woods he charged.
Galopin was the best of them, and he fell at Elye's feet.*

Douchement, de boin ceur, li a merchi proiet:
«Merchi,» dist il, «biaus Sire, por Dieu ne m'ochïés!
Je vous servirai, certes, par mout grant amistiet!" 1165

31.
Galopin fu li mieudres, se li vient a genos:
«Merchi,» dist il, «biaus Sire, je sui mout gentiex hon!
Je vous plevi ma foi orendroit a estrous!
C'onques ne me fu bel, li lai dire de vous*;
Encore ai .i. tressor en cel bos, la desous, 1170
U il a tant avoir et argent et mangons,
Et aubers et vers elmes et escus poins a flors,*
Boines armes et beles et auferans cointous.*
Se vous me laissiés vivre, che vous donra ge tout!»
Quant Elyë l'entent, forment le tient a prous. 1175

32.
Quant ore entent Elye qu'il n'est pas Sarasin,
Et qu'il croit bien en Dieu qui onques ne menti,
Il l'en a apelé; belement l'i a dit:
«Amis, con as tu non? Garde n'i ait menti!»
Et cil a respondu, «Biaus Sire, Galopin, 1180
Et si sui nés d'Ardane, fieus au conte Tieri;
Berrars si fu mes freres, li preus et li gentis.
A l'ore que fui nés, ceste paine m'avint:
.Iiii. feës i ot; quant vint al departir,
Li une me voloit a son eus detenir; 1185
Mais les autres nel vaurent endurer ne soufrir,
Et prierent a Dieu qui onques ne menti,
Que jamais ne creüsse, tous jors fuisse petis,
Se n'aïsse de lonc que .iii. piés et demi,*
Et s'alaisse plus tost que cheval ne ronchin. 1190
Certes, et je si fac, por voir le vous plevi.
Lors fu morte ma mere et mon pere autressi;
Mi parent m'orent vil, por chou qu'ere petis,*
Si me vaurent noier en le mer, el grant fil.

1172 ms e. point
1188 m c. tout, emended to the plural; see the above note.

Part Three

Quietly, with a good heart, he prayed to Elye for mercy:
"Mercy," Galopin said, "good sir, for God's sake don't kill me!
I'll serve you truly with deep, lasting friendship!"   1165

31.
Galopin was the best of them. He came to Elye on his knees:
"Mercy," he begged, "good sir, I'm truly a nobleman.
I pledge to you my allegiance now and forever more.
Never were the vile things said of you pleasing to me.
I still have a treasure in that woods over there,   1170
Where there's so much wealth in silver and gold coins
And hauberks and sapphire-studded helmets, and shields
   painted with flowers,
Powerful and handsome weapons and swift war steeds.
If you let me live, I'll give it all to you."
When Elye heard him, he thought him a very worthy man.   1175

32.
When Elye heard that this thief was not a Saracen,*
And that he firmly believed in God who never told a lie,
He called to Galopin and kindly said to him:
"My friend, what's your name? Take care not to lie!"
And the thief responded, "Good sir, it's Galopin.   1180
And I was born in the Ardennes. I'm the son of Count Tieri.*
Berrars was my brother, the brave and noble.
At the hour I was born, this tragedy befell me:
Four fairies were present.* When it came time to take leave,
One of them sought to keep me as her servant.   1185
But the others wouldn't endure or bear it,
And they prayed to God, who never told a lie,
That I'd never grow any more; that I'd always remain small;
That I'd not reach more than three and one half feet in height,
And that I'd run faster than a warhorse or packhorse.   1190
Believe me, I swear it's true.
Then my mother died, and my father as well,
My relatives held me in contempt because I was small,
They tried to drown me at sea, in the great current.

Elye of Saint-Gilles

Cist laron m'acaterent, que trovés avés chi,   [84v-a]   1195
Tant m'ont de lor mestier ensengiet et apris,
Sous siel n'en a chastel, dongon, ne roëllis,
Ne sor pilers de marbre, tant soit palais assis,
Que n'en traië l'avoir, tant parfont i soit mis.
Or devenrai vostre hom, si vous vaurai servir.»   1200
Galopin passe avant, son homage li fist,
Et joint ses mains petites, as Elyë les mist,
Et devint ses hons liges, et fïauté li fist.
Il li aura mestier, che quic, ainc mout petit.
Que Elyë esgarde tout .i. feré chemin,   1205
Et voit venir Ector, .i. felon Sarrasin,
Et Gosses d'Alixandre, Gautier l'amanevi;
Et quant les voit Elye, s'en a geté .i. ris.
De che fist il que faus, quant ne daigna fuïr.
A estal s'aresta, droit enmi le chemin,   1210
Et Hector laisse corre le destrier u il sist,
Et vait ferir Elye devant, en l'escu bis.
Le blanc auberc del dos desront et desarti,
Si que lés le costé, le roit espiel li mist,
Et li dui s'eslaisierent au chevalier gentil.   1215
Je que vous cheleroie? .iiii. plaïës i prist;
De toute la menor, ja deüst il morir,
Mais Jhesu le garda, qu'en sa garde le mist.
Ains k'eut traite* l'espee, i sorvint Galopin,
Et saissi .i. levier qu'il trova el chemin,   1220
Et vait ferir Gontier, rés a rés le sorcil.
La cervele en espant, mort l'abat el cemin,
Et il saissi l'espiel, qui des poins li cheï,
Et vait ferir Ector devant, en l'escu bis,
Si que parmi le cors, son roit espiel li mist,   1225
Et Jossés torne en fuie; navré l'a Galopin.

1202   ms j. mains; the hypometric verse is emended by the addition of the possessive pronoun.
1217   ms m. deust; the hypometric verse is emended by the adverbial expression characteristic before the subjunctive (cf. 546 and 762). Cf. R's emendation «en p.» and F's «ia m.».
1226   ms f. navra; the past participle is clearly intended.

Part Three

These thieves bought me, whom you found here. 1195
They taught and instructed me in so much of their trade
That beneath heaven, there's no castle, dungeon or palisade,
Nor palace seated upon marble pillars,
From which I can't extract its wealth, however securely it's
   been placed.
Now I'll become your man; I want to serve you." 1200
Galopin stepped forward and pledged Elye homage,
And his little hands joined, he slipped them between Elye's
And became his liege man and swore fealty to him.
Elye will need him, I think, in a very short time.
Then Elye looked down the paved road, 1205
And he saw Hector coming, a treacherous Saracen,
And Gosse of Alexandria and the adroit Gautier,
And when he saw them, Elye burst out laughing.
This proved to be a foolish act, when he did not deign to flee.*
He stopped right on the spot in the middle of the road, 1210
And Hector gave rein to his mount,
And rode to strike a frontal blow on Elye's painted shield.
The white hauberk Elye was wearing, Hector pierced and tore,
So that near the youth's ribs, Hector thrust his stout lance,
And the two of them charged on the noble knight. 1215
Why should I hide it from you? Elye sustained four wounds.
From the least of them, he ought to have died,
But Jesus protected him, who placed him in his keeping.
Before Elye had drawn his sword, Galopin came running
And seized a stout club that he had found in the road, 1220
And he went to strike Gautier right above the eyes.
Gautier's brains spurted out. Galopin struck him dead
   in the road,
And he seized the lance that fell from the pagan's hands,
And went to strike Hector with a direct blow on his painted
   shield,
So that through the pagan's body Galopin thrust his stout
   lance, 1225
And Gosse turned in flight — Galopin had wounded him.

Ne portera mes armes, si con moi est avis!
Et quant le voit Elye, cele part poignant vint;
Isnelement et tost, s'en vint a Galopin,
Tost et delivrement, sor* .i. ceval sailli, 1230
Plus tost qu'il onques pot, s'en vint a Galopin.* [84v-b]
Il l'en a apelé, belement li a dit:
«Certes, Sire conpains, bien l'avés deservi!»
«Sire,» che dist li leres, «por les saints Dé merchi,
Voir, je n'i montai onques, ne a ceval ne sis; 1235
Ne ne sai chevalchier, ne je nel ai apris.*
Ançois querroië* sempre, por voir le vous plevis,
Mais montés en chelui, qui vous vient a plaisir,
Et je menrai ces autres tout che ferré chemin.
S'il ne voillent aler, par les saints que Dieus fist, 1240
Jes aurai d'un baston afolés et conquis!»

33.
Quant Elyë entent que li leres fu tés
Qu'il n'ot soing de ceval, ne il n'i vaut monter,
So talent li lait faire; fache ses volentés.
En lor chemin s'en entrent, qu'il quident retorner; 1245
Une bruine lieve, ques a mout destorbé.
E les vous a Sorbrie, u furent escapé!
Devant le maistre porte encontrent Josüé;
Quant li paien les voit, ses reconnut assés.
Il met son caperon,* ses lait outre passer; 1250
Devant aus en entra, en la boine chité.
Quant il fu el palais, sel noncha Macabré,
L'amiral de Sorbrie, voiant tout son barné:
«Par Mahon, Amiraus, malement as ovré!
Ne verés mais Hector, que tant soliés amer, 1255
Ne Gontier, vostre dru, qui vous seut coroner!»*
Quant l'amiraus l'entent, le sens quide derver;
Il desfuble se cape, d'une part l'a jeté,

1251   ms e. entre; the hypometric verse is corrected by the use of the *passé simple*.

Part Three

He will never bear arms again, if you want my opinion.
And when Elye saw Galopin, he went riding in his direction;
Immediately and quickly, the youth came to Galopin.
Quickly and easily onto a horse he leaped   1230
As fast as he ever could, Elye rode up to Galopin.
Elye called to Galopin kindly and said to him:
"Truly, sir companion, you've well-deserved this!"
"Sir," said the thief, "it was only with the help of God's saints,
Believe me, I've never mounted a steed nor sat astride a horse.   1235
I don't know how to ride horseback, for I've never learned it.*
I'd never want to. I'm telling you the truth.
But you go ahead and mount this one you like so well,
And I'll lead these others all the way down the paved road.
If they don't want to go, by the saints God made,   1240
I'll have tamed and broken them with my club!"*

33.
When Elye heard that the thief was the kind
Who cared nothing for horses, nor wanted to ride,
He let him do as he liked, whatever he wanted.
They set out on a path they thought would lead them back home.   1245
A fog rose that disoriented them greatly.
Suddenly they found themselves back at Sorbrie, from which they had escaped!
In front of the main gate, they encountered Gosse.*
When the pagan saw them, he instantly had no doubt who they were;
He raised the hood of his cloak, and he let them pass by.   1250
He went straight ahead of them into the good city.
Once he was in the palace, he announced to Macabre,
The emir of Sorbrie, before all of his nobles:
"By Mahomet, emir, you've made a bad mistake:
You'll never see your beloved Hector again,   1255
Nor Gautier, your friend, who took part in your coronation."
When the emir heard him, he nearly lost his senses.
He took off his cloak; he cast it to one side,*

Puis se prist a .ii. poins, si se hurte al piler,
Por .i. poi que de lui ne fist les iex voler: 1260
«Tervagant, car pren m'arme, car je ai trop duré!»
U qu'il voit Sarrasin, si les a apelés:
«Alés or tost as pors, si pecoiés les nés;
Gardés que n'i remaigne sergant, ne bacheler!
Qui penra* les François, ses loiers en ert tés: 1265
Je li otroi ma terre, par che gant d'or brousdé!»
«Sire,» dist li paien, «mout grant tort en avés!*   [85r-a]
Por ques querrés plus loing, quant si pres les avés?
Devant ces maistres portes, desous cel pin ramé,
Ja vi ore les Frans, qui mout sont esgaré.   1270
Par le foi que vous doi, ne sevent u torner.»
Quant l'entent l'amiraus, grant joie en a mené;
Il a dit a ses homes, «Or tost ses amenés!
Tel justiche en ferai, con vous tuit loërés!»
Et cil ont respondu, «Si con vous loërés!»   1275
Isnelement et tost se corent adouber;
Et vestent les aubers, s'ont les elmes fremés,
Et çaignent les espees as senestres costés,
Et monterent es seles des destriers sejornés,
Et getent a lor caus les fors escus bouclés,   1280
Et prendent en lor poins les fors espies quarrés.
Jusc'a la maistre porte, en sont poignant alé.

34.
Or m'escoutés, Signor, que Dieus vous beneïe!
Cele nuit jut Elye soz le tor de Sorbrie,
Avoec lui, Galopins, sans plus de conpaignie.   1285
Il en a apelé, se li conmenche a dire:

1263   ms Ales tost; the hypometric verse is emended by the addition of the temporal adverb.
1269   ms De ces; We emend the verse on the model of 1248; F. emends similarly, while R emends «delés.»
1275   ms v. loeres; we emend on the model of this recurring hemistich; cf.. 2638, 2651, 2694, etc.
1280   ms. C. le; the plural is obviously meant; cf.1281.
1284   ms E. sor; emended on the model of 446.

Part Three

Then grabbed his head with both hands and threw himself
   at a pillar.
It nearly caused his eyes to fly out of his head.   1260
"Tervagant, now take my soul, for I have lived too long!"
He turned his gaze towards the Saracens and called to them:
"Go quickly to the ports and destroy the ships!
Make sure there's not a foot soldier or young knight remaining
   there!
Whoever will hang the Frenchmen will have this reward: 1265
I grant him my land, by this glove embroidered with gold!"
"Sir," answered the pagan, "you're so wrong!
Why keep seeking them far away, when you have them
   so near?
In front of the main gate under that boughed pine tree,
I just saw the Frenchmen who had completely lost their way.   1270
By the allegiance I owe you, they don't know which way
   to turn!"
When the emir heard him, it caused him great joy.
He said to his men, "Then quickly, bring them here!
Such justice will I do that you will all be praising it."
And they answered, "Just as you command!"   1275
Immediately and quickly, they rushed to put on their armor,
And they put on their hauberks, they laced on their helmets
And girded their swords on their left sides
And sprung into the saddles of their fresh warhorses
And hung around their necks their strong bossed shields   1280
And seized their strong, well-crafted spears.
Up to the city gate they spurred their mounts.

34.
Now listen to me, my lords, may God bless you!
That night Elye slept below the tower of Sorbrie.
With him was Galopin, without any other companions.   1285
Elye called to Galopin and spoke to him.

«Cha te trei, biaus conpains, Galopin,» dist Elye,
Veés ichi .i. castel de mout grant signorie:
Les ors et les abresces, les viviers et les vinges,*
Les maissons as borgois, et les gaïngeries! 1290
Sés tu or qui chou est? Con a non ceste vile?»
«Sire,» dist Galopin, «c'est la tor de Sorbrie,
Laiens est Macabré et ses fiex et se fille,
Rosamonde la bele, la plus gente mescine,
Qui soit des Alixandre dusc'as pors del Surie!» 1295
Quant Elyë l'entent, a poi n'esrage d'ire;
«Traï m'as, biaus conpains, Galopin!» dist Elye,
«Qui chi m'as amené, par ta grant felonie!
Plus me het l'amiraus que nul home qui vive,
Je li ocis son fil, Ataignant* de Sorbrie, 1300
Leres e! car en fui, car enblé m'as ma vie!
Mout est fiaus gentiex hom, qui en laron se fie!»
«Sire,» che dist li leres, «por les saints Dé, nel dites! [85r-b]
Ne vous dementés si conme veve caitive!
Faites bel contenant, franc chevalier nobile; 1305
Tant avés perdu sanc, le chiere avés palie.*
Nous nos vendromes chier, se Dieus me done vie!»*
Il est passés avant, s'a une espeë prisse;
Vers son signor se trait; vasaument li aïe.
Bien i fiert Galopin, entre lui et Elye,* 1310
.X. en ont geté mors, ains que mal li feïssent.
Paien orent grant forche, vasaument les requissent;
Desous Elye ont mort son destrier d'Orcanie,*
Lui navrerent el cors, et .vii. plaiës li fissent.
Or en a li ber .xi.; n'est conrois de sa vie.* 1315
Li doi baron s'en tornent; nes porent soffrir mie;
Ains passent d'un vivier les fossés et le rive,
Lés une barbacane, lés une roche antive.
La trovent .i. vergier qui fu tous fais d'olive,

1291   ms tu qui; the addition, on the model of 306, emends the hypometric verse.
1295   ms p. resrage; we emend with the formulaic expression; cf. 152, 238, etc.
1307   ms D. ne; we emend with the first person singular, rather than the plural, based on 1174. See note.

Part Three

"Come over here, good companion, Galopin!" said Elye.
"Look at this castle over here of very great nobility.
The gardens and the orchards, the ponds and the vineyards,
The burghers' houses and the pasture lands! 1290
Do you know what this is? What's the name of this city?"
"Sir," answered Galopin, "it's the tower of Sorbrie.
Macabre lives within and his sons and his daughter,
Rosamonde, the beautiful, the noblest maiden
From Alexandria to the ports of Syria." 1295
When Elye heard him, he spoke seething with rage:
"You've betrayed me, good companion Galopin,
Through your treachery you've led me here!
The emir hates me more than any man alive.
I killed his son, Ataignant of Sorbrie! 1300
Ah, you thief! Now flee, for you've cost me my life!
A nobleman is gravely mistaken who puts his trust in a thief!"
"Sir," said the thief, "don't say that, by God's saints!
Stop all your grieving. You're like a poor widow.
Cheer up and be of good mien, worthy noble knight. 1305
Your face is turning pale, you've lost so much blood.
We'll take a lot of them with us, if God gives me life!"
He stepped forward and seized a sword.
He drew close to his lord, providing knightly protection.
Galopin struck mighty blows. Between him and his lord, 1310
They slew ten Saracens before any harm came to themselves.
The pagans had great strength and valiantly attacked them.
They killed his Orkney warhorse right out from under Elye.
They wounded him, for they dealt him seven wounds.
Now the young knight had eleven: his life was in danger. 1315
The two knights retreated. There was no way they could
   hold out.
Instead they passed by the banks and moats of a garden,
Beside a barbican and close by an ancient rock.
There they found an orchard that was all planted with
   olive trees

Et de mout riches arbres, qui sont de mainte guisse, 1320
Li vergier fu jovenes, et li* anste* florie,
Et la nuit fu oscure; Dieus le vaut,* nostre Sire.
Et Sarrasin s'en tornent, nes porent coissir mie,
Il en portent les mors, et les navrés en guient.
Voient tout le barnage l'amiraus de Sorbrie; 1325
Quant le voit Rosamonde, se* conmencha a rire,
Et dist entre ses dens, que nus ne l'entent mie:
«De mort et de prison, desfenge Dieus,* Elye!
Si li conduie en Franche sain et sauf et delivre,
A Julïen, son pere, qui le pleure et dessire!» 1330

35.
Galopin et Elye s'en entrent el vergier;
.Xi. plaies ot grans, qui mout l'ont angoissié,
Plus de .vii. fois se pasme, sous l'onbre d'un pumier.
Galopin en apele, se li dist tout premier:
«Biaus conpains, car t'en fui! Dieu garisse ton cief! 1335
Prent conroi de ta vie, car de moi, ne me ciet;
Sarrasin m'ochiront, ains demain l'esclairier*!
Se tu ja passes mer, a nul jor desousiel,*
Et tu peus encontrer pelerin ne paumier,* [85v-a]
Qui en aut a Saint Gille, por l'apostle proier, 1340
Si me mande mon pere Julïen, le guerrier,
Et ma dame, ma mere, qui a son ceur irié,
Ja ne me veront mes, a nul ior desosiel,
Car Sarrasin m'ont mort, ochis, et detranchié!»
«Sire,» che dist li leres, «non ferai, par mon cief! 1345
Ja mes ne vous faurai, a nul jor desossiel!»
Quant Elyë l'entent, mout l'en prist grant pitié;
L'aige de ses biaus iex, les la fache li chiet.

1320   ms Et mout; the addition of the preposition goes with «fais de» of 1319 and «de mainte guisse» of 1320, correcting the hypometric verse. F emends with «s'ot».
1321   ms Et l.; the hypometric verse is altered by deleting the initial «et»; neither F nor R emend.
1326   ms s. li; deletion of the pronoun regularizes the hypometric verse.

Part Three

And many other kinds of luxuriant trees.   1320
And the orchard was young, and the bower was flowering.
And the night was dark; God willed it, our Lord.
And the pagans turned back. They couldn't see a thing;
They carried away their dead and helped their wounded limp away.
In sight of all the nobles stood the emir of Sorbrie.   1325
When Rosamonde spotted him, she burst out laughing
And whispered between her teeth, so that absolutely no one could hear her:
"From death and from prison, may God preserve Elye*
And lead him to France all safe and sound and free,
To Julien his father, who is weeping and longing for him."   1330

35.
Galopin and Elye entered the orchard.
Elye had eleven serious wounds, which caused him much anguish.
More than seven times, he fainted under the shade of an apple tree;
He called to Galopin, and he said to him right away,
"Good companion, you've got to flee immediately! May God protect you!   1335
Think of your own life, don't worry about me.
The Saracens will kill me before daylight tomorrow.
If you ever go overseas in your lifetime,
And you can meet a pilgrim or a palmer,
Who is going to Saint-Gilles to pray to the apostle,   1340
Send word for me to my father, the warrior Julien,
And to my lady, my mother, whose heart is in sorrow,
That they'll never see me again any day on earth,
For the pagans will have slain me, killed me, and slashed me to pieces!"
"Sir," said the thief, "I won't do it. I swear by my head!   1345
"Never will I fail you, any day under the heavens!"
When Elye heard him, great pity overcame him:
The tears from his fair eyes streamed down his face.

36.
Elyës li vassaus, qui seufre grant dolor,
Rapele Galopin douchement par amor: 1350
«Galopins, biaus conpains, por Dieu le creator,
C'or t'en fui, Galopins, ore aproche li jor!
Sarrasin m'ochiront orendroit, sans demor.»
«Sire,» che dist li leres, «por Dieu que jou aour,
Je devieng vostre hon lige, demain aura qart jor, 1355
Par Saint Denis de Franche, miex voil morir o vos,
Entre gent Sarrasine, et souffrir grant dolor,
Que repairier en Franche, a joie et a baudor!»
Quant l'entendi Elye, forment l'en tient a pros.
Et Sarrasin s'en issent, par son l'aube de jor; 1360
Bien en i ot .vii.xx. qui prissent lor adous,
Et vont querrant Elye, li felon traitor,
Mais nel troveront mie, se Dieu plaist, le signor,
Qu'il l'ont laissiet ariere, el vergier sous la tor.
Rosamonde s'estut sus el palais autor, 1365
Et vint a la fenestre, por oïr la douchour
Des oissellons menus, qui chantoient al jor:
L'eurïel et la merle ot chanter, sor l'aubor,
Le cri del rousingol, se li sovient d'amor.
«Vrais Dieus,» dist la pucele, «con tu es presïous! 1370
Tu fais croistre les arbres, porter foilles et flors,
Et le blé nous fais sourdre de la terre en amour!
Et en la Sainte Viergene, presis anonsion,*
Biaus Sire, et sanc et char i presistes por nous!*
Aussi con chou est voirs, Biaus sire glorïous, [85v-b] 1375
Desfendés le Franchois de mort et de prison!
Por la soie amistiet, renoierai Mahon,
Et guerpirai ma loi, que je voi que n'est prous!»
Et Sarrasin les quierent, qui vers Dieu n'ont amor;
Rosamonde les voit; tous les tient a bricon, 1380
Fierement lor escrie, «Fil a putain! glouton!
U devés vous aler? Mahomet vous confont!

1363 ms t. mi; we emend to the predominate orthography in the poem, since the meaning is the negative «not at all,» rather than «among, amidst»; cf. 806.

Part Three

36.
Elye, the knight, who was suffering harsh pain,
Called to Galopin again quietly, through deep affection: 1350
"Galopin, good companion, for God the Creator,
Get out of here right away, Galopin! Daylight is fast
  approaching;
The Saracens will kill me soon, without delay."
"Sir," said the thief, "for God whom I adore,
I became your liegeman four days ago tomorrow. 1355
By Saint Denis of France, I would rather die with you,
Among pagan people, and suffer great anguish,
Than go back to France in joy and rejoicing!"*
When Elye heard him, he held him in great esteem.
And Saracens came forth, at the break of day, 1360
There were a least seven score who took up their armor
And went searching for Elye, the cruel traitors.
But they'll find no trace of him, if it please the Lord God,
For they've left him behind, in the orchard below the tower.
Rosamonde was sitting up there in the palace, 1365
And she came to the window to hear the sweet sounds*
Of the little birds who were singing at break of dawn:
The oriole, the merlin, she heard singing up in the arbor.
The song of the nightingale reminded her of love.
"True God," said the maid, "how wonderful You are!* 1370
You make the trees grow and bear leaves and flowers,
And Your love for us causes wheat to sprout from the earth,
And in the Holy Virgin You took shape and form.
Dear Lord, You took on flesh and blood for us.
Just as this is true, dear glorious Lord, 1375
Preserve the Frenchman from death and from prison.
For love of him, I'll renounce Mahomet,*
And I'll leave my religion, which I know is worthless."
And the Saracens, who had no love towards God, kept
  searching for them.
Rosamonde saw them; she considered them all fools. 1380
Loudly she cried out to them, "Worthless scum! Whores' sons!
Do you have any idea where to look? Mahomet confound you!

Elye of Saint-Gilles

Por .i. seul chevalier, n'en vi tant en esrour!»
Galopins ot la noisse, le friente, le tabour,
Et l'esfroi des paiens, mout en ot grant paour; 1385
Venus est a Elye, si l'enbrache desous,
Si l'a mis a son col, si l'en porte a estrous,
Que li chiés li traine contreval, en l'erbous,
Et les jambes par tere, car Elye fu lons,
Car Galopin li leres estoit mout cours.* 1390
Rosamonde s'estut as fenestres, amont,
Fierement li escrie, «Biaus amis, valeton!
Tu as si peu de cors, et as si grant valour,
C'un chevalier enportes, o trestous ces adous!
Met le jus, biaus amis, si t'en fui a estrous! 1395
Et se tu ne le fais, tu feras grant folor,
Que tu troveras ja, teus .xm. conpaignon;
S'il te pevent trover, voirement t'ochiront!»
Quant Galopins l'entent, mout en ot grant paour;
U il vausist u non, si mist jus son signor. 1400

1384 ms n. et; eliminating the connective restores the hypermetric verse and also clarifies the use of asyndeton for a dramatic effect of accumulation.
1394 ms o trestout.

Part Three

For one sole knight, I've never seen so much uproar!"
Galopin heard the noise and the tumult and the drums,*
And he was seized by fear of the pagans. 1385
He came to Elye and threw his arms around his legs,
And he threw him over his shoulder and carried him off immediately
So that Elye's head was dragging along the ground in the grass
And his legs hanging down on the ground, because Elye was tall,
And Galopin the thief was very short. 1390
Rosamonde was sitting at the windows up above.
Loudly she called to him, "Good friend, small youth!
You have such a small body and such great valor*
That you can carry a knight with all that armor!
Put him down, good friend, and flee at once! 1395
If you don't, you'll be acting foolishly,
For you'll soon meet up with nearly ten thousand comrades in arms;
If they can find you, they will surely kill you!"
When Galopin heard her, he was seized by fear,
Whether he wanted to or not, he put down his lord. 1400

Elye of Saint-Gilles

Part Four

37.
Rosamonde la bele s'estut a la fenestre,   [86r-a]
Vestue ot .i. blïau d'un paile de biterne,
Afublé .i. mantel, a mervelles fu bele.
Tous les degrés avale, si est venue a tere,
Et desfreme .i. guicet d'une fauce posterne*;   1405
Par u ele sieüt issir, et les pucheles,
Quant vient el mois de mai, por colir la florete.
Venus est a Elye, qui se pasme sor tere;
Son cief li a lor mis par desous son brac destre,
Puis l'en a apelé, la cortoisse puchele: 1410
«Qui es tu, chevalier?» che li a dit la bele,*
«Aimes tu Mahomet, qui cest siecle governe?»
«Naië!» che dist Elye, «ne tout ciaus qui le servent!
Ains fui nés de Saint Gille, de Provence la bele,
Fieus Julïen, le conte a le kenuë teste.   1415
Avant hier m'adouba, che vous di, damoisele;
Illeuques me fu dit et conté tout a chertes,
Paien et Sarrasin essilloient la tere.
Je les ving sor requere, sor moi torna la perte*;
.Xi. plaïes ai grans, qui durement m'apressent!   1420
Je n'en quic escaper, que la vïe ne perge.»
«Amis, bien vous connois,» dist la franche puchele,
«Ces nostre gent se plaignent au matin et au vespre;
De nos millors amis nous avés fait grant perte.»
«Dame, laissieme ester,* perdus sui sans confesse;   1425
Certes, et mout me het, li rois de ceste terre,
Hier li ochis son fil, Ataignant d'Oliferne.
S'il me pooit tenir, por tout l'or d'Engleterre,*
Ne seroie esparngiés,* ne me tolist la teste.»
«Or ne vous esmaiés,» dist la franche puchele,   1430
«L'amiraus est mes peres, bien en quic le pes faire;

1429   ms s. esparengies; we emend to the Francien form, rather than the Picard, to correct the hypermetric verse.

A Chanson de Geste

Part Four

37.
The beautiful Rosamonde was seated at the window.
She had put on a tunic of striped Egyptian silk,*
And she had donned a mantel of wondrous beauty.
She came down all the steps to the ground floor,
And she unbarred the door of a hidden rear gate   1405
Through which she and her ladies would go out,
When the month of May came, to gather flowers.
She came up to Elye, who was lying unconscious on the ground,
She placed his head on her right arm.
Then the courtly maid spoke to him: 1410
"Who are you, sir knight," the beautiful maiden said to him,
"Do you love Mahomet, who rules this world?"
"No!" replied Elye, "nor all those who serve him!
On the contrary, I was born in Saint-Gilles, in beautiful Provence,
The son of Julien the hoary-headed count.   1415
I tell you, my lady, he knighted me the day before yesterday,
Then they told me and said quite truthfully
That pagans and Saracens were laying waste the land.
I came to confront them; it's been my undoing.
I have eleven gaping wounds, which are causing me intense pain.   1420
I don't think I'll escape here with my life."
"My friend, I know you well," said the noble young maiden,*
"From morning to night our people are lamenting
About our dear loved ones; you've caused us great losses."
"My lady, leave me alone; I'm going to die without confession!   1425
Truly, the king of this land hates me deeply.
Yesterday, I killed his son, Ataignant of Oliferne.*
If he could capture me, for all the gold in England,
I'd never be spared; he'd cut off my head."
"Don't despair," said the noble maid.   1430
"The emir is my father. I'm sure I can make peace.

Li enfes fu mes freres, li chevalier honestes.
Or* soiés a seür ja n'en aurés moleste.
Certes, je vous aim plus que nule riens en tere!
Venés ent avoec moi,» dist la franche pucele, 1435
«En tel lieu vous metrai, ains petitet de terme,
Que vous serés tous sains, ains que viegne li vespres!» [86r-b]
«E! Dieus,» che dist Elye, «conment pora chou estre?*
Che ne poroit nus faire, fors Dameldé chelestre!»
Galopins et Elyes vont aprés la puchele, 1440
En une cambre en entrent, qui fu toute sos tere*;
Mout fu bien pointuree a oiseus et a bestes.
En .i. lit le coucha, dont d'or est l'espondele,
D'un covertoir l'a cevre, por le caut qui l'apresse.
Rosamonde s'en torne, et son escrin deferme,* 1445
A ses mains qu'ele ot blances, en a traite .ii. herbes
Que Dieus ot sou ses piés, li glorïeus chelestre,*
Quant en crois le leverent, la pute gent averse.
En .i. anap de madre les souda la puchele,
Onques Dieus ne fist home, se le col en traverse, 1450
Que ne soit ausi sains con li pisson* sor tere.
Ele en dona Elye, .i. chevalier honestes*;
Li ber en a beü, por l'amor la puchele,
Tous fu sains et garis; Galopin en apele:
«Chaiens est paradis et la gloire chelestre! 1455
Je n'en quic mais issir, se tout jors i puis estre!»
«Sire,» dist Galopins, «por la Vierge puchele,
Mout par devés amer Rosamonde la bele!»

38.
Rosamonde la bele ama mout le vasal:
Tex .ix. herbes li done, qu`ele li destenpra, 1460
Puis qu'il en ot beü, et le col trespassa,
Tout fu sains et garris*; a mangier demanda.
Li gentiex hon en ot plus que il ne rova;
Li bains fu aprestés, u Elyës entra,
.I. tel baing li dona, quens ne dus tel n'en n'a!* 1465

1456   ms s. tout; we emend to the plural.

Part Four

That young noble was my brother, the honorable knight.
Now rest assured that you'll not be harmed.
Truly, I love you more than anything on earth."*
Then the noble maiden said, "Come in here with me.   1435
I'll keep you in such a place that before long
You'll be completely healed, before vespers come."
"My God!" Elye said, "How can that be?
No one could do that except the Lord God in heaven!"*
Galopin and Elye followed the lady.   1440
They entered a room, which was deep underground.
It was beautifully painted with birds and animals.
She laid him down on a bed, whose frame was made of gold.*
She covered him with a blanket to protect him from the
  oppressive heat.
Rosamonde went over and unlocked her chest.   1445
With her white hands she took out two herbs
That God had under His feet, the celestial glorious King,
When the evil enemy raised Him on the cross!
In a wooden chalice she dissolved them.
Never was man made, that if this potion went down
  his throat,   1450
He would not become as healthy as a fish in the sea.
She gave some to Elye, the honorable knight.
The youth drank some of it, for love of the lady;
He was completely cured and well. He called Galopin:
"This place is paradise and heavenly glory!*   1455
I don't think I'd ever leave if I could always stay here!"
"Sir," answered Galopin, "for the Virgin Mary,
You must love the beautiful Rosamonde very much!"

38.
Beautiful Rosamonde loved the knight very much.
Nine such herbs she gave him that she had infused.*   1460
When he drank some of the potion, and it went down his throat,
He was completely cured and well. He asked for some food.
The noble youth got more than he had asked for.
A bath was prepared, and Elye entered it.
Such a bath she provided him as no count or duke ever had!   1465

ELYE OF SAINT-GILLES

Puis li vest .i. hermin qui jusc'a val li a bat,
Heusses ot cordouänes, esperons a esmal.
Rosamonde la bele par les flans l'enbracha,
Sor .i. lit l'a assis, geteïs a cristal,*
.XI. fois li baisse et le vis et la char;   1470
Cil li guenchi la bouche, que il n'i adesa.*
«Galopin,» dist Elye, «vois quel feme chi a!
U roialme de Franche, si gente n'en aura! [86v-a]
Car pleüst ore a Dieu, qui le mont estora,
Je eüsse chaiens et Gautier et Gerart,   1475
Et Guimer l'amoreus, et le conte Aimart,
Et Hugon de Paris, et son conpaing Guichart,
Et Guillame d'Orenge, et son frere Bernart,
Et Julïen mon pere, le chevalier loial,
Et fussent adoubé d'armes et de cheval,   1480
Et fuissiemes* la sus, en el palais hautal:
Anqui le conperoiet li paien desloial!»

39.
Elyës li vasaus a le fiere poissanche
Fu .xv. jois tout plains laiens en .i. canbre,
Que paien ne le sorent, ne il ni ot doutanche...*   1485
«Gentiex fix a baron, vois con sui bele et gente!
.Vi. rois mout orgellous me quierent et demandent:
Clamador d'Abilant, et .i. rois de Brehaigne,
Et Hector et Turfier et Morin d'Abilande,
Lubïens de Baudas, a la barbe ferande!*   1490
Ichil en est li maistres, que il a plus poisance;
Entre lui et mon frere, en ont fait convenance,
A bataille fremee, par le fust de lor lances.
S'il l'ochist et afole, tous jors serai dolante;
Ains me prenge tés maus que il me face estendre,   1495
Que me parte li ceurs, et li cors, et li menbre,

1466   ms l. abat; we emend the hypermetric verse.
1467   ms c. esperon; the plural form is needed.
1494   ms a. tout; we emend to the plural.

Part Four

Then she dressed him in a full-length ermine robe,
Cordovan boots and enamelled spurs.
Beautiful Rosamonde hugged him.
She seated him on a bed cast in crystal.
Forty times she kissed his face and flesh. 1470
He turned his mouth away so that he wouldn't touch her.
"Galopin!" said Elye. "See what a maiden we have here!
In the kingdom of France you'll not find such a noble lady!
Now if God, who created the world, would only grant
That I had here Gautier and Gerart 1475
And Guimer the lover and count Aimart
And Hugh of Paris and his companion Guichart
And William of Orange and his brother Bernart
And Julien my father, the loyal knight,
And that they were fully armed with weapons and horses 1480
And that we were up above there in the palace,
Then the treacherous pagans would pay dearly!"

39.
Elye, the knight with noble power,
Remained fully fifteen days in the room,
And the pagans didn't find it out, nor did they suspect anything. 1485
"Noble knight's son, see how beautiful and high-born I am!
Six very proud kings have sought and asked for me:
Clamador of Abilant and a king of Brehaigne
And Hector and Turfier and Morin of Abilande
And Lubiens of Bagdad, with the iron-gray beard.* 1490
This last one is the master of all, because he has the most power.
He and my brother between them have made an agreement
To wage heated battle with the wood of their lances.
If Lubiens wounds and slays him, I'll be saddened forever.
I'd rather endure all the suffering they inflict on me, 1495
And have limbs, heart and body slashed in two,

Que Lubïens li vieus, a la barbe ferande,
Mon gent cors avenant ait ja nuit en sa canbre!»

40.
Elyës li vasal fist forment a prissier;
Dedens le canbre fu mout tres bien a aisiés,* 1500
Que paien ne li sorent, li quiver renoié!
Rosamonde le sert, de gré et volentiers,
Et s'amor li pressente, la bele au cors legier.
Macabrés l'amiraus fu assis al mengier,
Maisançois qu'il en lieve, ert dolans et iriés. 1505
Lubïen de Baudas, li chenus et li vieus,
Fu entrés en sa terre, a tout .xx.m. paiens;
Il fait gaster les vinges, et tos les blés soier.
Il a pris .i. message, al roi l'a envoiet, [86v-b]
Que il li doinst sa fille a per et a mollier, 1510
Et trestoute sa terre, ensi con il le quiert,
U son fil li envoit, Caïfas le proisiet,
U Jossé d'Alixandre, u Malpriant le fier.
Li qués d'eus qui en isse, mout ert mal engingiés,
Bien peut estre seür de le teste a tranchier. 1515

41.
Macabrés l'amiraus fu assis al disner,
Mais ançois qu'il en liet, ert dolans et irés.
Lubïen de Baudas, li viés kenus barbés,
A tout .xx.m. paiens, est en sa tere entrés.
A tant es le message sor* le palais montés, 1520
A sa vois qu'il ot clere, conmencha a crier:
«Macabré de Sorbrie, fai ta gent escouter:
Sés que mande mes peres, Lubïens li barbés,*
Que li doignes ta fille, Rosamonde al vis cler,
Et trestoute ta terre, ensi con ele apert, 1525

Part Four

Than let old Lubien, with the iron-gray beard,
Ever possess me at night in his chamber."

40.
Elye the knight behaved in a very praiseworthy manner.
In that room he felt completely at ease,   1500
Since the pagans, the abjured enemy, were not aware of
   his presence.
Rosamonde served him willingly and well,
And she offered him her love, the beautiful, slender maiden.
Macabre the emir was seated at dinner,
But before he rises, he'll know pain and sorrow!   1505
Lubien of Bagdad, the white-haired old man,
Had entered Macabre's lands with fully twenty thousand
   pagans.
He ordered the vineyards laid to waste and all the wheat
   mowed down.*
He chose a messenger and sent word to the king
That Macabre must give him his daughter as peer and wife   1510
And all of his land, just as Lubien asked,
Or else send out his son: Caifas the valiant
Or Joshua of Alexandria or bold Malpriant.
Whichever of them comes out, he will meet his doom:
He can be certain of having his head cut off.   1515

41.
Macabre the emir was seated at dinner,
But before he rose, he would know pain and sorrow.
Lubien of Bagdad, the old hoary-bearded man,
With over twenty thousand pagans, had entered
   Macabre's land.
Soon the messenger had gone up to the palace.   1520
In his loud voice, he began to announce:
"Macabre of Sorbrie, have your people listen!
Now hear this: my father, the bearded Lubien, sends
For you to give him your daughter Rosamonde with the
   beautiful mien,
And all your land, all that you possess,   1525

U ton fil li envoies, Caïfas, u José.
Li quel d'eus qui en isse, mal li ert encontré:
Bien peut estre seür de le teste a coper!»

42.
Macabré l'amiraus se lieve en son estage;
Il respont belement, et si dist al mesage: 1530
«Amis, cil vostre rois me mande grant outrage!
Chi sera o mes fieus o tel home en la place,
Qui li contredira le treü par ses armes!»

43.
Li messages s'en torne, le parolle ot bien dite*;
Macabré l'amiraus ne s'aseüra mie. 1535
Son fil en apela, Caïfas de Sorbrie:
«Tu feras cheste joste que por toi ai enprisse!»
«Sire,» dist Caïfas, «peciés le vous fait dire!
Bien a passé .iii. jors que la fievre m'est prisse;
Ne seroie en cheval, por a perdre la vie! 1540
Je ne puis chevalcier; la vigor m'est faillie!*
Mes donés li ma seur, que il vieut et desire,
Et trestoute la terre, ensi con il la quisse!
U peut ele miex faire? Trop est manans et riche!
Et s'ele le devee, la garche soit honie!   [87r-a] 1545
Mahomet me confonge, qui tout a enbaillie,
S'en avés ja par moi ne secor ne aie!»

44.
«Biaus fiex,» dist l'amiraus, «mout m'as mal engignié!
Porcoi pris je la joste encontre Lubïen?*
Que ne le vieus tu faire, mout t'en es avilliés! 1550
Ne m'en caut; ta seror li donra a mollier,
Et trestoute la terre, ensi con il le quiert.
Aprés ferai .i. plet, qu'en aurai .i. quartier,
Dont je vivrai a aisse, sans autre parçonnier,

1532 ms f. .i.; we emend for the «either...or» construction which the scribe began but did not complete. See note.
1545 ms l. deves; emended on the verb «dever» «to become angry». See note.

Part Four

Or send him your son Caifas or Joshua.
Whichever one of them rides forth will have met his doom.
He can be sure of having his head cut off!"

42.
Macabre the emir arose and stood up above the others on
   his dais,
He replied courteously and said to the messenger: 1530
"Friend, your king's demand has insulted me immensely.
There will be either my son or such a man on the field
Who will dispute this challenge by his arms!"

43.
The messenger headed back. He had spoken well.
Macabre the emir was in fear for his safety.   1535
He called to his son, Caifas of Sorbrie:
"You will fight this joust that I have committed you to."
"My lord," said Caifas, "it's a sin for you to make this
   commitment:
Three days ago I came down with a fever.
I wouldn't get on a horse if my life were on the line.   1540
I can't ride; my strength has failed me.
Go ahead and give him my sister, whom he wants and desires,
And all the land, just as he has demanded.
Where can she do better? He's so rich and powerful!
And if she refuses, shame on that bitch!   1545
May Mahomet damn me, who has all in his power,
If you'll ever get any help or aid from me!"

44.
"Good son," said the emir, "you've surely betrayed me!
Why did I agree to this joust against Lubien?
Since you refuse to do it, you've brought great shame upon
   yourself.   1550
It's no matter now. I'll give him your sister as a wife
And all the land, just as he demands.
Afterwards, I'll sue him to get a fourth of it,
Where I can live in ease without any other share.

Car li hom qui tout pert, doit estre coureciés. 1555
Ne je ne m'os conbatre, que poi ai chevaliers.»
«Sire,» dist Caïfas, «non feras, par mon cief!
Mieus aim ge estre povres, deshiretés, sans fiés,
Que je m'aille conbatre encontre Lubïen!
A l'espeë tranchant, me coperoit le cief!» 1560

45.
Quant Macabrés entent de son fil le corage,
Que ne voist chevalchier, ne ne se vaut conbatre,
N'encontre Lubïen n'ot cure de bataille,
L'amiraus se porpense, qui* fu cortois et sage.
Cil qui tranche son nés, il vergonge sa fache; 1565
Por che qu'il est ses fieus, si n'en vaut faire fable;
Josïen en apele: «Biaus amis, pren tes armes!
Tu feras cheste joste por moi, ceste bataille!»
«Sire,» dist Josïens, «volentiers i alaisse,
Mais jou ai tel ensoigne, que n'en doi avoir blame. 1570
Quant suï le François, aprés qui m'envoiastes,
Moi feri ens el cors; ore saine la plaie.
Mahomet me confonge, qui tout a en sa garde,
Se ja avés secor de moi, ne avantage!»
Quant l'amiraus l'entent, a poi que il n'esrage. 1575

46.
Quant l'amiraus entent le raisson de Jossé,
Qu'il ne si conbatra, ne il ni osse aler,
Ne faire le bataille vers le Turc desfaé,
Malpriant apela, «Biaus amis! cha venés!
Drus estes Rosamonde, nos le savons assés; 1580
Por la soie amistiet est vostre escus troués; [87r-b]
Vous en ferés bataille, volentiers et de gré!
Or porterés se manche en bataille campel;
Par itel convenant, vous alés adouber,
Et faites le bataille, et che roi me matés, 1585

1572   ms c. or; the hypometric verse is corrected by the form «ore».

Part Four

For the man who loses everything will end up being miserable. 1555
I don't even dare to fight, for I have too few knights."
"My lord," said Caifas, "you won't do it, by my head!
I'd rather be poor, disinherited and without fiefs,
Than go to fight against Lubien!
With his sharp sword, he'd cut off my head!" 1560

45.
When Macabre heard his son's reactions,
That he refused to ride, nor wanted to fight,
Nor had any intent to do battle against Lubien,
The emir, who was courtly and wise, uttered this reflection:
"He who cuts off his own nose, spites his face!"* 1565
Because Caifas was his son, Macabre would not make him
   a laughing-stock.
He called Joshua: "Good friend, take up your arms.
You'll fight this joust for me, this battle!"
"My lord," said Joshua, "I'd gladly go,
But I'm in such bad shape that I shouldn't be blamed. 1570
When I followed the Frenchman that you sent me after,
He struck me a fierce blow. Now the wound is bleeding.
May Mahomet punish me, who has all in his keeping,
If you'll get any help or assistance from me."
When the emir heard him, he almost went mad. 1575

46.
When the emir heard Joshua's arguments,
That he would not fight, nor did he dare ride forth
To do the combat with the treasonous Turk,
He called Malpriant: "Good friend, come over here.
You're Rosamonde's beloved, this we all know. 1580
For her affection, your shield has been pierced.
You'll fight this battle gladly and with pleasure.
Here now, wear this sleeve of hers onto the battlefield.*
It will serve as a sign of your agreement to go arm yourself
And do the battle and kill that king for me, 1585

Que jamais li treüs ne me soit demandés.
Je vous donrai ma fille, Rosamonde al vis cler,
Et trestoute la terre, ensi con ele apert.»
«Sire,» dist li paien, «par Mahon, tort avés,
Par tans aurés le los, al vilain rasoté, 1590
Que il hice son chien la u il n'ose aler!
Ains se tient a son huis, et lait avant aler,
Il n'en chaut quel part court, puisc'a son huis fermé!*
Si con vous estes sire de la terre clamés,*
Et rois et poëstis et les honors tenés, 1595
Si rechevés les joustes, et les estors canpés,
Et soufrés les grans plaies, et les cos endurés.
Mahomet me confonge, qui tout a a saver,
Se je monte en cheval, por mes armes porter!»
Quant l'entent l'amiraus, le sens quide derver; 1600
A sa vois qu'il ot clere, conmencha a crier:
«Fiex a putain, glouton! Mout vous voi esgaré!
Autretel me feïstes a l'issue des nés,
Quant laissastes Elye, le François, escaper!
Tervagant, sel eüsse,* bien me fust encontré! 1605
Cil feïst la bataille vers l'amiraus el pré!»
Mais il est en la cambre, qui bien les oï cler.
L'amiraus en apele son canberlenc privé,
«Alés moi de sa cambre Rosamonde amener,
Orendroit li donrai, ja n'en ert trestorné!» 1610
Dient li lecheor, «Mout avés bien parlé!
Chou est li mieudres plais que i puissons trover!»
Dusc'as huis de la cambre, en est venus Josés,
Il est passés avant, si a l'anel crollé.
Rosamonde l'oï, s'a le duc apelé: 1615
«Jentiex fieus a baron ja seres afolé,
Je quic qu'espïé estes, cha dedens encussé!* [87v-a]
Mes peres vous vieut faire tous les menbres coper!»
«Hé! las!» che dist Elye, «que ne sui adoubés!*
C'or n'en ai en mon dos mon blanc auberc safré, 1620

1607   ms Mais est; the copyist omitted the subject pronoun, creating a hypometric verse.

Part Four

So that never will tribute be asked from me.
I'll give you Rosamonde with the bright countenance
And all the land that belongs to her."
"My lord," said the pagan, "by Mahomet, you're wrong!
You're trying for cheap praise like an idiot peasant   1590
Who sends his dog out where he doesn't dare go himself.
Instead, he stays behind a locked door and lets it go ahead.
He doesn't care where it runs, since his door is safely fastened.
Since you are the proclaimed lord of the land,
And you hold kingship and power and the honors,   1595
Then you take on the jousts and the single combats,
And you endure the harsh blows and suffer the great wounds!
May Mahomet, who has all knowledge, destroy me,
If I mount on a horse and bear arms!"
When the emir heard him, he thought he would lose
   his mind.   1600
In his loud voice, he began to shout:
"Whore's son! Coward! I see that you're a pathetic case!
You did this self-same thing when we landed the boats,
When you let Elye, the Frenchman, escape!
Tervagant! If I only had him, then I'd be in luck!   1605
He'd enter into combat against the emir on the battlefield!"
But Elye was in the room and clearly heard them all.*
The emir called his private chamberlain*:
"Go bring Rosamonde from her room for me.
I'll give her to Lubien right away. I won't be dissuaded."   1610
And the cowards replied, "Well said!
This is the best argument that we could ever come up with!"
Joshua came up to the door to her room.
He came forward and pounded the door knocker.
Rosamonde heard him, and she called to the duke: 1615
"Noble knight's son, now you're in harm's way!
I think they've spotted you here, and your presence has
   been betrayed.
My father wants to have all your limbs cut off!"
"What a shame," said Elye, "that I'm not armed!
If only I were wearing my white orphreyed hauberk,   1620

Et laciet le vert elme, l'espee a mon costé,
Et li vaires d'Espaigne me fust chi aprestés!
Con vous me veriés* ja de ruistes cos doner,
Et mon fier vaselage fierement esprover!»
Et respont la pucele, «De folië parlés, 1625
Par Dieu, de le bataille, n'i aura mot soné!
Que paien ont grant force, tost seriés maté,
Et .i. hom vers .xx.m., conment poroit durer?»
«Ne sai,» che dist Elye, «quel consel me donrés?»
Et respont la pucele, «Consel aurés assés*; 1630
A enfant vous tenrai, se plus me demandés!
Vasal, en chele cambre laiens vous en entrés,
Par cel guicet la jus, que vous des iex veés*;
La troverés .iii. lis de cristal tresjetés,
Li pavemens en est tous a fin or ovrés; 1635
Les colombes d'ivoire qui tienent les pilers,*
Ains ne furent veües plus rices en chités!
.Iii. chevalier en coste i pevent bien ex aler,
Tout lor lances levees, sor les destriers armés.
Trespassés les abarges, et gardins et fossés,* 1640
La verés vous les huis et le palais torner;
Et les vieutres detraire et les ors encainer,
Et les pisons noians, et le ciel estelé,
Et toute riens en tere, conme l'arce Noé,
Ai ge fait en ma canbre a fin or pointurer. 1645
S'i a une richece dont vous ne vous gardés:
.Iiii.c. chevaliers, as manteus engoulés,
Et sont home ton pere, ne le quier plus cheler,
Julïen de Saint Gille, qui tant fait a loer.
Bien quide l'amiraus que soient mort geté, 1650
Mais je fac les François en ma cambre garder,
Les haubers et les elmes, les escus fors et lés,
Et cascon tient s'amie par l'ermin engoulé, [87v-b]

1640   ms l. abarge; the «s» has been inadvertently omitted by the scribe.
1652   ms l. hub's; the «a» has been left out; we emend with the usual orthography of this manuscript

Part Four

And had my emerald-studded helmet strapped on, my sword
   at my side,
And if my dappled Spanish steed were ready here,
Then you'd see me already out there dealing devastating blows
And boldly testing my noble knighthood!"
And the young maiden answered, "What an insane idea!*   1625
For God's sake, I'll hear no talk of fighting.
Since the pagans are so strong, you'd be quickly killed.
How could one man ever hold out against twenty thousand?"
"I have no idea," said Elye. "What advice will you give me?"
And the maid answered, "You'll get plenty of advice!   1630
You'll seem like only a child to me, if you keep asking
   me questions!
Sir knight, go into that inner room,
Through that gate down there that's right before your eyes.
There you'll find three beds of finely cast crystal.
The pavement of the floor is all worked in fine gold.   1635
The columns of ivory, which hold up the pillars —
Never were more rich pillars ever seen in a city!
Three knights side by side could easily pass through them,*
All their lances raised high, wearing armor, on warhorses.
Continue on by the bowers, moats and gardens.   1640
There you'll see doors and the turning palace*
And sporting greyhounds and chained bears
And swimming fishes and the starry sky
And everything on earth, just like Noah's ark,
I've had painted in my room in fine gold!   1645
And there is a treasure there you don't expect:
Four hundred knights with furred mantels,*
And they're your father's men — I don't want to hide it longer —
Julien of Saint-Gilles, who did so many praiseworthy deeds.
The emir thought that they had been thrown in prison
   to die,   1650
But I had the Frenchmen hidden away in my room,
Their hauberks and their helmets, their strong broad shields,
And each one holds his beloved by her ermine robe.

Qui est fille de conte, de duc, u d'amirel,
Et si que la plus vieile* n'a pas .xxx. ans passé.　　　　1655
Quant il vieut, si le baisse douchement et soëf,
Qui vous aideront bien, se mestier en avés.»
«Dame,» che dist Elye, «v.c. merchis et grés!»
«A val, par devers destre, quant vous i enterés,
Troverés le chiterne,* a fin or pointuré,　　　　1660
Et le mien lit demaine, mout bien connisterés.»
«Ne sai,» che dist Elye, «boin consel me donés.»
Et respont la puchele, «Encor vous dirai el;
Trespassés tous les autres, devant vos iex gardés,*
Par art de ningromance, sont li limon fondé;　　　　1665
Aussi siet avenant, con s'il fust conpassé.
Si a .i. vermeil paille galasïen ovré,
Del plus fin or d'Arabe, i a .c. mars saudés;
Si a .m. clokete qui pendent d'or fin cler.
Touchiés i de vo doit, .i. petitet assés,　　　　1670
Amis, en tant de terme con .i. hons peut aler,
Mais qu'il soit auques lons, .xxx. piés mesurés,
Vous sonera li lis, menuement soëf.
Ne harpe, ne vïele, ne route, ne jougler,
Ne nus oiseus qui soit tant sache de chanter,　　　　1675
Plus volentiers n'orois, je vous di par verté.»
Elye entre en la cambre, .iii. tans i a trové,
Que la puchele n'ait de bouce devissé.
Galopin le petit ont defors oublié.
Rosamonde la bele li va l'uis defermé.　　　　1680
Signor, tout premerains i entra Josüé,
Li quiver d'Alixandre, qui tout confonge Dé,
Qui Galopins avoit et cachiet et navré.
U qu'il voit le baron, s'el reconnut* assés.
«Cuiver,» dist la puchele,* «c'avés vous en pensé,　　　　1685
Qui entrés en ma cambre, sans congiet demander?

1654　　ms u. damiel; the «r» was omitted and is restored, correcting the hypometric verse.
1655　　ms plus n., rendering the verse hypometric; the word «viele» has clearly been omitted and we restore with the orthography of *Aiol,* 1513. See note.
1663　　ms p. encore; the hypermetric verse is corrected by use of the alternate form.

Part Four

Each lady is the daughter of a count, of a duke or of an emir,
And the oldest one is not yet thirty.   1655
When he wants, she gently and softly kisses him.
They'll be of great help, if you need it."
"My lady," said Elye, "five hundred thanks!"
"Down there, on the right, when you enter,
You will find the cistern painted in fine gold,   1660
And my bed, you'll recognize it right away."
"I don't know," said Elye, "if you're giving me good advice."*
And the lady answered, "Here's still more to come:
Go beyond all the others right before your eyes.
By the art of necromancy, the bed frame is held together.   1665
It stands as firmly as though it had been set by compass,
And it has a vermillion cover with Galician embroidery,*
Sewn with a thousand marks' worth of the finest gold
    from Arabia.
And hanging there are a thousand tiny tiny bells made of fine
    white gold.*
Touch it with your finger, ever so slightly,   1670
My friend, in so much time as a man can go
Thirty measured feet, even if he is tall,
The bed will ring softly for you.
No harp nor viol, rote nor minstrel,
Nor any bird that might exist, no matter how well he sings,   1675
Would you listen to more gladly. I am telling you the truth."
Elye entered the room. He found there three times as much as
What the lady's lips had described.
They had forgotten Galopin the short and left him outside.*
Rosamonde went back and opened the door.   1680
My lords, right away Joshua entered,
That despicable traitor from Alexandria, may God punish him,
Whom little Galopin had pursued and wounded.
As soon as he saw him, the knight immediately recognized
    him.
"Worthless creature," said the maid, "What could you be
    thinking,   1685
That you could simply come into my room without asking
    permission?

Elye of Saint-Gilles

Pres va je ne te fac tous les menbres coper,
U ferir, u bien batre, u loier a .i. pel!»
«Dame,» dist li paien, «mout grant tort en avés!   [88r-a]
Vostre peres vous mande c'alés a lui parler!»   1690
Et respont la pucele, «Je ne li puis veer.»
Ançois qu'ele vausist de la canbre torner,
S'est faite la puchele gentement atorner.
En son dos a vestu .i. hermin engoulé,
D'une lasnete d'or ot estrais* les costés;   1695
Unes cauches mout riches, solers bien pointurés.
Un mantel covoitous ot a son col jeté:
Uns rices amiraus l'i ot fait presenter.
.Iii. ans mist on a faire, ains que fust parovrés,
Et fu d'un cabetenc* tout environ ourlés.   1700
Richement ot la bele son gent cors acesmé;
De plus bele pucele n'oï nus hon parler,
Les ances ot bassetes, et estroit les costés,
Et la bouche bien faite, et les dens ot igués,*
Et sont fait par conpas, con s'il fuissent planté.   1705
Li alaine de li par flaire tant soëf,
Que n'es .i. encensiers de mostier enbrasé.
Onques Dieus ne fist home qui de mere soit nés,
Se il tres bien le garde, que n'en soit trespensés.
Faucon ne nus ostoir, ne oiseus d'outremer,   1710
Ne porte si bias ieus, ne de si grant biauté,
Con porte la pucele, qui tant a de biauté.
Or s'en va la pucele, a son pere parler.

47.
Signor, quant la puchele en entra en la sale,
Rois Macabrés le prent, li vieus, entre ses bras,*   1715
Delés lui l'a assis, et si l'acole et baise:
«Fille,» dist l'amiraus, «mout estes convenable*;
Por vostre cors me croist mout dolereus damages!

1695   ms o. estrais; we use the usual orthography of this form of «estraindre», as found at 4287. See note.
1697   ms u. maltel; we use the normal spelling, as found at 2157.

Part Four

I'm almost ready to have all your limbs cut off
Or have you tied to a post and thoroughly whipped or beaten!"
"My lady," said the pagan, "you are greatly mistaken.
Your father has ordered you to go to speak to him."   1690
And the maid anwered, "I can't refuse him this!"
But first she wanted to return to her room,
And she had herself nobly attired.
She put on a collared ermine robe —
With a golden cord she had bound the sides —   1695
And wore rich hose and exquisitely-painted slippers.
She put around her neck an envy-inspiring cloak
A gift from a powerful emir.
It was seven years in the making before it was completed.
Its expensive cloth was embroidered all around.   1700
What a wonderful outfit the beautiful maid chose for herself!
No man ever heard tell of a more lovely maiden.
She had low-slung hips, and she had a slim waist
And a well-formed mouth, and with straight, regular teeth,
And evenly spaced, were they placed.   1705
And from her mouth her breath smelled as sweet
As lighted incense in a church's censer.
Never did God make a man born of a mother,
Who, upon contemplating her beauty, would not fall into
   a trance.
No falcon, hawk nor bird from overseas   1710
Had such lovely eyes nor such great beauty
As that maid, who posssessed such great loveliness.
Now she went off to speak to her father.

47.
My lords, when the young maiden entered the room,
King Macabre, the old man, took her in his arms,   1715
He seated her beside him, and he hugged and kissed her.
"My daughter," said the emir, "you are very becoming.
Because of you, an increasingly distressing problem is
   besetting me!

Elye of Saint-Gilles

Lubïen de Baudas, a le chenue barbe,
Est issus de sa terre, s'est entrés en mes marces; 1720
De ton cors le vaillant li ai fait otriage.
Mes il me jureraançois que de moi parte,
Coroneë serés, ains le feste de Paske.»
«Sire,» dist la pucele, «ains me prenge li rage,
U male fondre,* Sire, m'eüst ançois toute arse, [88r-b] 1725
Que Lubien de Baudas, a le chenuë barbe,
Mon gent cors avenant ait ja nuit en sa garde,
Ne grate le sien dos, ne que sente se barbe!»

48.
Rosamonde la bele, qui preus fu et nobile,
En apela son pere, se li a pris a dire: 1730
«Biaus pere, donés moi,» dist la franche mescine,
«.I. vallet voil avoir touset de barbe prime;
Je ne quier que il ait que l'espeë forbie,
Qui por amor de moi fache chevalerie.
N'ai cure de viellart, qui le pel ait froncie, 1735
Peres, il a le loi a le pume porie,
Qui par desors est verde, et par dedens, vermine!*
Ne poroië soufrir la soie char flairie*;
Miex m'en fuiroië, voir, conme une autre caitive,*
Ens en .i. autre tere, a deul et a martire, 1740
Que Lubïen li fel, a le barbe florie,
Mon gent cors avenant eüst en sa baillie!»

49.
«En la moië foi, Sire,» dist la bele al vis fier,*
«Caïfas, li miens frere, qui tant fait a prisier,

1722 ms me jura; emending to the future corrects the hypometric verse. See note.
1725 ms ancois arse; the verse is hypometric, and the sense calls for «toute».
1734 ms a. del; the article standing alone does not make sense and is omitted.
1737 ms p. dens; the scribe accidentally omitted the «de» of dedens; the error created a hypometric verse.
1738 ms p. soufri; the infinitive is needed after the modal auxiliary. See note.
1743 ms v. cfer, with a dot under the "c," where he began to write «cler» but emended to expunctuate the «c» and alter the «l» to an «f».

Part Four

Lubien of Baudas, with the white beard,
Has left his realm and has entered my kingdom.   1720
To him I have granted your worthy person.
But he will swear to me before he leaves with you
That you will be crowned before the Easter feast."
"My lord," said the young maid, "I'd rather be consumed
   by madness
Or burned up, sir, by devastating lightening,   1725
Before Lubien of Bagdad with the white beard
Ever possesses all my charms every night
Or that I ever have to scratch his back or feel his beard!"

48.
The beautiful Rosamonde, who was noble and worthy,
Addressed her father and began speaking to him: 1730
"Dear father, give me," said the noble young maiden,
"A youth. I want a very young man with his first beard.
I don't want him to have anything except a sharp sword
Who, for love of me, would perform acts of chivalry.
I have no desire whatsoever for an old man whose skin
   is wrinkled!   1735
Father, he looks like a rotting apple*
Whose outside is green and inside is wormy.
I couldn't bear the smell of his withered flesh.
Truly, I'd rather flee as a wretched, exiled woman,
To another land, in martyrdom and grief,   1740
Than for that treacherous Lubien, with his long straggling
   beard,
To ever have me in his governance."

49.
"By my faith, my lord," said the beauty with the bright face,
"Caifas my brother, who has done such worthy deeds,

113

Elye of Saint-Gilles

Ne Jossé d'Alixandre, ne Malpriant le fier,   1745
Encore n'ont il gaires Lubïen essaiet,
Ne son grant vaselage prové, ne acointié.
Par mon cors seulement vous i quidiés paier;
Mais par icel Mahon qui tout a a baillier,
Iceste grant paor ne vous vaut .i. denier.   1750
Envers .i. autre afaire, vous en quic conmenchier:
Je manderai en Franche, les barons chevaliers,
Des plus haus pers de France, qui servent por denier;
Certes, je vous ferai tous ces murs trebucier,
Et toutes ces parois cheoir, devant vos piés!   1755
Venés avant, biaus pere, si me chees as piés,*
Et si me proiëroiés, et manaide, et pitié.
Je quic avoir ains vespre .i. itel chevalier,
Qui ert de paienie u ert de crestïens,
Qui fera la bataille encontre Lubïen!»   1760

50.
«En la moie foi, Sire,» dist la bele al vis cler,   [88v-a]
«Or me dites, biaus peres, par Mahomet no dé,
Se je vous pooie ore .i. tel home trover,
Qui feïst la bataille vers l'amiral el pré,
Li feriés vous tous de son cors seürté,   1765
Que il n'i eüst garde au venir ne a l'aler,
Ne qu'il ne fust mal mis, ochis, ne afolés?»
«Fille,» dist l'amiraus, «de folië parlés!
S'il m'avoit d'un espiel par mi le cors navrés,
Ne auroit il ja garde, n'al venir n'a l'aler!»   1770
Et respont Rosamonde, «Premier, le me jurés!»
«Voire,» dist Macabrés, «.c. fois, se vous volés!»

1753   ms De plus; we emended the scribal oversight of the omitted «s» for the plural.
1754   ms f. tout; although scribal variation is fluid throughout, we emend to the plural for the context, since agreement is made by the scribe in the following verse.
1757   ms m. proieroie; we emend by adding «s». See note.
1759   ms u de; the verse is hypometric and «ert» has no doubt been omitted by the scribe.
1765   ms vous de; the hypometric verse is emended by adding «tous». See note.

Part Four

Nor Joshua of Alexandria, nor the proud Malpriant   1745
Have ever even challenged Lubien in battle
Nor tested nor been acquainted with his great skills in
    knighthood.
You are thinking about buying him off solely with me!
But, by that Mahomet who has all in governance,
This great fear of yours is baseless.   1750
I believe I can show you another way out of this bind.
I'll send to France for nobles and knights.
With the help of the highest peers of France, who serve as
    mercenaries,*
Truly, I'll bring down all your walls
And make all of these ramparts fall before your feet.   1755
Come forward, dear father, and fall at my feet,
And if you were to beg my aid and pity,
I think that before vespers I'll have found such a knight
Be he of pagandom or of Christendom,
Who'll do battle against Lubien!"   1760

50.
"In my faith, lord," said the beauty with the bright face,
"Tell me, dear father, by Mahomet our god,
Now if I can find you such a man,
Who'd fight against the emir upon the field of battle,
Would you grant him safe passage,   1765
So that he would not have to worry, either coming or going,
About being mistreated or killed or harmed?"
"My daughter," said the emir, "you're talking nonsense!
Even if he had wounded me with a lance through my body,
He'd have no worries for his safety, either coming or going!" 1770
And Rosamonde answered, "First swear it to me."
"Of course," said Macabre, "One hundred times, if you want."

Il a fait Mahomet el palais aporter,
Desor .i. vermeil paile galasïen ovrés;
Le pieres presïeusses getoient grant clarté. 1775
La jura l'amiraus quan qu'ele ot devissé,
Paien et Sarrasin, et li boin, et li mal.*
Rosamonde le voit; grant joie en a mené;
Arier vint en la canbre; Elye a apelé.

51.
Rosamonde la bele s'en entra en la cambre; 1780
A haute vois escrie, «Sire Elyë de Franche!
Des or parlés en haut, que il n'i ait covranche!
Vous ferés la bataille au fer de vostre lanche;
Gentiex fieus a baron, con puis estre dolante!
Lubïen de Baudas, a la barbe ferrande, 1785
Est issus de sa terre, s'est venus en no lande.
Au riche roi mon pere, me requiert et demande;
Portera m'ent, li fel, a Baudas, en sa cambre,
Se je ne puis trover home qui me desfenge.
Gentiex fieus a baron, voi con sui bele et gente, 1790
Mout ferés bel scrviche, s'a Dieu rendés .i. ame.»
«Dame,» che dist Elye, «ne sui pas a aprendre;
Salemon si prist feme, dont sovent me ramenbre,
.Iiii. jors se fist morte, en son palais meïsme,*
Que onques ne crola, puing, ne pïé, ne menbre. 1795
Puis en fist .i. vasaus toute sa consïenche.
Par le foi que vous doi, fole cose est de feme; [88v-b]
Certes, con* plus le garde, donques le pert on senpre!»

52.
«Sire,» dist la puchele, «n'ai soing de ranproner,
Gari vous ai des plaies, savoir m'en devés gré. 1800
Feré vous la bataille, dites, u le lairés?
Se vous vers Lubïen me volés contrester,

1779   ms Ariere; yields a hypermetric verse, corrected by dropping the «e».
1795   ms c. puing; a negative particle is missing which, when added, corrects the hypometric verse.

Part Four

He had Mahomet brought into the palace
On an embroidered vermilion Galician cloth.
The precious gems gleamed with great brightness.   1775
There the emir swore to whatever she said,
And also all the pagans and Saracens, the good and the evil.*
Rosamonde observed it, which brought her great joy.*
She went back to her chamber; she called Elye.

51.
The lovely Rosamonde went back into her room.   1780
Aloud, she cried, "Lord Elye of France,
From now on, speak aloud, and let there be no concealment!
You'll do battle with the steel tip of your lance!
Noble baron's son, how saddened you must feel!
Lubien of Bagdad with his steel gray beard   1785
Has come out of his land and has come into our country;
From the powerful king, my father, he asks and demands me.
This evil man will carry me away to Bagdad, to his chamber,
If I cannot find a man who'll defend me.
Noble knight's son, see how beautiful and noble I am.   1790
You will do a very great service, if you deliver a soul to God!"
"My lady," said Elye, "I'm not easily influenced.
Solomon* did take a wife, I think of this often.
For four days she feigned death in their palace,
When she never moved a hand, nor foot, nor limb.   1795
Then a knight did his will with her.
By the allegiance I owe you, a woman is a mad thing:
Truly, the more you watch over her, the sooner you'll lose her!"

52.
"My lord," said the young woman, "I don't need insults.
I cured you of your wounds; you should be grateful to me!   1800
Tell me: will you fight the battle, or will you refuse it?
If you're willing to fight against Lubien for me,

Ja ançois ne verés Pentecouste passer,
Que vous quic de Sorbrie faire roi coroné.»
«Dame,» che dist Elye, «car me laissiés ester! 1805
Che n'est mië marchiet por l'argent deviser;
Je ne prendrai jor feme, se ne croit en mon Dé;
Mais por l'amor des plaies dont vous garri m'avés,
Se vous cheval et armes me volïés doner,
Je m'en istroië fors por mon cors deporter, 1810
Encontre l'amiraus dont je vous oi parler.
Quant partira de moi, se il osse joster,
Ja ne s'en gabera, se Dieus me vieut salver!»

53.
«Par mon cief, damoisele,» dist Elyë de Franche,
«Chanpïon avés boin por droit porter sa lanche; 1815
N'a paien en Espaigne de si riche poissanche,
Se il vous a dit cose qui vous tort a pessanche,
Et jel puis encontré* par le fer de ma lanche,
Quant il partra de moi, ja n'en aura beubanche.»
«Sire,» dist la pucele, «mout me faites joianche, 1820
Et je guerpi Mahon por la vostre creanche;
Por la vostre amisté, m'en irai jou en Franche!
Mais quant che venra senpre, que vous venrés ensanble,
Gardés vous de cheoir, qui qu'en sele remaigne.
Li glous a .i. destrier, il n'a si boin en Franche, 1825
C'est Prinsaus l'Aragon, qui fu nés d'Orïande;
Quant il vient en la presse, que la bataille est grande,
Lors saut de .iiii. piés, et brait, et fiert des jambes!»
Galopin saut en piés, quant oï la loanche,
Et vient a son signor, sans nule demoranche; 1830
Maintenant li a dit, li leres sans doutanche,
«Gentiex fieus a baron, de coi avés doutanche?
Faites querre les armes beles et avenantes, [89r-a]
Dites la damoisele qu'ele vous baut sa lanche,

1807   ms jor se; the scribe has omitted the word «feme» which restores the meaning and the hypometric verse.
1810   ms i. fros; an accidental metathesis emended to the correct spelling.

Part Four

Before you ever see Pentecost go by,
I'm certain I'll have you crowned king of Sorbrie."
"My lady," said Elye, "stop bothering me.   1805
We're not in a marketplace haggling over money.
I'll never ever wed a woman, if she does not believe in my God.
But in recognition of those wounds from which you cured me,
If you're willing to give me a horse and weapons,
I'll ride out to enjoy some exercise,   1810
Against the emir of whom I heard you speak.
After we separate, if he dares to joust,
He'll never joke about it, if God will protect me."

53.
"I swear by my head, my lady," said Elye of France,
"You have a good champion to bear his lance for you as is
    the custom.   1815
There's not a pagan in Spain* of such mighty power
That if he said something that wrongly caused you pain,*
And if I could meet him with the iron tip of my lance,
After I'm through with him, he'll have no reason to boast."
"My lord," said the maid, "you fill me with joy, 1820
And I'll give up Mahomet for your belief,
And for your sake, I'll go to France.
But when it happens soon that you two join in battle,
Be careful not to fall. No matter what, stay in the saddle!
That worthless pagan has a horse — there is none so good
    in France —   1825
Prinsaus, the Aragonese, who was bred in Oriande.
When it gallops into the press and the battle is raging,
Then it jumps up with all four feet, and neighs and
    strikes with its forelegs."
Galopin jumped up when he heard these words of praise,
And he came to his lord without delay.   1830
Now the thief said to him without hesitation:
"Noble knight's son, what are you afraid of?
Have your fine, handsome arms brought.
Tell the young lady to give you her lance.

Ançois la mië nuit, que li premiers cos cante, 1835
Vous rendrai le destrier, qui qui en ait pessanche!
Orendroit je vois quere, sans nule demorance,
Nel lairai por paien, que li cors Dieu cravente,
Que je nel vous amaing, soiés ent a fïanche!»
Et respondi Elye, «Jhesu t'en doinst poissanche!» 1840
Lors parla la puchele a Elyë de Franche.

54.
«Par mon cief, Sire Elye,» ce dist la damoisele,
«Li destriers est si boins, il n'a millor en terre;
Des grans bontés de lui vous dirai tout acertes.
Il n'est home en cest siecle, si le prent par le resne, 1845
Se il le prent au frain et il monte en la sele,
S'il n'en est mout hardis, que il n'en jete a tere!*
Et bien ne set joster, et droit porter la teste!»
Galopins saut en piés quant oï la novele,
Et afuble une cape, n'ot que .iii. piés sor terre; 1850
Prist .c. saus de denier, entor lui les areste.*
Viseus fu mout li leres de sa besoigne faire.
Et d'ileuckes s'en torne, que il plus n'i arcstc,
Fors de la cambre vait, a l'uis de la posterne;
Trés par desous la tor, illeuques trove .i. eue. 1855
Maintenant entra ens; n'a paor que il perde;
Il a passé a no; d'autre part vint a tere.
Lors passa .i. vergier, et trestoutes les estres,*
Dusc'au tref l'amiraus, ne fine ne ne cesse.
Cha defors l'a trové, par defors les herberges. 1860
A tant es le laron, por conter ses noveles,
U qu'il voit Lubïen, gentement l'en apele:
«Icil grant Mahomet qui le siecle governe,
Cil saut l'enpereor* et tout cil qui le servent!»
Et Lubïens respont, que il ne s'i areste, 1865

1858   ms e. trestoute; the plural form is needed, and usually observed.
1864   ms l'enperereor; the scribe used the normal abbreviation, but proceded to spell out the word; neither F nor R noted the error. We emend to omit it.
1864   ms et tout; the plural form is needed.

Part Four

Before midnight, when the first cock crows,   1835
I will bring you that charger, no matter who objects.
Right away I am going to get it, without any delay.
I won't fail because of any pagan — may God cause him harm —
To bring you that steed. Count on it!"*
And Elye answered him, "May Jesus give you strength!"   1840
Then the maiden spoke to Elye of France.

54.
"I swear by my head, Lord Elye," the lady then said,
"This warhorse is so good, there's no better on earth.
Here's the truth about its qualities:
There is not a man on earth, if he takes it by the reins,   1845
If he seizes its bridle, and he mounts in the saddle,
That if he is not extremely bold, it won't throw him to the ground!
And it knows how to joust well, and how to carry its head high."
Galopin jumped up when he heard these words,*
And he fastened on a cape, although he was only three
    feet tall,   1850
And he took a hundred coins worth a denier. He secured them
    about him.
The thief was very careful to do his task well,
And then he started out so that he would no more delay.
Out of the room he went to the postern gate.
Far below the tower, there's a river.   1855
He jumped right in. He was not afraid of losing his life.
He swam to the other side, and he came to the shore.
Then he passed through an orchard and all the moats.
As far as the emir's tent, he did not stop or halt.
He found him out front, outside the tents.   1860
The thief appeared before him to tell his story.
When he saw Lubien, he nobly called to him:
"May that great Mahomet, who rules the whole world,
Save the emperor and all those who serve him!"
And Lubien replied without delay,   1865

Elye of Saint-Gilles

«Amis, et cil saut toi! Dont es et de quel terre?»
Galopins li respont, qui estoit mout fors leres,
«Sire, d'outre mer sui, del val desous Luiserne!
Marcheans ere riches, encore ersoir al vespre; [89r-b]
Une barge menoie, ains hon ne vit tant bele! 1870
Tant i avoit argent et de l'or de Palerne,
Manteus, et siglaton, et paile de Biterne;
.Xx. destriers i avoit, et .xx. mules mout beles!
Celes vous envoioit li sires de no tere,*
Car il vous aime mout, et si le fait a certes! 1875
Macabré me taut tout, et mes nés et mes barges,*
Et mes homes a mors, et moi geté en l'aigue.
A vous vieng, Sire rois, que droiture me faites!»
Quant l'entendi li rois, por .i. poi qu'il ne derve;
Il se drecha sor pies, mist se main sor sa teste, 1880
«Mar le pensa, li glous, par ceste barbe bele!
Vostre avoir raverois, et vo* barges refaites!
Et del sien, .xv. tans, ains que fine la guerre!
Se jou ai la mescine, tes avoirs torne a perte!*
Et se n'ai la pucele, dont conmenche la guerre! 1885
Jamais ne finerai, si l'aura cha fors traite!»

55.
«Sire,» che dist li leres, «de l'avoir ne me chiet,
Car j'en aurai assés; je sai bien gaignier.
Mes des destriers me poisse, c'avoië forment cier!
Que .i. en i avoit, qui mout fist a proisier, 1890
.I. vairet mout tresient, .i. hermin montenier;
Il a maigre la teste, et l'oil apert et fier,
Petites orilletes, si a le crin deugié,
Les jambes longes, si ot coupé le piet.*
En nul pais qui soit n'en a nul plus legier! 1895

1891 ms .i. vaire't; the poet unnecessarily abbreviated, on the pattern of the following word; cf. 1864. We emend to the attested form of the noun. See note.

Part Four

"Friend, and may he save you too! Where are you from?
   What land?"
Galopin, who was a most clever thief, answered him*:
"My lord, from overseas, from the valleys near Luiserne.
I was still a rich merchant last night at vespers.
I was hauling on a barge, no one ever saw such a beautiful one,   1870
So much silver and gold from Palermo there was on it,
So many cloaks and rich clothes, rich bedspreads from
   Biterne,
Twenty warhorses there were, and twenty very fine mules.
These the lord of our land was sending to you,
Because he loves you greatly, and this he was truly doing.   1875
Macabre took it all from me — my ships and my barges —
And he killed my men, and he threw me in the water.
I come to you, lord king, so that you can render justice for me!"
When the king heard him, he nearly lost his mind.
He stood up on his feet and put his hands on his head: 1880
"He'll rue the day he ever thought of it, by this handsome
   beard!
You'll have your wealth back and your barges replenished,
And fifteen times their wealth, before this war ends.
If I get the maiden, your riches turn to losses;
If I don't get the maiden, a war will break out.   1885
I won't stop waging war until you've regained your wealth."

55.
"Sire," the thief replied, "I'm not concerned about my riches,
Because I'll have enough. I'm an expert at earning it back.
But it saddens me about the warhorses. I was very attached
   to them.
For there was one of them that had done many fine deeds,   1890
A most noble, dappled-gray horse, an Armenian of
   the highlands.
It had a small, slim head and proud, flashing eyes
And tiny little ears and a very dainty mane
And long legs; its feet were delicate.
None lighter on its feet was ever born in any other land.   1895

Mieudres destrier ne fu onques por gerroier,
Quant estoit en bataille, et en estor plenier,
Et il trovoit a terre abatut chevalier,
Tant le foloit des piés, que tout ert debrisiés!
De baston ne d'espee, ne covenoit touchier!» 1900
«Tai, glous!» dist l'amiraus, «lai ester ton pladier!
J'ai encore tel cens que miex fait a prisier*;
Je nel donroië pas, por .m. livres d'or mier!
S'avoiés asamblé des tiens .xv. millier,
Et trestout ciaus de Franche quan qu'en a u resnier, [89v-a] 1905
Ne querroië tout ciaus por ichestui cangier!
Orendroit le veras, ja trestorné ne n'ert.»*
«Sire,» che dist li leres, «por coi le veroie* ge?
Je ne sai riens de che, ne ne connois destriers,
Puis que jel voi troter, a mout isnel le tieng. 1910
Mieus ameroi .i. peu, s'il vous plaist, a mangier.
Tant ai esté en l'aigue, tout le cors ai molliet!»
Et respont l'amiraus, «Par mon cief, vilain es!»*
«Sire,» che dist li leres, «or ne vous courechiés!
Puis que vous le volés, jel verai volentiers!» 1915
L'amiraus se corouche, s'a bouté l'eskekier,
Mieus venist l'amiraus c'a son giu entendié!*
Tart estoit Galopins, que l'eüst aprochié.
Les aises au cheval vous doië dire bien:
Il ert en .i. travail* bien saielé d'achier, 1920
Le menor des estaches ne menast .i. somier.
Il ne remuïst mie, por le keue a tranchier.
A .iii. kaïnes d'or fu par le col loiés,*
.Iiii. paires de buies ot li chevaus es piés;
Par dedens sont feutrees, por le poil que ne ciet. 1925
Del feure et de l'avaine ot desi al poitrier,
Et boit a une nef* entailliié d'or mier.
L'aige li cort devant, a canel a aisiet.
.Xxx. gardes i a, qui gardent le destrier;

1906 ms q. tout; we emend to the plural.
1926 ms De, emended here with the enclitic particle for parallel structure.
1927 ms u. nes; emended to «nef», used throughout.

Part Four

A better steed there never was for warfare.
When it was in battle, and in the full furor of combat,
And it found on the ground a fallen knight,
It would trample him so much with its feet that all his bones
   would be broken.
You didn't need to touch him with sword nor mace."   1900
"Quiet, impudent braggart!" said the emir, "Enough of your talk!
I have a better one in my stables that does far more fine deeds!
For a thousand pounds of pure gold, I'd never give it up!
If you had fifteen thousand pounds of gold, together with
   all your own gold,
And all the gold in France, or any kingdom whatever,   1905
I would not trade all that gold for my horse!
You'll see it right away now. There's no putting it off."
"Sir," replied the little thief, "what good would it do me to look at it?
This is something I know nothing about, nor do I know
   warhorses!
If I see one trotting, it looks fast to me!   1910
If you please, I'd rather have something to eat!
I've been in the water so long, I'm soaked to the skin!"
And the emir answered, "By my head, what a peasant!"
"Sire," said the little thief, "now don't get angry!
Since that's what you want, I'll be glad to take a look at it!"   1915
The emir got angry. He kicked his chessboard over.*
He'd have had better luck if he'd paid attention to his game!
Galopin was only stating the obvious, when he'd
   approached him.
About the luxurious lodgings of the horse, I must tell you now.
It was in a cage well reinforced with steel.   1920
The least of its harnesses would not lead a sumpter mule.
It could not move at all, even if its tail were cut off!
With three chains of gold, it was tied around the neck.
Four pairs of shoes, the horse had on its feet.
They were padded with felt all inside, so its hair wouldn't
   be rubbed off.   1925
It had hay and oats all the way up to its chest,
And it drank from a large vessel sculpted from pure gold.
Water ran freely through a channel in front of it.
Thirty guards there were who watched over the steed,

Et quant li .xv. dorment, les .xv. esteut vellier. 1930
Il n'en i a .i. seul, tant orgelleus et fier,
S'il le treve dormant, ja meche autre loier.
Ja n'i metra escange, fors que les iex del cief!
Forjurer li fait ot* le terre et le renier,
Et lui et ses* lignages fors del pais cachier. 1935
.Iii. chiereres i ardent, qui mout font a prissier.*
L'amiraux le descevre, s'ot le costé delgié,
La teste fu bauchande, et tout li .iiii. piet.
Il a dit au laron, «Ere li tien si chier?»
«Nenil!» che dist li leres, «ja celer nel vous quier, 1940
Ne vi mais nul si bel, ne si bien estachié!»   [89v-b]
Et dist entre ses dens, que nus ne l'entendié:
«Male garde en ferois, ains le jor esclairier,
Je le vous enblerai, se jel puis esploitier,
Anuit en ceste nuit, ja si bien n'ert gaitiés! 1945
Sire Elyë de Franche, se cestui aviiés,
U roialme de France, vanter* vous en poriés,
C'ains hom de vo lignage ne fu sor tel destrier!
Mais mout est* en fort lieu; ne sai conment che ert,
Or en penst Dameldé, qui tout a a jugier, 1950
Par l'ame de mon pere, autant aim cel destrier,
Con s'il fust la defors, a .i. arbre atachiet!»

Part Four

And while fifteen men slept, the other fifteen remained
   on guard.   1930
There was not a single one of them so arrogant and proud
That if he were found sleeping, he'd not get another kind
   of reward.
Not even the eyes in his head could he trade for it.
He would have to leave his lands and the kingdom,
And he and his lineage would be driven from the land.   1935
Three torches burned in there, which were very costly.
The emir took off the steed's horse blanket; its flanks were svelte.
Its head was palest white, as well as each of its four feet.
He said to the thief, "Was yours so valuable?"
"No," said the thief, "I won't try to hide it from you.   1940
I've never seen any mount so beautiful, nor so well guarded!"
And he added, between his teeth, so no one could hear:
"I'll make sure it's poorly guarded before the break of day,
And I'll steal it from you — if I can pull it off —
At nightfall this very evening, no matter how well it's
   guarded!   1945
Lord Elye of France, if you had this one,
In the kingdom of France, you'd be able to boast
That no man of your lineage was ever on such a charger!
But it's in such a stronghold, I don't know how things
   will turn out.
Now may the Lord God grant His blessing, Who has
   dominion over all;   1950
By my father's soul, I love this warhorse as much
As if he were out there tied up to a tree!"

Elye of Saint-Gilles

Part Five

56.
Des puis que Galopins ot veü le cheval,
Ne n'ot* bien, ne repos, ne aillor ne pensa.
Sarrasin s'estormissent; venu sont as ostaus;   1955
Il demanderent l'aigue, al mengier vont sear.*
Aprés, s'en vont dormir, que ne pensent nul mal,
Que del petit laron, ne s'en donent regart.
Galopins ne s'oblie; venus est au travail;
Il s'apuie a le trelle, si garde le cheval;   1960
Dameldé reclama, le pere esperital:
«El ventre del pisson, garistes Saint Jonas,
Les .iii. enfans garistes, que il ne furent ars;
Sainte Marië, Dame, donés me che cheval,
Que ne me puist blechier, ne ne me fache mal!»   1965
Tant entent au proier, Galopins li vasal,
De l'aleine de lui, esfreë* li cheval.   [90r-a]
Il saut de .iiii. piés, si abat le traval;
Les gaites le coisirent, si saillent cele part,
Et saisirent lor lances, et gaverlos* et dars,   1970
Et kierent par le canbre, .vii.xx. bien par esmal.
Galopins fu en l'onbre, qui petit les douta*;
Tant vont pres del laron, que cascon le frota.
S'il ot adont paor, je ne m'en mervel ja!
Quant il ne trevent riens, s'asient as escas,   1975
Et dist li uns a l'altre, «C'a senti chis chevals?»
«Par mon cief,» dist li maistres, «sejornés est et cras,
De mout petite cose, li chevaus s'esfrea!»
Galopins ot une herbe des puis de Garnimas,
Que Basin ot tolu, quant Garin encanta,   1980
Quant li fain de la loge si fort les engresa;
Signor, che fu la nuit que Karles i ala.
Mist se main a sa bourse, l'erbe fort en geta;

1956   ms i. demandent. The hypometric verse is corrected by the use of the *passé simple*.

A Chanson de Geste

Part Five

56.
Ever since Galopin had seen the horse,
He was constantly agitated and thought of nothing else!
The Saracens made a great ruckus. They came into their lodging. 1955
They asked for water. They sat down to eat;
Afterwards, they went off to sleep, since they didn't anticipate
    any harm,
They paid no attention to the little thief.
Galopin wasted no time; he went straight to work.
He leaned against the cage's grating and looked at the horse. 1960
He prayed to the Lord God, our heavenly Father*:
"In the belly of the fish, You saved Saint Jonas;
The three children You protected, so they wouldn't be burned.
Saint Mary, our Lady, give me this horse.
Don't let it hurt me or do me harm." 1965
Galopin the valliant was so intent on praying,
That the sound of his breathing frightened the horse.
It sprung completely off the ground and crashed against its cage.
The guards were alerted, and they hurried in its direction.
They seized their lances, javelins and darts, 1970
And they thoroughly searched the room over and over again.
Galopin, who had little fear of them, was in the shadows.
They got so close to the thief that each one brushed against him:
If he was afraid then, it wouldn't surprise me!
When they found nothing, they sat back down to their
    chess game 1975
And said to each other, "What made that horse do that?"
"By my head," said the master, "it's well rested and well fed.
Just any little thing would make that horse nervous."
Galopin had an herb from the hills of Garnimas,
Which Basin had stolen when he enchanted Garin,* 1980
When they were gnawed by hunger in their tent:
My lords, that was the night when Charles went there.
Galopin put his hand into his pouch. He drew out the
    strong herb;

Elye of Saint-Gilles

Tant le frota li leres, que li odeurs en saut,
Par entre .ii. les grailles,* l'a lanciet el travail;   1985
Les gardes s'endormirent; lors fu seus li cevals.
«Par mon cief,» dist li leres, «conquis estes et mas*!
Tout soit fel l'amiraus se ne vous pent et art!»
Puis a fait ses engiens, si desfait le travail;
Il le prist par les grailles, si le trait d'une part.   1990
Hé, Dieus! che fu mervelle quant il le remua!
Tant par a fait li leres, que il vint al cheval,
Les costés li planoie, que mener l'en quida.
Li chevals n'el connut, as dens si le conbra,
Puis le fiert contre terre, et en haut le leva,   1995
Grans .xv. piés pleniers, le jeta contreval,
Si le fiert a .i. pel, por poi que nel creva!
Li leres fu blechiés; .iiii. fois se pasma,
Lors a jure Jhesu, ja mais nel baillera;
Soef, entre ses dens, Elyë reclama: 2000
«Hé, Elyes de Franche, perdut as le cheval!»
Li leres se dolut del grant cop que il a;
Lors a rejuré Dieu que point ne le laira,   [90r-b]
Pour Elyë de Franche, qui le don en dona.
Au pooir que il ot, avala contreval;   2005
Il trova .i. baston, le gros en enpuigna,
Par les costés c'ot gros, .xxx. cos li dona,
Tout le fait estre cois, et l'orgeul en abat.*
N'onques puis ne se mut, ne les piés ne crola.
Galopins li escrie, «Ne vous movés, vous ja!   2010
Folië feriés, se Dieus ait en moi part!»
Lors a pris une sele qui pendoit d'autre part,
Se li mist sor le dos, belement le çaingla;
Le frain li mist el cief, les caïnes abat,
Par son estrier* senestre, Galopins i monta.   2015
Il ne sot chevalcier, de chou fist con musart!
Li chevals passe avant, et il ciet a .i. fais,*
Por .i. peu, ne se brisse les costés et les bras.

1985   ms les railles; we emend to «grailles,» as in 1990.
1990   ms I. les, emended to the singular pronoun, as used in the second hemistich.

Part Five

The thief rubbed it so much that it gave off an odor.
In between the two bars, he threw it into the cage.   1985
The guards fell asleep. Then the horse was alone.
"By my head," said the thief, "it's check and mate!
The emir is so evil, he'll hang you and burn you!"
Then he used his skills, and he unfastened the sides of
    the cage.
He took it by the bars and drew it to one side.   1990
Oh, God! It was a great marvel that he moved it!
So skillfully did the thief work that he got to the horse.
He stroked its flanks. He intended to lead it out.
The warhorse didn't know him: with its teeth it seized him,*
Then it struck him against the ground and lifted him up   1995
A good, full fifteen feet then it threw him back down,
And it dashed him against a post and nearly killed him.
The thief was wounded; four times he fainted.
Then he swore to Jesus that he'd never give it up.
Quietly between his teeth, he called upon Elye;   2000
"Oh, Elye of France! You've lost the steed!"
The thief was suffering from the mighty blow he'd received.
Then he swore again to God that he would not give it up
For Elye of France and that he would give Elye this gift.
With all the strength he had, he crawled along the ground.   2005
He found a club and seized its thickest part.
On its massive flanks, he gave the steed thirty blows.
He made it become meek, and he beat down its pride.
It didn't move again, nor kick its feet.
Galopin called to it, "Don't you dare move!   2010
You'd be completely crazy, if God takes my side!"
Then he took a saddle that was hanging over on a wall
And put it on the charger's back. He girded it firmly on.
He put the bridle on its head, then unfastened the chains.
Using its left stirrup, Galopin mounted,   2015
He didn't know how to ride: this was a stupid thing for
    him to try.
The steed moved forward; Galopin fell off abruptly.
He came close to breaking his ribs and his arms.

Elye of Saint-Gilles

Lors rejure Jhesu, jamais n'i montera,
Ne ne set chevalchier, jamais nel aprendra.*   2020
S'il eüst une corde, as arçons se loiast,
Or l'amaine* aprés lui, soävet, tout le pas.
Assés s'en vait plus tost que li chevaus ne fait.

57.
Vai s'ent li petit leres, s'enmaine le destrier;
Li chevaus nel connut, en grant vieuté le tient,   2025
Petit le voit, ne la gaires proisiet.*
Il joint les .ii. orelles, si regete des piés,
Hauche devant le destre, et Galopin refiert:
Cheïr l'a fait a tere, mes nel a pas bleciet.*
Galopins fu legiers, si resailli en piés*;   2030
Neporquant si l'ataint par desous le braier,
Par le mien ensïant, se bien l'eüst consui,*
Jamais li petis leres n'enblast le boin destrier.
Prist un baston d'une ausne, si repaire au corsier;
Par les costés c'ot gros, .xl. cos l'en fiert,   2035
Tout le fait coi ester, ne s'emeut li destriers;
Se li tranble li cors con feulle de lorier.
«Certes,» dist Galopins, «justiche a boin destrier!*
Ne vous movés! Ja folië feriés!*   [90v-a]
Si m'aït Dieus de gloire, bien tost le conperiés!»   2040
Puis a pris une corde, el col li a lachiet;
Ensus de lui le maine, que durement le crient.
Jusc'au tref l'amiraus ne se vaut atargier;
Il le trouve dormant, en son pavellon cier,
Delés lui pent s'espee al poing d'or entaillié.   2045
Quant Galopins le voit, s'en fu joiant et lié*;
Andeus ses mains en tendi vers le ciel*:
«Haï, Pere de gloire, Tu soiés grasïés!»*
Puis a passé les aigues et les viviers,*
Enfressi en la cambre pointuree a or mier,   2050

2022   ms l. soaves; we emend from the adjectival to the more logical adverbial form.
2034   ms b. dun; the gender of «ausne» is feminine.
2043   ms. J. tres; the word is clearly meant to be «tent».

Part Five

Then he swore again to Jesus that never again would he
   mount.
Not only did he not know how to ride, but he'd never learn.   2020
If he had a rope, he'd tie himself to the saddlebows!
Now he led the charger after him, quietly at every step.
He went much faster than the warhorse did.

57.
The little thief started out, and he led the mount away.
The steed didn't know him: it held him beneath contempt.   2025
It saw that he was little, so it had no respect for him at all.
It laid back its two ears and again it kicked its feet.
It raised its right front foot and struck Galopin again.
It made him fall down to the ground, but it didn't injure him.
Galopin was nimble, and he jumped back to his feet.   2030
Nonetheless it struck him beneath his arm.
It seems to me it could well have done him in,
So that the little thief might never have stolen the good steed.
He seized a club a yard long, and he went back to the animal,
On its broad flanks, he struck the horse with forty blows.   2035
He made it be still: it didn't move
And its body trembled like laurel leaves.
"Truly," said Galopin, "the good steed has been dealt justice!
Don't move! That would be a foolish thing for you to do!
If God of glory helped me, you'd soon pay dearly for it!"   2040
Then he took a rope; he tied it around the animal's neck;
He led it walking in front, for he feared it greatly.
He wouldn't pause until he got to the emir's tent.
Galopin found the emir sleeping in his luxurious pavillon.
Beside the pagan hung his sword, its hilt richly sculpted
   in gold.*   2045
When Galopin saw this sword, he was joyful and happy.
Both his hands he lifted towards heaven:
"Thanks be to You, oh Father of glory!"
Then he passed by the waters and ponds,
All the way back to the room painted in fine gold   2050

Ou Elyës se dort, ains qu'il fust esvelliés,
Li fu pres li chevaus que tant a covoitié.
Et quant le voit Elye, joians en fu et lié;
Andeus ses mains en a tendues vers le ciel:
«Haï, Pere de gloire, Tu soiés grasïés!» 2055

58.
Al matin par son l'aube, quant li jor lor esclaire,
Jusc'al tref Lubïen en vienent les noveles;
.I. Sarrasins li conte, destruite soit sa geste,*
«Par Mahon, Amiral, or est trop grant la perte!
En Prinsaut l'Aragon, ne meterés mes sele! 2060
Or le vous a enblé, et vo gardes desfaites!
Cha fait li petis leres, qui hier vint devant vespre;
Leres ert et espie, bien sot conter la besse.
Par l'ame Tervagant, boine le nous a faite!
Plus de .c. mars d'argent en vaut hui vostre perte! 2065
Amirals orgellous, a demain ert* li termes;
Que tu te dois conbatre s'avoir veus la pucele!»
Quant l'entent l'amiraus, por poi que il ne derve!

59.
«Signor,» dist l'amirals, «mout m'est mal avenu!
Mon destrier qui m'aidoit ai par pecié perdu! 2070
Mais aportés mes armes, ains que soit parcheü!»
Et il si firent senpres, ne s'atargierent plus.
Son auberc li vestirent .iiii. roi mescreü,
Puis li çaingent l'espee, Murgale de Sor fu.*
Le destrier li amainent Beraut de Valodru*;   [90v-b] 2075
Lubïen i monta, prist le lance et l'escu.
Devant le maistre porte de Sorbrie est venu;
A haute vois escrie, «Biaus amis, que fais tu?
Car me ren la bataille que tant ai atendu,
U je te ferai prendre en ton castel la sus!»* 2080

Part Five

Where Elye was sleeping. Before he would awaken,
Nearby him stood the warhorse that he had desired so greatly,
And when Elye saw it, he was joyful and happy.
Both his hands he lifted towards heaven:
"Thanks be to You, oh Father of glory!" 2055

58.
In the morning at the crack of dawn, when the day broke for them,
All the way to Lubien's tent, came the news of the theft.
A Saracen told him about it, may his lineage be destroyed.
"By Mahomet, emir, surely the loss is immense!
On Prinsaut the Aragonese, you'll never be saddled again! 2060
Now he's been stolen from you, and your guards have been outwitted!
The little thief did this, who came here last night before vespers.
He was a thief and a spy; he could really spin a yarn!
By Tervagant's soul, he's really put one over on us!
Today you've lost the equivalent of a hundred marks
  of silver!* 2065
Proud emir, tomorrow was the appointed time
For you to do combat, if you want to get the maiden!"
When the emir heard him, he nearly went out of his mind.

59.
"My lords," said the emir, "I've suffered great misfortune!
My trusty warhorse through my own fault I've now lost,* 2070
But bring me my arms before its absence is discovered!"
And they did so quickly; they delayed no more.
Four heathen kings then put Lubien's hauberk on him,
Then girded on a sword; it belonged to Murgale of Sorbrie.
The steed they brought him belonged to Beraut of Valodru. 2075
Lubien mounted it; he took his lance and shield.
Before the main gate of Sorbrie he came.
In a loud voice he cried, "Good friend, what are you doing?
Come on! Give me the battle I've been waiting for so long
Or I'll have you imprisoned in your castle up there." 2080

60.
Lubïen de Baudas dessendi a la tiere;
Il atent la bataille: Dieus, il aura si pesme!
Or vous dirons noveles du bacheler Elies.*
Rosamonde l'adoube en sa cambre sous tere,
Puis li vest .i. auberc dont a or est la maille, 2085
Par deseure .i. blïaut qui li pent jusc'a tere;
Qui ferist le hauberc a .i. espiel a tere,
Ne l'enpirast il ja le monte d'une nesple.
A tant es Galopins, qui fu preus et honestes;
U que il voit Elye, cortoisement l'apele,* 2090
Et tenoit en son poing l'espeë toute traite:
«Sire, chaingiés cesti; quens ne rois n'ot plus bele!
Par itel convenant le çaingiés a senestre,
Que Dieu vous doinst barnage, et proeche, et poeste,
Et foi contre tous homes et estenance entere, 2095
Et vous meche en talent que prengiés la pucele
Qui si vous a gari en le canbre sous tere!»
«Par foi,» dist Rosamonde, «tel proeche avés faite,
Dont vous serés mout riches ainsque viegne li vespre!»
Rosamonde li çaint a son flanc le senestre; 2100
Par desor la ventaille li a lachiet .i. elme,
A .xxx. las d'or fin li lache la pucele,
Et ot hanste de fraine et ot fer de Castele,
A .iii. claus de fin or .i. pengon i ventele.
Voit Prinsaut l'Aragon, qui fiert del piet a terre,* 2105
De .xv. piés pleniers, ne pot consentir beste;
Et quant le voit Elyes, tous li ceurs li sautele,
De la joie qu'il ot, est sallis en la sele;
Quant li destrier le sent, se li saut plaine perche,
Mais cil le conduist bien, qui le tient par le resne; 2110
Onques nel sorporta vaillant une chenele.   [91r-a]
«Par mon chief,» dist Elye, «chevalier doi je estre!»
«Voire,» dist Galopins, «onques n'en poi tant faire;
Encore n'a il gaires qu'il me mostra la tere!»

2100   ms R. li; the direct object is needed, since the possessive is used in the second hemistich.

Part Five

60.
Lubien of Bagdad dismounted.
He's waiting for the battle. God! He'll have the worst of it!
Now we'll give you the news of the young knight Elye.
Rosamonde armed him in her underground room.
She put on his hauberk, whose chainmail was made of gold;   2085
Over it a tunic that reached all the way to the floor.
Whoever struck the hauberk with a lance
Could not damage it a single bit.
Galopin arrived, who was worthy and honorable.
When he saw Elye, he addressed him in a courtly manner   2090
And held in his hand his fully drawn sword:
"My lord, now gird this on. No count, nor king had one more
  handsome!
By such a covenant, gird it well on your left side.
May God give you strength and valor and prowess
And faith against all men and total support,   2095
And may He inspire in your mind the desire to wed the maiden
Who healed you in her underground chamber!"
"In faith," said Rosamonde, "you've done a mighty deed*:
It will make you rich, before vespers come!"
Rosamonde girded the sword on Elye's left side.   2100
She laced on a helmet over his ventail.
The maid secured it with thirty laces of fine gold,
And Elye had a lance of ashwood with a point of Castilian steel.*
A pennon fluttered from it, attached with three nails of fine gold.
Elye saw Prinsaut the Aragonese, who struck the ground with
  its hoof —   2105
It could not stand any creature within fifteen feet of it —
And when Elye saw it, his heart leaped in his breast.
His heart brimming with joy, he vaulted into the saddle.
When the warhorse felt him, it bounded forward an entire
  furlong.
But the knight handled it well, keeping a tight rein.*   2110
Elye wouldn't put up with anything the steed might try.
"By my head," said Elye, "now I must be a knight!"*
"That's true," said Galopin, "I couldn't ever do so much.
It's just awhile ago that it had me on the ground!"

61.
Lubïen de Baudas fu a la porte armés; 2115
A haute vois escrie, «Car t'en is, Macabrés!
Ou m'envoiës ton fil, Caïfas u Jossé,
U Malpriant qu'est tiers, el ne voil demander!»
Quant l'amiraus l'entent, le sens quide derver;
Il en a apelé ses canbrelens privés, 2120
Qui sont de sa maisnie, et de son parenté:
«Alés tost a ma fille, que n'i ait aresté!
.I. chevalier devoit en l'angarde amener,
Ne sai de paienie u de crestïenté,
Et s'ele chou ne fait con vous ai devissé, 2125
Lubïen la donrai, le viel kenu barbé!»
Et respondent paien, «Mout avés bien parlé!
Chou est li mieudres ples que i puissiés trouver!»
Jusc'a l'uis de la canbre en sont trestout alé,
Et sont passé avant, et sont l'anel crollé. 2130
Rosamonde l'oï, s'a tost l'uis desfermé.
«Dame,» che dist Elye, «en la car vous traiés!*
Veés icel cheval, qui mout est esgarés;
Si m'aït Dieus del ciel, jel criem mout d'afoler!»
«Vassal,» dist la pucele, «allés a vostre Dé! 2135
Dieus garisse ton cors de mort et d'afoler!»
Il a laskiet le resne, lait le ceval aller;
Le gonfanon de soie lait al vent venteler,
Et li destriers li saut .xxx. piés messurés,
Que le fu et le flanbe fait del marbre voler! 2140
Quant le voient paien, tout en sont esgaré,*
Meïsmes l'amirals en a .i. ris jeté:
«Mahon, je rai ma terre, bien t'ai servi a gré!
C'est Elyë de Franche, li gentiex et li ber!
Chil fera la bataille, ja n'en ert trestorné!» 2145

2126 ms L. li; the direct object pronoun is more appropriate, as in 2100.
2133 ms v. cel; the hypometric verse can be remedied with the form «icel».

Part Five

61.
Lubien of Bagdad was armed at the gate. 2115
In a loud voice he cried, "Come on out, Macabre!
Or send me out your son, Caifas or Joshua,
Or Malpriant who's the third. I'll ask nothing else."
When the emir heard him, he thought he'd go insane.
He called his personal chamberlain, 2120
Who belonged to his household and his lineage*:
"Go quickly to my daughter. Let there be no delay!
She was supposed to bring a knight to the advance guard.
I don't know if he's from pagandom or from Christendom,
And if she doesn't do just as I've told you, 2125
I'll give her to Lubien, the old white-bearded man."
And the pagans answered, "Well spoken!
This is the best argument that you could ever find!"
They all rushed to the chamber door,
And they stepped forward and pounded the door-knocker. 2130
Rosamonde heard it and promptly unlocked the door.
"My lady," said Elye, "stand back in a corner now.
Look at this horse, who is very upset.
So help me God in heaven, I'm afraid to get him upset!"
"Sir knight," replied the young woman, "may your God go with you. 2135
May God protect you from death and from all harm!"
Elye then loosened the reins, and he let the charger run.
The silk standard he let flutter in the wind.
And the steed sprang forward with him a full thirty feet,
So that it caused sparks and flames to fly from the marble. 2140
When the pagans saw him, they all were dumbfounded.
The emir himself burst out laughing:
"Mahomet, now I'll get my land back! I've served you well and willingly!
It's Elye of France, the noble and the brave knight!
He'll fight the battle. There's no getting around it!" 2145

62.
«En la moië foi, Sire,» dist la bele al cler vis,
Sor Mahon me jurastes vous et vostre Arabi,   [91r-b]
Que il ne aroit garde n'a l'aler n'al venir!»
«Non aura il, ma fille, por voir le vous plevis!»
Il ovrirent la porte, si le laissent issir;   2150
Macabré de Sorbrie, et Jossés, et Malpris,*
En montent el palais, regardent le meschin.
Rosamonde la bele va veïr son ami;
En son dos a vestu .i. pelichon hermin,
Et en son puing senestre, tenoit .i. esmeril,   2155
Ele le vait paissant d'une ele de pertris.
Et evre son mantel, si que Elye le vit.
De la joië qu'il ot, fait le cheval saillir;
Li destrier s'en repaire contreval le lairis.
Onques Dieus ne fist beste, que s'i puïst tenir,   2160
Cers, ne dains, ne aloe, faucon ne esmeril!
Caïfas le regarde, a son pere la dit:
«Cuidiés vous, Sire rois, que bataille feïst?
Ja s'en fuira, li glous, quant venra al ferir!
Rosamonde vous a vergondé et honni;   2165
.Iiii. jors l'a tenue,* s'en a fait ses delis,
Remesse en est enchainte, por voir le vous plevi!
Mahomet vous confonge, qui tout a atenir,
S'en .i. feu, n'en est arsse, anuit u le matin!»
Quant l'entent la puchele, si ot le ceur mari,   2170
U qu'ele voit son frrere, fierement li a dit:
«Par mon cief, Dan traïtres, vous i avés menti!
Onques ne fuië* pute, ne on nel me requist!
Mais je le fuisse, certes, si il tres bien vausist,
Qu'il est boins chevaliers coragous et hardis,   2175
Et vous estes couars, et malvais et faillis!
Ceste jouste qu'il fait, deüssiés maintenir!
Se Sarrasin me croient, et mon pere autressi,
En une cambre basse vous meterons tout vif!»

2156   ms p. dun; the feminine form of the indefinite article is needed.
2158   ms c. saillier; the scribe expunctuated the "e" with an underlying dot.
2171   ms f'rre; the scribe inadvertently used both the abbreviation and the double «r».

Part Five

62.
"On my faith, my lord," said the beautiful, bright-faced maid,
"By Mahomet, you and all your Arabs swore to me
That he wouldn't have to be on guard, either coming or going."
"Nor will he, my daughter; you have my solemn pledge!"
The pagans opened the gate, and they let Elye ride out. 2150
Macabre of Sorbrie and Malpriant and Joshua
Went up into the palace. They watched the youth;
Rosamonde the beautiful went to watch her friend.
She was dressed in a fur-lined ermine cloak,
And on her left wrist, she was holding a small merlin falcon.* 2155
She was feeding it with the wing of a partridge,
And she opened her mantel, so that Elye could see it.
From the joy that he felt, he caused the horse to leap.
The steed galloped down to the bottom of the hill.
Never did God make a creature who could keep up with it: 2160
Neither deer nor stag nor lark nor falcon nor merlin.
Caifas looked at Elye. To his father he said:
"Do you believe, my king, that he'll really fight the battle?
The coward will flee as soon as it comes to blows!
Rosamonde has shamed and dishonored you.* 2165
He kept her for four days and did his will with her.
It will turn out that she's pregnant. I swear to you that it's true!
May Mahomet punish you, who has all in his dominion,
If she's not burned in a fire by tonight or in the morning!"
When the maiden heard him, her heart was heavy. 2170
She faced her brother and said to him proudly,
"By my head, lord traitor, you've lied about this.
I was never a whore. It was never asked of me.
But I'd be one for him, truly, if he wanted me to.
For he's a good knight, courageous and brave. 2175
And you're a coward, both evil and a failure.*
This joust that he's undertaking, you were supposed to
   have fought.
If the Saracens believe me, and my father as well,
Deep down in a prison cell we'll close you up alive!"

Elye of Saint-Gilles

Ele lait le parler; par les temples le prist,   2180
Des cheveus a sachiet, quanque la bele en tient.
Caïfas s'en retorne, ens es dens le refiert,*
Que la levre li tranche; le sanc en fait saillir. [91v-a]
Hé! Dieus, mar le toucha! De pute ore le fist,*
Car ançois qu'il soit vespre, l'en convenra morir,   2185
Car Galopins l'esgarde, qui n'a pas mescoisi,
Quel nonchera Elye, le chevalier gentil!

63.
Or fu li bers Elye* ens el pre contreval,
Apoiés sor sa lance, bien resanble vasal.
Li Sarrasin le voit, vers lui en vait les saus: 2190
«Cuiver,» dist Lubïen, «u preïs mon cheval?
Qui le te mist as mains, onques jor ne t'ama!
Che fist li petis leres, qui ersoir le m'enbla!
Tervagant, que nel soc, il fust pendus a hart!
Or laisse cele jouste, si me rens mon cheval,   2195
Si en vien avoec moi, a la chit de Baudas;
Si seras de mes vins serjans et boutellas,*
.Iiii.m. Sarrasin* en ton ficf en tenras.
J'ai une bele fille, que tu espouseras,
S'a non Esclabonie, sossiel plus bele n'a,   2200
Ne mais que Rosamonde, ne sai s'ele le vaut.»
«Sarrasin,» dist Elye, «je n'ai soing de vo gas!
Tu ne sés qui je sui, aparmain, le seuras;
Sodoiers sui de Franche, dont cis rois m'amena,
Et fui pris desous Arle, en l'estor conmunal.   2205
.I. miens conpains petis me dona ce ceval,
Rosamonde la bele hui matin m'adouba;
Si me çaint ceste espee a mon lés de decha.
Se je te puis ochire, je sui rois de Baudas!

2181   ms s. q'nq'q'; we delete the second «q'» as a scribal oversight which would yield a hypermetric verse.
2184   ms d. put; the feminine form of the adjective is needed.

Part Five

Then she stopped speaking and by the temples she
 grabbed him.   2180
She seized her brother by the hair, by all the hair the
 beautiful maid could grasp.
Caifas turned around. He hit her on the mouth
So that he cut her lip and made the blood spurt out.
Oh, God! Woe to him, that he touched her! It was in an
 evil hour he did it!
Because before vespers, he'll have to die for it,   2185
Because Galopin, who saw him, understood exactly what
 happened,
And he'll tell Elye, the noble knight.

63.
Now the noble Elye was on the battlefield down in the meadow.
Leaning on his lance, he looked like a mighty knight.
The Saracen saw Elye and went riding towards him.   2190
"Worthless scum!" said Lubien. "Where did you get my charger?
Whoever gave it to you had no love for you.
This was the work of the little thief who stole it from me
 last night.
Tervagant! If I'd known, he'd be hanged with a noose.
Now call off this battle, and give me back my warhorse.   2195
So come along with me to the city of Bagdad,
And you'll be my wine steward and butler.
Four thousand Saracens you'll hold in your fief.
I have a beautiful daughter, whom you'll marry.
Her name is Esclabonie. There's none more beautiful on earth,   2200
Unless it's Rosamonde. I don't know if she's equal to her."
"Saracen," said Elye, "I've no interest in your mockery.
You don't know who I am, but you'll soon find out:
I'm a mercenary from France, from where this king brought me,
And I was captured below the walls of Arles during a
 great battle.   2205
A little companion of mine gave me this steed.
The beautiful Rosamonde armed me this morning,
And she girded this sword on me, here at my left side.
If I can slay you, I'm king of Bagdad!

De s'amor sui tous fis; certes, n'i faillerai!» 2210
Quant l'entent li paien, por poi qu'il n'esraga:
«Es tu dont crestïens, c'a moi es venus cha?
Je t'en jur Mahomet, qui cest siecle estora,
Je ne mengerai mes, tant con tu vis seras!»
Et respondi* Elyes, «Iche ne sera ia! 2215
Certes, bien poroit estre voire parolle ja!»

64.
Quant ot li Sarrasin, que il est crestïens,
Onques puis n'i ot resne ne tenu ne laissiet,
Il laisent par vertu randoner les destriers,* [91v-b]
Et Prinsaut l'Aragon lait aler les .ii. piés. 2220
Elyës saut a lui de la lanche qu'il tient;
.I. poi li mist trop haut, desor l'elme vergié,
Et li paien le fiert, ne l'a pas esparngiet.
Grant cop li a doné en l'escu de quartier,
Desor la bende d'or li a fraint et brisié; 2225
Le blanc auberc del dos desront et desmaillié,
Parmi le flanc senestre, li conduist son espiel,
Enpoin le par vertu, si l'abat del destrier.
Signor, n'est mië mors, mes il est mout bleciés!
Et Elyës saut sus, qui le cors ot legier; 2230
Si est saillis mout tost sor le corant destrier,*
Il a prisse sa lance et l'escu de quartier,
Vait ferir le paien, si grant cop esforchié,
Que sa lanche pechoie, s'il l'abat* del destrier.
Quant li paien le voient, mout en sont esmaié; 2235
Premerains a parlé Tornebrans et Turfier,
Et Gontable d'Orlie, et Garlans l'envoisié,
Et autres avoëc, qui firent a proissier*;

2217 ms q'l; the enclisis, however, would result in a hypometric line.
2220 ms l. lai; the third person singular is needed.
2221 ms E. faut; the meaning of this verse is like that of 2230 and is emended accordingly.
2223 ms p. esparengiet, which yields a hypermetric verse.
2238 ms firent et; the preposition «a» is needed with the infinitive; «et» is a scribal oversight.

Part Five

I'm sure I can rely on her love. Truly, I will not fail!" 2210
When the pagan heard him, he nearly lost his mind.
"Does that mean that you're a Christian who's come against me here?
I swear to you, Mahomet, the ruler of this world,
That I'll never eat again, so long as you're alive!"
And Elye answered him, "That will never happen! 2215
Indeed, those could be true words!"

64.
When the Saracen heard that Elye was a Christian,
No longer did he draw rein or hold his charger back.
They let the warhorses boldly gallop freely,
And Elye let Prinsaut the Aragonese come within two feet
 of the pagan, 2220
Elye thrust at him with the lance that he held,
But placed it a little too high upon the burnished helmet,*
And the pagan struck Elye — he gave no quarter —
A great blow he struck on Elye's quartered shield.
Upon the band of gold, he pierced and tore it. 2225
The white hauberk the youth was wearing, the pagan split
 and tore.
Into Elye's left side Lubien thrust his lance;
Lubien thrust his lance deep and struck him down from
 his horse.
My lords, he's not dead at all, but he is gravely wounded.
And Elye jumped up, because he was nimble, 2230
And mounted the swift steed quickly.
He took his lance and quartered shield.
He rode to strike the pagan. He dealt such a mighty blow.
That it shattered Lubien's lance and knocked him off his
 charger.
When the pagans saw this, they were greatly dismayed. 2235
First of all, Turfier and also Tornebran spoke,
And Gontable of Orlie and the joyous Garlans
And the other worthy knights who were with them.

Cis .vii. furent tout roi, les corones es ciés,
Et dist li un a l'autre, «Mal somes engingié! 2240
Mors somes et vencu, si perdons Lubïen!
Par Mahomet, Signor, alomes li aidier!»
Et cil ont respondu, «De gré et volentiers!»
Il vestent les aubers, s'ont les elmes lachiés,
Et çaingent les espees a lor flans senestriers, 2245
Et monterent es seles des boins corans destriers,
Et prisent en lor poins les rois tranchans espiés.
Parmi .i. val s'acoillent corant tous eslaissiés.
Dieus en garrisse Elye, qui en crois fu drechiés!
N'i a cel, nel manache de la teste a trenchier! 2250

65.
Lubïen de Baudas se senti a la tere;
Voit Prinsaut l'Aragon, qui traïne ses resnes,
De .xv. piés pleniers ne pot consentir beste.
Il le pleure et regrete con chevalier honeste:
«Hé! chevals ravineus, por coi me meus tu guerre?* [92r-a] 2255
Je t'ai soëf nori, et le crupe coverte,
Et doné a mangier et del fain et del herbe!*
Or sus me veus chi coere, por chou que sui a tere!
Ja ne soit mes nus hom qui mes se fit en beste,
Se tant non con il l'a, et il le tient acertes. 2260
Chevalier, mout es preus, par le loi de ma tere!
Car me ren mon cheval, dont je chaï, caële;
Por amor Rosamonde, qui t'esgarde as fenestres!»
«Sarrasin,» dist Elye, «maldite soit ta geste!
Va, si pren ton cheval, por amor la pucele; 2265
N'i auras hui mes garde, si seras en la sele!»
Il meïsmes li rent, par anbedeus les resnes.
Lubïen i monta, qu'es archons ne s'areste,*
Des plaïes qu'il ot grans, ne li ramenbre gaires;
Or poés vous bien croire, diäbles le governe! 2270
Le main mist a l'espee, fors del feure l'a traite,

2257 ms de fain; the enclisis is necessary and parallels the second hemistich.
2258 ms or me; the hypometric verse is emended by the addition of «sus» for the expression «corrir sus» found at 2358. See note.

Part Five

Those seven were all crowned kings,
And one said to the other, "We had this all wrong. 2240
We're all dead and defeated if we lose Lubien.
By Mahomet, lords, let's go and help him!"
And the others answered, "Let's get going!"
They put on their hauberks and laced on their helmets,
And on their left sides, they girded their sharp stout swords 2245
And mounted upon the saddles of the good swift warhorses,
And they took in their hands stiff sharp lances.
Through a valley they charged, giving their mounts full rein.
May God, Who was hung on the cross, protect Elye,
From the pagan menace and from having his head cut off. 2250

65.
Lubien of Bagdad found himself on the ground.
He saw Prinsaut the Aragonese, who was trailing its reins.
The charger wouldn't allow any creature within fifteen feet of it.
Lubien wept over the steed and lamented like an honorable
   knight:
"Ah! Impetuous horse, why are you waging war on me? 2255
I have taken good care of you and covered your croup
And gave you hay and fodder to eat.
Now you want to attack me because I'm down on the ground.
Let there be no man who ever trusts in a beast again,
Unless he has it and holds it securely! 2260
Sir knight, you are very worthy, by the law of my land.
Please give me back my horse, from which I fell,
For love of Rosamonde, who's watching you from the windows."
"Saracen," said Elie, "cursed be your lineage!
Go and get your horse, for the love of the maiden. 2265
You don't need to be on guard until you're back in the saddle."*
Elye himself gave the steed back to the pagan, by both its reins.
Lubien mounted it; he didn't stop until he was between the
   saddlebows.
He scarcely was conscious of the grievous wounds he had.
Now this will show you that he was possessed by the devil: 2270
He put his hand on his sword and drew it from its sheath

Et va ferir Elye droit par desor son elme,*
Qu'il en a abatu et les flors et les pieres.*
Li brans est trestornés par de devers senestre;
Il li trancha les guices et les quirs* jusq'en tere. 2275
Sel conseüst en char, sa fin en eust faite!
«Par mon cief,» dist Elye, «vostre espee m'apresse!
Mon escu m'as tranciet, s'en est moië la perte;
Par le mien ensïant, j'en rai chi une bele,
Je quic qu'ele fu vostre, Sire amirals de Perse! 2280
Galopins le me çaint, mes conpains li honeste;
De meïsme vo cosse, vous doi je honte faire!»
Il l'en drecha amont, si l'en feri sor l'elme*;
Qu'il en a abatu et les flors et les pieres,
Tout le va porfendant enfressi en la sele; 2285
Le ber estort son cop, mort l'abat a le terre.
Rosamonde le voit, qu'estoit a la fenestre;
U qu'ele voit son frerre, fierement l'en apele:
«Or venés cha veoir, malvais couars superbes!
Si verrés les grans cos que li paien set faire!* 2290
Car pleust ore Mahom, qui cest siecle governe, [92r-b]
Que vous fuissiés la fors, avoec lui, sor cele herbe,
Et seüst le grant honte que pour lui m'avés faite!
A s'espeë tranchant, perderiés ja la teste!»*

66.
Quant Elyës ot mort Lubïen de Baudas, 2295
Prist le cheval as resnes, que mener l'en quida,
Quant li .vii. Sarrasin li essorbent* d'un val,
Et quant les voit Elyes, mervelles l'enpessa;
Jhesu le nostre pere douchement reclama,
«Se tés sont tout cil .vii. con estoit li viellars, 2300
Par le mien ensiant, n'en quic estordre ja.
A quel cief que il tort, tout le premier ferai!»

2292   ms s. cel; the feminine form of the demonstrative adjective is needed.

Part Five

And went to strike Elye right on top of the helmet,
So that he knocked off its flowers and gemstones.
The blade was turned towards the left.
He sliced the shield straps and leather so they fell to
   the ground.   2275
If it had reached the flesh, it would have been the end for Elye.
"By my head," said Elye, "your sword's wounded me!
You've split my shield, and the loss is mine.
But it seems to me I have another fine sword here.
I think it was yours, lord admiral of Persia!   2280
Galopin girded it on me, my companion, the man of honor,
With a weapon from your own side, it's my duty to cause you
   shame!"
He raised it high and then brought it down on the helmet
So that he knocked out of it both flowers and gemstones;
He split the Saracen all the way down to the saddle.   2285
The knight struck his blow; he knocked Lubien dead to
   the ground.
Rosamonde saw it, who was at the window.
She turned toward her brother and proudly called him:
"Now come and see this, evil and arrogant coward,
And you will see what great blows the pagan can deal!   2290
If it only had been Mahomet's will, who rules this world,
That you had be out there with him on that field,
And you'd experience the great shame you have caused me
   because of Elye.
By his sharp sword, you'd soon lose your head!"

66.
When Elye had finally slain Lubien of Bagdad,   2295
He took the horse by its reins, because he intended to lead
   it away,
When the seven pagans emerged from a valley to block his way.
And when Elye saw them, he was intensely grieved.
To Jesus our Father, he prayed quietly:
"If all these seven are like the old man was,   2300
In my opinion, I don't think I'll be defeated yet.
Whoever sticks his neck out first, I'll strike him first."

Elye of Saint-Gilles

Le premier qu'il encontre, onques ne s'en loa,
Si le fiert de l'espee, qui par mi le copa.
A l'autre iouste en apres, autre .ii. en abat. 2305
Et Jonacles s'en fuit, a esperon s'en va,
Et li rois Malvergiés .iiii. mos s'escria:
«Par Mahomet, Signor, cis hon est Satenas!
Il fu fieus Luchibus de la roche Baudas,
Qui conquist en Espaigne Feraon et Judas,* 2310
Et le viel Salatré, et Costantin Macars!
Si fera il nous tous, ja piés n'en estordra!
Mais guerpissons les loges, et entrons el arnas!»*
Et il si fissent senpre, li glouton desloial;
Il guerpirent les loges, dont .iiii.m. i a, 2315
En la mer sont venu, s'en entrent es canas.
Elyës les encauche, qui seoit sor Prinsaut,*
Il se feri en l'aigue, jusc'al col del cheval;
Puis a traite l'espee, lor ancre lor trencha.
Li vens se fiert es voiles, qui les Turs esfondra, 2320
Or noent Sarrasin et a deul et a mal,
Que de .iiii.m., un seus n'en escapa.*
Li faucon Lubïen fu devant l'estandart;
Il connut le destrier, forment le regarda,
.Vii. fois s'est esvolés, que aler s'en quida, 2325
Quant li giet le retienent, dont a or sont les las.
Quant Elyës le voit, grant joie en demena, [92v-a]
Deslië le faucon, sor son puing le porta;
Sel donra Rosamonde, qui le hui adouba.*

67.
Or s'en va li valés, qui bien set mener guerre, 2330
S'enmainne les destriers anbedeus par les resnes;
Venus est a Sorbrie, si dessent en la presse.
Encontre sont venu la pute gent aversse;

2305   ms j. en; to correct the hypermetric verse, we omit the scribal error of the superfluous «en» of the first hemistich.
2316   ms l. sont; a word is obviously missing, causing a hypometric verse. «Mer» is added; see note.
2329   ms hui ladouba; we emend to «le hui adouba».

Part Five

The first pagan Elye encountered never lived to brag of it:
Elye struck him with his sword which sliced him in two.
At the second joust, he struck down two others,   2305
And Jonacles fled — he rode off spurring fast —
And King Malvergie then shouted these words:
"By Mahomet, my lords, this man is Satan.
He was the son of Luchibus of the rock of Bagdad,
Who conquered in Spain Pharaoh and Judas,   2310
And old Salatre and Constantine Macars!
And he'll do it to us all. Soon no one will escape!
But let's abandon the tents and board the ships quickly."
And they did it — quickly did so — the treacherous cowards.
They abandoned their tents — there were four thousand
   of them.   2315
To the sea they rode and boarded their ships.
Elye pursued them, mounted on Prinsaut.
He plunged into the water up to his charger's neck,
And then he drew his sword. He severed their anchor line.
The wind filled the sails, which capsized all the Turks.   2320
Then the Saracens drowned in evil and in grief,
For out of four thousand men, not one escaped.
Lubien's falcon was in front of the standard;
It recognized the horse. It peered at it closely.
Seven times it took flight as it tried to get free,   2325
But the line held it fast, whose laces were of gold.
When Elye saw it, great was his joy:
He untied the falcon, on his wrist he carried it,
And he'll give it to Rosamonde, who armed him that day.

67.
Now the young knight rode off, who knew well how to
   wage war,   2330
And he led both horses by the reins.
He came to Sorbrie, and he rode down into the throng.
The foul enemy people came to meet him.

Le faucon Lubïen tent a le damoisele,
Il le trova enbronche et encline sor terre. 2335
Il li a demandé, «Qui vous fist che, Dansele?
Qui si vous a baillie, mes amis ne veut estre!»
A tant es Galopins, qui l'en dist la novele:
«Elyës, biaus dous sire, mout devés dolans estre!
Por vous, l'a Caïfas a tel honte detraite, 2340
Et batue, et ferue, et le bouche desfaite!
Se tu ne l'en fais drois, ja ne tienges tu terre!»
«Amis, et che ne fache, ne place au roi celestre!»

68.
Or s'en torna Elyes, qui a Saint Gille fu nés,
Et tenoit son branc nu, qui fu ensanglentés, 2345
L'Arrabi a hurté des esperons dorés,
Tout droit enmi sa voie a Caïfas trové.
.I. grant cop li dona, mout la bien asené,
Que les flors et les pieres fist del elme* voler;
La coife del auberc ne li pot contrester, 2350
Enfressi el menton li fist le branc couler.
Elye estort son cop, et li glous est versés,
Et li cors estendi; l'ame en porte malfé.*
Amont a la fenestre, ert li rois acoutés;
Macabré de Sorbrie a ses gens apelés: 2355
«Signor,» che dist li rois, «ne la porons durer!*
Ichou est Begibus qui nous a enchantés!
Car li corons tout sus, Sarrasin et Escler!
Trestous mes mal talens vous ert ja pardonés!»
Lors s'en ceurent as armes Sarrasin et Escler; 2360
Bien furent .xxx.m. quant il furent armés.
Parmi le mestre porte s'en vont abandoner;
Por la mor Caïfas* qui jut enmi le pré,   [92v-b]

2344   ms s. tourne; to correct the hypometric verse, we change the tense to «torna». See note.
2345   ms f. ensangletes; the scribe omitted the nasal bar.

Part Five

Lubien's falcon he held out to the young woman.
He found her with her head lowered, bent over towards the
    ground. 2335
He asked her, "Who's done this to you, my lady?*
Whoever has mistreated you, doesn't want to be my friend!"
Suddenly Galopin appeared, who told him all about it:
"Elye, good, kind lord, you have reason to grieve:
Because of you, Caifas brought great shame upon lady
    Rosamonde. 2340
He beat and struck her and split her mouth.
If you don't exact justice for it, may you never hold land!"*
"My friend, may it never please our heavenly King that I
    neglect do to it."

68.
Now Elye started out, who was born at Saint-Gilles,
He was holding his unsheathed sword, which was still
    bloodied. 2345
He spurred his Arabian with golden spurs.
Straight ahead in the middle of his path, he found Caifas.
A great blow he gave the pagan. He struck him very hard,
So that the flowers and gemstones flew off his helmet.
The chain-mail hood of the hauberk could not withstand
    the blow, 2350
All the way down through the chin, he drove his blade.
Elye dealt his blow; the coward fell over backwards
And lay flat on the ground. A demon carried his soul away.
High above, leaning out the window, the king was watching.
Macabre of Sorbrie called his people: 2355
"My lords," said the king, "we can't endure this!
This is Beelzebub, who has bewitched us!
Let's all attack him, Saracens and Slavs!
All my griefs against you will be pardoned."
Then they ran to arms, Saracens and Slavs.* 2360
There were over thirty thousand, when they were all armed.
Through the main gate they rode at full speed,
Inspired by the death of Caifas, who lay dead upon the
    battlefield.

Sont issu de Sorbrie, li quiver parjuré,
Et encauchent Elye qu'a Saint Gille fu nés. 2365
Li vasaus tint le branc qui a or fu letrés,
De pitiet a plouré, s'est forment gaimentés:
«Hé! pere Julïen, jamais ne me verrés!*
Ahi! oncle Guillame, je vous conmanc a Dé!»
Quant Galopins le vit, li preus et li senés, 2370
Rosamonde la bele a congiet demandé,
De la tor avala les marberins degrés;
En la bataille entra, coureçous et irés.
En sa main le baston u tant a richetés,*
Que les feës ovrerent en .i. ille de mer. 2375
Lors peüssiés veoir tant ruiste cop doner,
Tant brac, tan puing, tante teste voler,*
Et tant cheval cheoir, trebuchier et verser!
Bien i feri Elyes del branc forbi letré;
Et Galopins aussi, del grant baston quarré. 2380
Hé! Dieus, con grant damage ne poront afiner,*
Car li nostre sont poi, et Sarrasin plenté!
Karles Marteus le dist .i. ior en reprover*:
Selonc que dist la letre, la forche paist le pré!

Quant Rosamonde les prist a regarder,* 2385
A genollons se mist la pucele al vis cler,
Et a jointes ses mains, Dieu prist a apeler:
«Glorïeus Sire Pere, qui te laissas pener,
Et fesistes la lune et le solail* lever,
Et les estoiles, les poissons en la mer,* 2390
Gardés ces crestiiens d'ochire et d'afoler!
Baptisier me ferai, et en sains fons lever,
Et trestoute ma loi ferai crestïener*;
Puis penrai le baron, se me vieut espouser.»
Estes vous Galopins, le preu et le sené, 2395
La u il voit Elye, sel prent a apeler:
«Conpains,» dist Galopins, «nes porons endurer!
Veés vous la les os? Pensons del cheminer!
Car faites une cose que m'orés devisser: [93r-a]

Part Five

The treasonous cowards rode forth from Sorbrie,
And they pursued Elye, who was born in Saint-Gilles.   2365
The knight brandished his gold-lettered sword,
From pity he wept, and he sorrowfully lamented:
"Ah! Julien, my father! You'll never see me again!
Ahi! Uncle William! May God grant you His protection!"
When Galopin saw him, the worthy and wise man,   2370
He asked leave of the beautiful Rosamonde.
He ran down the marble steps of the tower,
He entered the battle, angry and sorrowful.
In his hand was the richly decorated staff,
Which fairies had made on an island in the sea.   2375
Then you'd have seen so many blows harshly dealt,
So many arms, so many hands, so many heads go flying,
And so many warhorses stumbling, falling and rolling over!
Elye struck well with his strong, lettered blade,
And Galopin also, with his big, stout cudgel.   2380
Ah God, even with as much damage as they're inflincting,
   they won't be able to win,
Because our men are few, and there are hordes of Saracens!
Charles Martel said one day by way of a proverb,
Thus it is written, "The scythe devours the meadow!"

When Rosamonde first saw them   2385
   The bright-faced maid fell to her knees;
Her hands joined, she began to pray to God:
"Glorious Lord Father, who let Yourself be tormented
And made the moon and sun rise
And the stars in the sky and the fish in the sea,   2390
Protect these Christians from being killed or harmed.
I'll be baptised and raised at the holy font,
And all of my kingdom I will Christianize.
Then I'll take the knight, if he wants to marry me."*
Then Galopin appeared, the worthy and the wise man,   2395
He turned towards Elye and began to speak to him :
"Companion," said Galopin, "we can't hold out!
Do you see that army? Let's get out of here!
Let's do something, which you will hear me lay out for you:

Que hurtés l'Arabi des esperons dorés, 2400
En cel vergier laiens, nous irons reposer.
Je desfendrai mout bien le pont et le fossé;
La dedens vous metrai, qui qu'en doië pesser!»
«Conpains,» che dist Elye, «si con vos conmandés!»
Lors hurte le destrier des esperons dorés, 2405
Et la gentil puchele vint le pont avaler,
Et destachie* les caines, dont i ot a plenté;
Et Elyës i entre, qu'a Saint Gille fu nés,
Et Galopins ausi ne si vaut arester.
Ferment la bare et le pont ont levé.* 2410
Quant furent la dedens, s'ont grant joië mené!
Elyës dessendi del destrier sejorné,
Rosamonde la bele le corut acoler;
.Iiii. fois li baissa la bouche et le vis cler.*
En une croute a vaute ont le destrier mené, 2415
Del feure et del avaine* li donent a plenté.
Puis vienent el planciet, en le tor sont monté,
Si ont veü les os qui sont acheminé.*
Macabré de Sorbrie a se gent apelé:
«Signor,» che dist li rois, «la ne porons durcr! 2420
Tout che me fait ma fille, que s'i m'a encanté!»
As armes sont coru Sarrasin et Escler;
Bien furent .xxx.m. quant il furent monté,
Asallent de la tor les pans et les pilers.
Elyes se desfent,* qu'a Saint Gille fu nés, 2425
Grans pieres et grans fus laissent aval aler;
Bien en font .iiii.c. reculer el fossé.
Hé! vous poignant Corsaut, .i. felon parjuré,*
Rois fu de Tabarie, si ot mout richeté,
Et ot en sa conpaigne .xx.m. Turc armé! 2430
Il asaillent la tor, s'ont grant noise mené,
Et pikent, et machonent conme gent forsené.*
Quant Galopins les voit, s'a Elye apelé:

2407 ms d. de caines; we emend to the definite article.
2410 ms fierement; we emend to «ferment»; the verse is clearly the contrary of 2619 «desferment». See note.
2410 ms p. sus; we emend to «ont», after 2619; a decasyllabic verse results.

Part Five

It's that you spur your Arabian steed with golden spurs   2400
Into that orchard nearby, where we'll go to gather our strength.
I'll stoutly defend the bridge and the moat.
I'll get you inside there, no matter what."*
"Companion," said Elye, "Whatever you say!"
Then he spurred on his steed with his golden spurs,   2405
And the noble maiden went to lower the drawbridge
And unfastened the chains — there were many of them —
And Elye, who was born at Saint-Gilles, went inside
And also Galopin. He refused to stop.
They barred the door and raised the drawbridge.   2410
Once they were inside, they felt great joy.
Elye dismounted from his spirited warhorse.
The beautiful Rosamonde ran to embrace him:
Four times she kissed his mouth and his bright face.
They took the charger to a vaulted crypt.   2415
Plenty of hay and oats they fed it.
Then they entered the room above and went up to the tower
And they saw the armies, which had ridden up.
Macabre of Sorbrie addressed his people:
"My lords," said the king, "we can't put up with this!   2420
All this my daughter, who bewitched me so, has done to me!"
To arms rushed all the Saracens and Slavs.
There were more than thirty thousand of them, when they were all mounted.
They attacked the pillars and walls of the tower.
Elye defended himself, who was born at Saint-Gilles.   2425
Huge stones and much fire, too, they dumped down below.
They forced at least four hundred pagans to fall back into the moat.
Oh no! Here comes Corsaut riding up, a lying evil man.
He was the king of Tabarie and had great wealth,
And he had in his force twenty thousand armed Turks.   2430
They attacked the tower, and they raised a great din.
Like madmen, they thrust their pikes to undermine the masonry.
When Galopin saw them, he called Elye:

«Conpains,» dist li vasaus, «ne la porons durer!»
Elye et Galopin sont forment esfreé.* [93r-b] 2435
«Signor,» dist Rosamonde, «por coi vous desmentés?
Ceste tor est trop riche u nous somes entré!
Li quarrel en sont fort, a chiment conpassé;
Chaiens a assés armes et destriers sejorné,
Et fors elmes agus, et boins brans* acherés: 2440
.Iiii.c. chevalier en peut on adouber!
Chi dedens avons char, et puiment et claré,
Et boin pain de forment, et flors avons assés;
Jusc'a .vii. ans tous plains, i poons sejorner,
Que ja n'i entera Sarrasin ne Escler!» 2445
Elyë de Saint Gille a grant joië mené,
U qu'il voit Galopin, si l'en cort acoler,
En l'orelle li dist, coiëment a chelé:
«Galopins, biaus conpains, bien nous est encontré!
Chaiens est paradis, je nel quier mais celer!»* 2450
Estes vous .i. vasal qui est d'outre la mer,
Godefroi ot a non, ensi l'oï nomer;
Cil ot nori Elye petit en son ostel,*
Vienent de la montaigne, al port sont arivé.
Quant Galopins le voit, s'a Elye apelé: 2455
«Vois tu la .i. vasal qui revient d'outre mer?
Car alons a la porte, savoir et demander,
De quel pais il sont, et u doivent aler!»
Et Elyë respont, «Si con vous conmandés!»
Al brestekes* des murs est Elyes acostés; 2460
Les barons en apele, si les a salués:
«Signor,» che dist Elye, «de quel terre estes nés?
Dont venés? U irés? Quel part devés torner?»
Et Godefroi respont, «A Valence fui nés,
Senescau Julïen, le franc duc honoré, 2465
Et venons del sepulcre, u fumes por ourer.
Contreval paienie ai .vii. ans converssé;
Or irai en ma terre, se Dieu l'a destiné.»

Part Five

"Companion," said the knight, "we can't hold out!"
Elye and Galopin were very much afraid.   2435
"My lords," said Rosamonde, "Why are you so upset?
This tower that we have entered is extremely solid:
Its stones are set in cement, well engineered.
Inside there are enough arms and fresh horses
And strong, pointed helmets, and good, sharp swords   2440
That four hundred knights could be armed here!
Here inside we have meat, spices and claret
And good wheat bread; and we have enough flour.
For seven whole years, we can stay in here,
For no Sarracen nor Slav will ever enter!"   2445
Elye of Saint-Gilles felt great joy.
He turned towards Galopin and ran to embrace him.
Into his ear he whispered quietly in secret,
"Galopin, companion, for us it's turned out well.
It's paradise in here. I won't deny it any longer."   2450
Then a knight appeared, who was from overseas,
Godefroi was his name, that's what I have heard him called.
This knight had raised young Elye in his lodgings.
They came from the mountains and arrived at the port.
When Galopin saw this knight, he called Elye: 2455
"Do you see that knight out there, who's returning from overseas?
Now let us go to the gate to find out from them
What country they're from and where they're going!"
And Elye answered, "We'll do as you say!"
Elye leaned out over the wall's parapet.   2460
He called to the knights and greeted them:
"My lords," said Elye, "in what land were you born?
Where are you coming from, and where are you going, in what direction?"
And Godefroi answered, "I was born in Valence,
The seneschalsy of Julien, the noble, honored duke,   2465
And we're coming from the Holy Sepulchre where we went to worship.
I've lived among the Saracens for seven years;
Now I'll go to my land, if God has willed it."

Quant Elyë l'entent, s'a grant joië mené*;
A la vois qu'il ot clere, conmencha a crier: 2470
«Godefroi,» dist Elye, «fai ta gent escouter! [93v-a]
Tu iras a Saint Gille, a mon pere parler!
De par Dieu et de moi, mout bien le salués,
Et me secore chi, si fera mout que ber:
Cha sus en ceste tor, m'ont paien enseré, 2475
Il sont bien .xxx.m. fervestu et armé!»
Quant Godefroi l'entent, s'a de pitiet ploré,
Les maroniers apele, belement et soef:
«Signor,» dist Godefroi, «.i. petit m'entendés:
Se vous a seche terre me poés amener, 2480
Tant vous donrai avoir con vous prenre en volés,
Et riche coupes d'or, et boins bacins dorés.
Ne serés jamais povres, se le savés garder!»
Quant cil l'ont entendu, se li ont creanté;
Lor cinglent et governent au ciel esperitel, 2485
Tant ont lor rices barges coru et ceminé,
Qu'il vinrent a Brandis, au port sont arivé,
Et montent es chevals qui furent sejorné.
Lors trespassent les teres et les anples renés,
Et vienent a Saint Gille tout le chemin feré. 2490
Parmi le mestre porte sont en la vile entré,
Et vienent el palais qui fu a or listé.
La trevent Julïen, qui dessent des degrés,*
Aimeri de Nerbone, et sen riche barné,
Et Hernaut le vaillant, et Bernart l'aduré, 2495
Et Garin d'Anseune, et le franc Aimer,
Bevon de Conmarchis, et Bertran le sené,
L'archevesque de Rains, et le grant richeté,
Qui tienent parlement de la crestïenté.
Elyë voillent querre, nel sevent u trover. 2500
Estes vous Godefroi, qui les a salués,

2481 ms v. penre. The scribe has inadvertently omitted the «r».
2487 ms a Braidis; we emend to the spelling at 2540.

Part Five

When Elye heard him, his heart was filled with joy.
In his strong voice he began to call,   2470
"Godefroi," said Elye, "have your people listen!
You'll go to Saint-Gilles to speak to my father.
On God's behalf and on mine, you'll greet him warmly,
And you will do a very worthy deed and help me here:
Up here in this tower, pagans have beseiged me.   2475
There are at least thirty thousand of them steel clad
   and armed!"
When Godefroi heard him, from great pity he wept.
He called to the mariners quietly and calmly:
"My lords," said Godefroi, "listen to me a moment.
If you can take me to the mainland,   2480
I'll give you as much wealth as you can possibly carry
And rich cups of gold and good, gilded bowls.
You'll never be poor again, if you can hold on to it!"
When they heard him, they believed him.
They set their sails and steered by the heavens.   2485
They sailed and traveled so long in their mighty ships
That they came to Brindisi, and at the port they arrived.
Then they mounted fresh horses
And passed through many lands and vast kingdoms —
All the way on the paved road — and they came to
   Saint-Gilles.   2490
Through the main gate, into the town they entered,
And they came to the palace with its bold-banded
   chamber walls.
There they found Julien, who was coming down the steps,
Aymeri of Narbonne and his powerful entourage,
And Hernaut the valiant and Bernart the brave,   2495
And Garin of Anseune and the noble Aimer,
Bevon of Conmarchis, also the wise Bertrand.
The archbishop of Reims and all the immensely powerful
   nobility
Were holding a council of Christendom.
They wanted to search for Elye, but they didn't know where
   to find him.   2500
Godefroi appeared before them and greeted them;

Godefroi les salue, conme hons bien apensés:
«Cil Dameldé de gloire qui en crois fu penés,
Saut Julïen le conte et son rice barné,
Aymeri de Nerbone, et tout son parenté! 2505
De par son fil Elye, le gentil et le ber,
Par moi vous mande tous, foi que vous mi* devés, [93v-b]
Dedens Sorbrie esrant, que vous le secorés!
Par dedens une tor l'a assis Macabrés;
N'i a que Rosamonde, sa fille o le vis cler, 2510
Et Galopin aussi, qu'en Ardane fu nés!»
Quant Julïens l'entent, s'a de pitiet ploré;
A tere chiet pasmés, ne pot sor piés ester.
Beves de Conmarchis, li gentiex et li ber,
Aymeri de Nerbone est cele part alés, 2515
«Biaus sire,» dist li quens, «.i. petit m'entendés!
Or fera ge mes homes maintenant asambler;
Si mandrai Loëys a Paris la chité,
Et Rainewart ausi, qui porte le tinel,*
L'archevesques i ert,* cil de Rains la chité, 2520
Et seront .xxx.m. de la crestïenté!
Dessi jusc'al sepulcre, ne quier mes arester,
De la ferai mes grailles et mes tabors soner,
Et si diront encore Sarrasin et Escler,
C'Aymeris est venus, por paien esfraer!» 2525
«Pere,» che dist Guillames, «grant amoisne ferés!»
Trestous ses messagiers a li quens apelés;
Il fait ses letres faire, s'a ses homes mandés,
De toute Franche a fait son barnage asanbler.
Illeuques fu Bernars, et Hernaut l'aduré, 2530
Bueves de Conmarchis, et Bertram li senés,
Et Garin d'Anseüne, et li caitis Aimers,*
L'archevesque de Rains, quan que pot asambler.
Rois Loëys repaire de Paris la chité,
Et ot en sa conpaigne Rainewart au tinel. 2535

2502 ms h. apenses; the hypometric verse is emended with «bien»; see note.
2507 ms p. foi; we emend to «moi» on the model of 2582.
2517 ms h. maintenant; the scribe omitted the nasal bar, cf. 2661.

Part Five

Godefroi greeted them as a judicious man would:
"May that God of glory Who was hung on the cross
Save Julien the count and his powerful noblemen,
Aymeri of Narbonne and all his lineage! 2505
On behalf of his son Elye, the noble and the worthy,
Through me, he asks you all, by the allegiance you owe me,
To help him by hurrying to Sorbrie
Where Macabre has beseiged him in a tower.
With him is only Rosamonde, Macabre's daughter with the
    bright face, 2510
And also Galopin, who was born in the Ardennes."
When Julien heard him, from pity he wept.
He fell in a faint to the ground; he could not remain standing.
Beves of Conmarchis, the brave and noble,
And Aymeri of Narbonne rushed over: 2515
"Good Sir," said the count, "listen to me a moment.
I'll have my men assembled,
And I'll send for Louis in the city of Paris
And for Rainewart also, who carries the cudgel.
The archbishop of the city of Reims will be with us, 2520
And there'll be thirty thousand from Christendom!
From here to the Sepulchre, I won't stop.
There, I'll have my horns and my drums sound,
And once again the Saracens and the Slavs will say
That Aymeri has come to terrify the pagans!" 2525
"Father," said William, "you'll perform a great service!"
All of his messengers the count summoned.
He had his instructions written, and he sent orders to his men.
From all over France, he had his nobles assemble.
First of all there was Bernars and the strong Hernaut, 2530
Bueves of Conmarchis and the wise Bertrand
And Garin of Anseune and the exiled Aimers,
The archbishop of Reims and as many as the count could
    assemble.
King Louis arrived from the city of Paris,
And he had in his force Rainewart with his cudgel. 2535

Ains si riches* barnage ne fu mes asamblés,
Qui por le boin Elye vauront le mer passer!
Godefroi les conduist, u pais ot esté,
Il sot mout bien les marces et le latin parler.
Lors vienent a Brandis, les os font sejorner. 2540
Des dromons et des barges i vienent a plenté,
La dedens se sont mis nostre franc bacheler,
Et singlent et governent, et pensent de l'esrer,* [94r-a]
Et voient de Sorbrie les murs et les pilers,
Les brestekes, les tors, et les palais listés. 2545
Godefrois li sachans a grant joië mené,
Julïen en apele, qu'a Saint Gille fu nés:
«Sire,» dist Godefrois, «mout t'est bien encontré!
Vois tu or cele tor, a cel plonc crestelé?
Laiens laissai ton fil a mout grant poverté; 2550
Galopin, l'Ardenois, et la dame al vis cler!»
Quant Julïens l'entent, s'a de pitié ploré;
Il sont venu al port, des vaseus sont torné,
Puis montent es destriers, dont i ot a plenté,
Si drechent les ensenges, si pensent de l'esrer. 2555
Quant Galopins les voit, c'as murs fu acostés,
La u il voit Elye, si l'en a apelé:
«Haï!* Sire conpains, bien nous est encontrés!
Veés ichi les ensenges de la crestïenté,
L'oriflambe le roi de Paris la chité, 2560
Aymeri de Nerbone, le viel quenu barbé,
Julïen de Saint Gille, au dragon enpené!
Amis, fai une cosse que te voil deviser*:
Que vous vestés l'auberc et l'ïaume fremés,
Et si çaingiés l'espee au senestre costé, 2565
Montés en Marchegai, le destrier abrivé,*
Et g'irai la defors, a Loëys parler!»
Rosamonde la bele va congiet demander,

2536 ms si grans barnage; we emend the hypometric verse to «riches» on the model of 2745. See note.
2555 ms l. enseges; the scribe has omitted the nasal bar. We emend to the word, as in 2559.

Part Five

Never before had such powerful nobility been assembled
Who, for noble Elye, sought to cross the sea!*
Godefroi was leading them: he had been to that land;
He knew the countryside well and how to speak the language.
When they came to Brindisi, they allowed the armies to rest.   2540
There came a great number of warships and barges.
Our noble knights boarded them and embarked,
And they started out, then sailed and steered to make the voyage.
And they saw the walls and the pillars of Sorbrie,
The parapets and the towers and the ornate palaces.   2545
Godefroi, the judicious man, felt great joy.
He called Julien, who was born at Saint-Gilles,
"My lord," said Godefroi, "you're in good fortune!
Do you see now that tower crenelated with lead?*
I left your son inside in dire straits   2550
With Galopin from the Ardennes and the bright-faced maid."
When Julien heard him, from pity he wept.
They entered the port; they sprang from the vessels.
Then they mounted on their steeds, which were abundant,
And they raised their standards and set out on the journey.   2555
When Galopin, who was leaning over the walls, saw them,
He turned towards Elye and called out to him:
"Look! Sir companion, it's turned out well for us!
Here are the standards of Christendom,
The Oriflamme of the king from the city of Paris,   2560
Aymeri of Narbonne, the old and hoary-bearded,
Julien of Saint-Gilles with his banner with the dragon!
My friend, here's what I advise you to do:
Put on your hauberk and lace on your helmet
And then gird your sword on your left side;   2565
Mount on Marchegai, the swift steed,
And I'll go out there to speak to King Louis."
He went to ask leave of the beautiful Rosamonde,

Et ele li dona, volentiers et de gré.
Par le fausse posterne, issi de la chité.   2570
Il lait ester le pas, si se prent au troter,
Tant que il vient en l'ost, ne vaut onques finer.
Il salue le roi, si con oïr porés:
«Cil Dameldé de gloire, qui fist crestïentés,
Saut le roi Loëys, et son riche barné,   2575
Aymeri de Nerbone, qui li siet au costé,
Julïen de Saint Gille, et Bernart l'aduré!»
«Amis,» che dist li rois, «Dieus te puisse saver!
Conment as tu a non, et de quel terre es nés?»   [94r-b]
«Sire,» dist Galopins, «en Ardane fui nés,   2580
Et si sui* fil Tieri, le franc duc honoré;
Par moi vous mande Elye salus et amistés!»
Quant li baron l'entendent, s'ont grant joïe mené;
Enqui illeuc s'adoubent, con ja oïr porés*:
Il vestent les aubers, s'ont les elme fremés,   2585
Et pendent a lor caus les fors escus bouclés,
Ens en lor poins ont pris les fors espiels quarrés,
Et montent es destriers corans et abrivés.
De .iiii. pars ont leus assise la chité,
Mout par i ot drechiés de tentes et de trés.   2590
La fu grans li asaus de la crestïentés,
Li paien se desfendent qui as murs sont montés.*
Quant Galopins d'Ardane a Guillame apelés,
Julïen de Saint Gille, et le caitif Aimer.*
El vergier Rosamonde s'en sont cil .iiii. entré;   2595
Rosamonde les voit, si lait le pont aler,
Et cil entrent dedens, qui grant joie ont mené.
Elyë vit son pere, si le cort acoler*;
Plus de .xx. fois, li baisse et le bouche et le nés.
«Signor,» dist Galopins, «bien vous est encontré!   2600
Or seromes nous .v. fervestu et armé,
Quant vous verois l'asaut de la crestïenté,
Et g'irai a la porte, por paien destorber,
L'Enpereor de Franche voil les huis defermer.»

2592   ms s. desfende; the plural form is needed.

Part Five

And she granted him leave willingly and gladly.
Through the hidden postern gate, he left the city. 2570
He stopped walking and began to trot along.
Until he reached the army, he refused to stop.
He greeted the king, just as you'll now hear:
"May that Lord of glory, Who created Christianity
Save King Louis and all his powerful nobles, 2575
Aymeri of Narbonne, who is seated beside him,
Julien of Saint-Gilles and Bernart the strong."
"My friend," said the king, "May God save you!
What's your name, and in what land were you born?"
"My lord," said Galopin, "in the Ardennes I was born, 2580
And I'm the son of Tieri, the brave and much-honored duke.
Through me, Elye sends you his greetings and friendship!"
When the nobles heard him, their hearts were filled with joy.
Then they armed themselves, just as you will hear:
They put on their hauberks, they laced on their helmets, 2585
And they hung at their necks their stout-bossed shields.
In their hands they took their strong, stout lances,
And they mounted on swift, rapid warhorses.
From all four directions, they laid seige to the city.
Everywhere there had been many tents and pavillons arrayed. 2590
Mighty was the assault of all of Christendom!
The pagans, who'd climbed up to the walls, defended themselves
When Galopin of the Ardennes called William
And Julien of Saint-Gilles and the wretched Aimer.
Into Rosamonde's orchard these four entered. 2595
Rosamonde saw them, and she let down the drawbridge,
And they all went in, who felt great joy.
Elye saw his father, and he ran to embrace him:
More than twenty times he kissed his mouth and nose.
"My lords," said Galopin, "you've come at the right moment! 2600
Now there'll be five of us, steel clad with weapons!
When you see Christendom's assault,
And when I go to the gates to attack the pagans,
I want to unlock the doors for the emperor of the French."

Quant Julïen l'entent, s'a grant joie mené; 2605
Rosamonde la bele avale les degrés,
Et vint a s'aumoniere, s'en a trait une clef,
Au tressor est venue, s'a les huis desfermés.
La prendent les escus, et les aubers safrés,
Et montent es destriers corans et abrivés. 2610
Aymeri de Nerbone asailli la chité,
L'arcesvesque de Rains, et tous ses parentés.
D'autre part, fu li rois, a tout .m. home armés.*
Grant joië* demenerent Sarrasin et Escler;
Et desfendent forment les murs et les fossés.   [94v-a] 2615
Estes vous Galopins qui s'est abandonés,
Guillames li marchis, cil li fu al costé,
Jusc'a .xxx. paien i ont mort et tués.
Puis desferment le bare, s'ont le pont avalé;
Galopins conmencha hautement a crier: 2620
«Saint Denise de Franche, tuit serés ostelé!»
François, et Borgengon sont la dedens entré,
Flamenc, et Beruier, dont i ot a plenté;
Espeës toutes nues, sont ens acheminé,
Mout par fu grant la noisse de la crestïenté. 2625
La peüssiés veöir tant riche cop doné,
Tant brac, tant puing, tant pié, tante teste caper,*
Tant Sarrasin morir, trebuchier et verser!
Es vous poignant Bernart de Brubant la chité,
Et a brandië l'anste del roit espiel quarré; 2630
Desor l'escu a or, vait ferir Macabré;
L'escu li a perchié, et le hauberc faussé,
Tant con anste li dure, l'a del destrier hurté.
Il n'est pas encor mors, mes il est craventé!
Par le brac l'a saissi, si l'a amont levé. 2635
U qu'il voit Galopin, si l'en a apelé:
«Petis hon,» dist Bernars, «c'est prison m'egardés!»
Et cil li respondi, «Si con vous conmandés!
En le chartre parfonde le m'esteut avaler,

2627   ms t. test caper, emended to «teste», as in 2377.

Part Five

When Julien heard him, he felt great joy.   2605
The beautiful Rosamonde ran down the steps,
Went to her alms purse and took out a key;
To the treasury she went, and she unbarred the doors.
There they took the shields and the burnished hauberks,*
And they mounted on swift, rapid warhorses.   2610
Aymeri of Narbonne attacked the city
With the archbishop of Reims and all his lineage,
And on the other side was the king with a thousand men.
The Saracens and Slavs shouted with great joy,
And they stoutly defended the walls and the moats.   2615
Galopin arrived, who went at full speed.
William the marquis was right at his side.
They killed and slayed over thirty pagans.
Then they unbarred the door and lowered the drawbridge.
Galopin began to shout loudly: 2620
"By Saint Denis of France, there's room for everyone inside!"
The French and Burgundians went in,
The Flemish and the many knights from Berry.
With unsheathed swords, they made their way inside.
Mighty was the din raised by all those Christians!   2625
There you'd have seen many rich blows dealt:
So many arms, so many hands, so many feet, so many heads
    cut off,
So many Saracens stumbling and keeling over and slain!*
Then came riding up Bernart from the city of Brubant,
And he brandished the hilt of his stout, well-shaped lance.   2630
He rushed to strike Macabre upon his gilded shield.
The shield he pierced, and he tore the hauberk.
Thrusting the lance to its breaking point, he hurled the pagan
    from his courser.
Macabre was not yet dead, but he was gravely wounded.
By the arm Bernard seized him, and he raised him up.   2635
He turned towards Galopin and called out to him:
"Little man," said Bernart. "Guard this prisoner for me!"
And Galopin answered him, "Just as you command!"
"In the deep prison, I must have him lowered.*

Bos, culevres* i a, sachiés, a grant plenté, 2640
Qui li mengeront senpre les flans et les costés!»
Lors a drechiet amont le grant baston quarré,
Parmi outre le teste, a feru Macabré,
Le teste li pechoie, li oilg en sont volé,
Et li cors estendi, l'ame en portent mal fé.* 2645
Estes vous Loëys, qu'est arier retorné,
Si fist pupler le vile de la crestïenté.*
Es vous venus Bernart de Brubant la chité,
U qu'il voit Galopin, si l'en a apelé:
«Petis hon,» dist Bernars, «mon prison me rendés!» 2650
Galopins respondi, «Si con vous conmandés!» [94v-b]
Par les jambes le prent, si l'a amont levé.
«Amis,» che dist Bernart, «tu le m'as conraé!
Il n'est pas ore iteus, quant le toi conmandé!»*
«Sire,» dist Galopins, «il ne voloit aler; 2655
Por chou qu'erre petis, si me tint en vieuté!»
Et quant Bernars l'entent, s'a grant joië mené.
Lors montent el palais li demainne et li per,
Et font tantost les fons beneïr et sacrer;
Rosamonde i menerent, la bele o le vis cler, 2660
Tout maintenant le fissent beneïr et sacrer.
Dieus, con riche pressent i ot le jor doné!
Aymeri de Nerbone i courut au lever,
Julïen de Saint Gille, et Loëys li ber,
Guillame li marcis, et li franc .xii. per. 2665
Quant Elyës les voit, s'est cele part alés;
Isnelement et tost est courus au lever,
Hé! Dieus, con grant damages, pere de majesté,*
Por chou le perdra il ne le pot espouser!
El palais en monterent les marberins degrés, 2670
Elyës vit le roi, sel prist a apeler:
«Signor,» che dist Elyes, «m'amië m'espousés,
Rosamonde la bele, qui tant jor m'a gardé,
En cest palais de marbre, des menbres a coper!»

2656   ms m. tient; we emend to the *passé simple*. See note.

Part Five

There are many lethal toads and snakes there, you may
 be sure, 2640
Who'll soon gnaw at his flanks and eat his sides!"
Then he raised aloft his huge well-shaped cudgel,
He struck Macabre over the head.
He split his head open — the eyes flew out of it —
And the body lay there. Devils bore off his soul. 2645
Louis arrived then, who had turned back to them,
And he had the city populated and occupied by Christians.
Then there appeared Bernart from the city of Brubant.
He turned toward Galopin and called to him,
"Little man," said Bernart, "give me back my prisoner." 2650
Galopin answered, "Just as you command!"
By the legs he took him, and he raised him up.
"My friend," said Bernart, "you've really taken care of him!
He wasn't like this just now, when I gave him to you!"
"My lord," said Galopin, "he refused to go. 2655
Because I was little, he held me in contempt!"*
And when Bernart heard him, his heart was filled with joy.
Then the lords and the peers went up to the palace,
And rapidly they had the fonts blessed and sanctified.
They led Rosamonde there, the beautiful maid with the
 bright face. 2660
Right away they had her blessed and made holy.
God, what a rich gathering there was that day!
Aymeri of Narbonne hurried to the baptism,
Julien of Saint-Gilles and Louis the noble,
Guillaume the marquis and the twelve brave peers! 2665
When Elye saw them, he went over to them;
Immediately he hastened to the baptism.
Oh God! What a great misfortune, Father of majesty!
Because of this sacrament, he will lose her and will not be able to
 marry her!
At the palace, they went up the marble steps. 2670
Elye saw the king, and he called out to him:
"My lord," said Elye, "marry me to my beloved,*
Rosamonde the beautiful, who protected me for so many days
In this marble palace from having my limbs cut off!"

«Vasal,» dist l'archevesque, «de folië parlés! 2675
Che ne poroit soffrir sainte crestïentés!
Voiant nos ieus trestous, l'as aidiet a lever,
Et es saintismes fons beneïr et sacrer!»
Quant Elyë l'entent, s'a de pitiet ploré,
Rosamonde, autressi, ne pot sor piés ester, 2680
Ains cheï a la tere, et se prist a pasmer,
Et Guillames d'Orenge l'en corut relever.
«Bele,» che dist li rois, «envers moi entendés!
Veés vous el palais trestous les .xii. pers?
Certes mout richement vous vaurai marïer: 2685
Tel home vous donrai, con volés deviser!»
«Signor,» dist la puchele, «tout che laissiés ester! [95r-a]
Puisc'ai perdu Elye, que tant jor ai amé,*
Por l'amor del baron, Galopin me donés!»
Quant li baron l'entendent, cele par sont alé; 2690
Aymeri de Nerbone i fu as fois doner,
Sor les saintes reliques font Galopin jurer
Qu'il penra la puchele a mollier et a per.
Et Galopins respont, «Si con vous conmandés!
Jamais en douche Franche ne me verés entrer; 2695
Ains conquerrai de cha, sainte crestïenté,
Et ferrai les asmoines et les messes canter!»
Elyë de Saint Gille a de pitié ploré,
L'Enperere meïsmes est cele part alés:
«Vasal,» dist l'Enperere, «envers moi entendés! 2700
En Franche no pais, ensanble o nous venrés,
Mout richement, amis, vous vaurai marïer!
Ma seur vous donra je,* Avisse o le vis cler,
Et vous donrai assés castieus et fermetés,
Orliens, et tout Behorges, qu'est dame des chités, 2705
Et me riche oriflanble devant moi porterés.»
Quant Elyë l'entent, s'a de ceur sospiré,
«Sire,» che dist Elye, «.v.c. merchis de Dé!»
Enqui donent les fois, et li a creanté
Qu'il aura sa seür, al gent cors honoré. 2710

Part Five

"Sir knight," said the archbishop, "you speak nonsense!*   2675
Holy Christendom could never allow it!
Before all our eyes, at her baptism, you helped raise her
And bless her and sanctify her in the most holy font!"
When Elye heard him, he wept from pity.
Rosamonde, as well, could not remain on her feet.   2680
She began to faint, and she fell to the ground.
And William of Orange ran to lift her up.
"Beautiful lady," said the king, "listen to me a moment:
Do you see all of the twelve peers here in the palace?
Believe me, I want to arrange a very advantageous
    marriage for you.   2685
I'll give you the high-born man of your choice."
"My lord," said the girl, "please let all that happen.
Since I've lost Elye, whom I have loved for so long,
For the love of that knight, give me Galopin."
When the nobles heard her, they went over to Galopin.   2690
Aymeri of Narbonne was present at the plighting of the troths.
On holy relics, they had Galopin swear
That he would take the maid as wife and as peer.
And Galopin answered, "Just as you command!
Never will you see me enter sweet France.   2695
Rather, I'll conquer lands here for Holy Christendom,
And I will have alms given and masses sung."
Elye of Saint-Gilles wept from pity.
The emperor himself went to him.
"Noble knight," said the emperor, "listen to me: 2700
To France our land you will come with us.
My friend, I'll want to arrange a very advantageous
    marriage for you.
I'll give you my sister, Avisse with the bright face,
And I'll give you many fortresses and castles,
Orleans and all of Bourges, which is the queen of cities!   2705
And before me, you'll bear my magnificent Oriflamme."
When Elye heard him, he breathed a heart-felt sigh.
"My lord," said Elye, "five hundred thanks be to God."
Soon they swore oaths of fidelity, and Louis pledged to Elye
That he would have the emperor's noble, honored sister,   2710

Et trestout li baron ont grant joïë mené,
Et Julïen ses peres, li vieus kenus barbés.
Lors tienent parlement de le crestïenté;   [95r-b]
Galopins prist la dame a mollier et a per;
.Iii. jors durent les noches, dedens cele chité.   2715
L'Enperere de Franche ne vaut plus demorer,
Ne li autre baron, dont i ot a plenté;
Ains iront au sepulcre, por lor ames saver.
Rosamonde la dame les prist a esgarder,
Pour chou que il devoient en sus de lui aler,   2720
Tenrement a ploré, et del ceur souspiré;
A Chelui les conmande, qui en crois fu penés.
Galopins les conduist, qu'en Ardane fu nés,
Quant che vint au partir, grant deul ont demené;
Meïsmes Galopins au gent cors honoré,   2725
Por son signor Elye, que il ot tant amé.
A tant s'en sont parti, et pensent de l'esrer;
Et Galopin revint a sa feme al vis cler.
Et no baron chevauchent, que Jhesu puist saver!
Il trespassent les teres et les anples resnés;   2730
Les pais avironent, qui sont et grant et lés,
Mout trevent le pais plain de grant poverté.
Godefroi les conduist, c'ot el pais esté.
Tant ont par lor jornees esploitiet et esré,
Passent prés, et boscages, et grans desrubans lés,   2735
Qu'il sont tout al sepucre venu et arivé.
Et quant il furent la, si l'ont tout aoré.
Quant ont fait lor offrande, si sont tout retorné,
Tout droit, vers douche Franche, se sont acheminé.
Tant ont et nuit et jor chevalciet et esré,   2740
C'a Paris sont venu, l'amirable chité.
Encontre sont venu li viel et li barbé,
Et dames et pucheles, serjant et bacheler;
Cel jor font mout grant joie del riche coroné.

2731   ms Le pais; we emend to the plural, as in 2730. See note.
2737   ms t. aorné; we emended to the sense of «worship» («aorer»), rather than the incorrect «ornament, decorate» («aorner»).

Part Five

And all of the nobles felt great joy,
With Julien his father, the old, white-bearded man.
Then they held a council of all Christendom.
Galopin took the lady as wife and peer.
Three days the wedding festivities lasted in that city.　　2715
The emperor of France did not want to stay longer,
Nor did the other nobles, of whom there were many.
Instead, they wanted to go to the Holy Sepulchre, to save
　their souls.
And lady Rosamonde began to look at them,
Because they had to be separated from her.　　2720
Tenderly she wept and gave deep heartfelt sighs.
To Him Who was hung on the cross, she then commended them.
Galopin led them out, who was born in Ardennes.
When it came time to part, they were all greatly saddened,*
Even Galopin, the noble and honored,　　2725
For his lord, Elye, whom he had loved so much.
Then the knights left and started out on their journey,
And Galopin returned to his wife with the bright face.
And our nobles rode forth, may Jesus save them!
They journeyed through many lands and vast kingdoms.　　2730
They went through countries that were vast and wide.
They found these lands full of great poverty.*
Godefroi led them, for he had been to that country.
They travelled and journeyed for so long,
Past meadows and woods, great wide ravines,　　2735
That they finally arrived at last at the Holy Sepulchre.
And when they were there, and they had worshipped at all
　the holy places,
And when they had made their offering, they turned back
　towards home.
Straight toward sweet France, they made their way.
They rode and journeyed so much by day and night　　2740
That they came to Paris, the wondrous city.
The old and the bearded came out to meet them,
The ladies and maids, servants and young squires.
That day they celebrated in joy the mighty crowned king.

.Viii. jors tient li rois cort, et son rice barné,* 2745
Mout fu grande la feste el palais princhipel.
Li boins rois Loëys, qui tant fait a loer,
A fait venir sa seur, Avise o le vis cler, [95v-a]
Elyë le dona a mollier et a per,
Et il l'a recheüe, volentiers et de gré. 2750
Se les noches sont grans, nel esteut demander!
Maint riche vasel d'or i fu le jor doné;
Menestrel s'en loërent, quant vint al dessevrer,
Ensi dona li rois sa seror al vis cler
A Elye le preu, fil Julïen le ber, 2755
Qui fu dus de Saint Gille, si con oï avés.
D'Elyë vint Ayous, si con avant orés.
Ichi faut li romans de Julïen le ber,
Et d'Elyë, son fil, qui tant pot endurer.
Cil engenra Ayoul, qui tant fist a loer, 2760
Si con vous m'orés dire, sel volés escouter.

EXPLICHIT LI ROMANS D'ELYE

Part Five

For a week the king and his powerful nobility held court.   2745
Very great was the feast in the king's main palace.
The good king Louis, who did so many worthy deeds,
Sent for his sister Avisse with the bright face.
To Elye he gave her, as wife and as peer.
And Elye received her, willingly and gladly.   2750
There's no need to ask if the wedding feast was great!
Many luxurious golden vessels were on that day given.
The minstrels praised the festivities, when it came time to part.
Thus the king gave in marriage Avisse, his bright-faced sister,
To Elye, the noble son of worthy Julien,   2755
Who was duke of Saint-Gilles, as you have already heard.
From Elye came Ayoul, as you will hear presently.*
Here ends the story of Julien the noble
And of Elye his son, who had to endure so much!
Elye will beget Ayoul, who did so many praiseworthy deeds,   2760
Just as you'll hear me tell, if you want to listen.

HERE ENDS THE STORY OF ELYE

ILLUSTRATIONS
From BNfr25516

Fol. 76r   Ichi commenche li vraie estoire de Juliens de saint Gille le ques fu pere Elye du quel Aiols issi ensi con vous orés el livre.

Fol. 82r   C'est chi ensi con Sarrasin ont pris Elye et l'ont mis en une nef.

Fol. 84r   Ch'est chi ensi que Elyes ochist les larons et con Galopin li pria merchi.

Fol. 85v   Ch'est chi ensi con Galopin en porta son signor navre el vergier et con la puchele le vit.

Fol. 89v   Ch'est chi ensi con Galopins enbla le boin destrier.

Fol. 95r   Ch'est chi ensi con Galopin espousse Rosamonde l'amie Elye.

1. Here begins the true story of Julien of Saint-Gilles who was the father of Elye, of whom Aiol was born as you will hear in the book. (fol. 76r)

Elye of Saint-Gilles

2. This is how Saracens seized Elye and put him in a boat. (fol. 82r).

3. This is how Elye slays the thieves and how Galopin begs him for mercy. (fol. 84r).

Illustrations

4. This is how Galopin carried his wounded lord into the garden and how the maiden saw it. (fol. 85v).

5. This is how Galopin stole the good war-horse. (fol. 89v).

6. This is how Galopin weds Rosamonde, the friend of Elye. (fol. 95r).

NOTES
by line number

3   *Vers* has multiple meanings, including "poem" or "parts of a poem." Here the expression *3 vers* likely refers to the three parts of the so-called *geste de Saint Gille* (a title invented for convenience by critics but never referred to in the poems themselves). These sections relate to the First and Fourth Crusades and the Reconquest, all of which deeply involved the House of Flanders (Kelly 28–31, Martin 43, Chailley 28).

4   *Conte* has a dual meaning in this context, alluding to similar word play on homophones meaning both "count" and "story" in Chrétien de Troyes' prologue of *Erec et Enide* 13–22. The *Elye* poet refers both to the birth of the literary character, Count Julien de Saint-Gilles, and to the story itself, generated from the *faille* or break in the story at *laisse* 50 of the *Couronnement de Louis*. See Introduction and 1085.

18 *Biauland* is a fictional region in the south of France associated especially with the William of Orange cycle and one of its characters, Hernaut. This toponym occurs also in some manuscripts of the *Chanson de Roland*.

41 Langlois suggests that Piereplate (var. Pierrelate, Pierrelange), originally referred to the city of Nice (*Couronnement de Louis* 79). Piereplate was a southern city conquered by William in the *Couronnement de Louis* (2026) just prior to his defeat of Julien of Saint-Gilles. (See also Frappier 2: 207 n). This place name may also refer to the actual southern city of Pierelatte.

42 *Jovenes* can be monosyllabic in Picard; Gossen notes that the "e" of "ve" is atonic (Gossen 81.26).

42 The legal age for marriage in northern France, including Flanders and Hainaut, was twelve for girls and fifteen for boys (Wolff 284, Warlop 2: 155).

47 The topos that opposes *clergie/chevalerie* is common to vernacular narrative, occuring prominently in the *Couronnement de Louis* 94–97, and in the Oxford version of the *Chanson de Roland* 1877–83. F noted the originality of this analogy of the monk *(moine reclus)* in the choir stall and the warhorse *(destriers en garde)* in the stable stall. See Jenkins 144 and n 1881, and Fawtier, "Notes" 99–100.

49 The cathedral cities of Paris and Chartres were located within the domains of the king of France; Chartres was a seat of the house of Blois and Champagne. The latter was connected with the kingdom of Navarre, whose king was the father of Blanche of Champagne, mother of Thibaut IV le Chansonnier, or the Song Writer, who became the king of Navarre at his majority. See Introduction.

54 The scribe mistakenly wrote *chastieus* after the numeral, probably influenced by the expression *.iiii. chastieus* in the previous line. He expunctuated the mistake by underlining the entire word, a technique used systematically in the West in elimination of whole words since the fifth century (Prou 267).

54 The *freté* (usu. *ferté*) was a fortified castle.

55 The identity of this *apostle* has been subject to various interpretations due to the difficulty created by the word *arche*. R (185) queried whether it could refer to Saint Jacques de Compostelle, who in the New Testament is Saint James the Greater, son of Zebedee,

183

although in the *Prise d'Orange* William swears by God, by Saint James and by the apostle of the ark (1380–81), suggesting that the latter is other than Saint James. Langlois surmised that it could refer to Rome and Saint Peter's (*Couronnement de Louis* gl.). F noted the affinity of *l'arche* with *l'arce* and Noah's ark, referred to later in *Elye* (1644).

56   The entire opening episode alludes to *Les Narbonnais* 37 ff., where Aymeri of Narbonne distributes his estates and sends forth his sons to win their own fiefs.

65   Trapes has been hypothesized by R as Trebizonde (203); its usage here echoes the *Couronnement de Louis*, var. ms C, 441. This toponym is found in the Venice 4 manuscript of the *Chanson de Roland* as well as in Jean Bodel's *Chanson des Saisnes* 2: 94–95.

66   Aimer is a character who is prominent in the William of Orange cycle where he appears as one of William's brothers; he vows never to sleep under a roof but to fight the Saracens as long as he lives. He is traditionally referred to as *le chétif*, (lat. *captivum*), "the captive" or "the exile" or "wretched," a term associated in Old French with the "terminology of repentance" (Brault 1: 221 and 430 n 12 and 13; *Couronnement de Louis* 826).

67   Anseïs de Cartage seems to be a composite character in *Elye*; the geographic reference may allude to the forty-ninth *laisse* of the *Couronnement de Louis*, where William subjugates Dagobert of Carthage. The name *Anseïs* is associated with one of Charlemagne's twelve peers in the *Chanson de Roland*, who is killed by a Saracen (1594–1604.). In *Elye* the poet has constructed a role reversal, and Anseïs becomes a Saracen killed by a Christian. R's glossary (196) mistakenly identified the name as a reference to the later eponymous *chanson de geste*, but he subsequently corrected the error in his introduction (xxi n 4).

70   A *quintaine* or "quintain" (lat. *quintana*) was a piece of equipment designed to train young knights in jousting and the use of the lance. Its construction varied but often consisted of a shield set up between two posts or stakes. The name was derived from the area in a Roman army camp between the fourth and sixth divisions of a legion where training exercises were held. (Ascherl 274 and 294 n 17).

71   Of all of the poems that comprise the Old French epic corpus, *Elye* contains the sole reference to "Navarese shields" (Langlois, *Table* 482), as well as to the king of Navarre. Navarre was not synonymous with the manufacture of arms. In fact, the primary centers were northern Italy, Germany and urban areas of Flanders, while Toledo was famous for its steel swords. The reference in *Elye* may allude to the *escut de Tolette*, or shield of Toledo, of Malquidant, slain by Turpin, in the *Chanson de Roland* (1611). As is the case with *Elye*, the *Chanson de Roland* contains the sole reference in the epic canon to a shield made in Toledo (Langlois, *Table* 644). The close association of Navarre with the Parisian court at the time of our poem may account for the pointed, unusual reference; see 49. (Gaier 179, 193; Ascherl 293 n 7).

78   A *denier* was a widely-used monetary unit in medieval Europe from the Carolingian era on; it was a piece of silver that weighed about two and one-half grams in 1096 (*Gesta Francorum* 36 n. 1), but its value varied. Today it might be metaphorically compared to a penny.

80   Hereditary succession in the most illustrious noble houses could occur either through the legitimate son or daughter. The reference to Julien's possible female successor might have been of interest in the context of *Elye*, because Jeanne of Constantinople, or Flanders, at her majority succeeded to the feudal domain or county of Flanders and that

NOTES

of Hainaut. During the lengthy imprisonment of her husband after his loss to the French king in the Battle of Bouvines in 1214, her rule as countess initiated a long period of rulership of the county by women. (Wolff 284).

84   "Nero's fields" or gardens was the name of the location in Rome identified with the martyrdom of Saint Peter. At the time when *Elye* was composed, Rome was the second most favored pilgrimage site (after Jerusalem).

88   *Meïsme* (lat. *met* + *ipsimu*) is a Picard form frequently found in literary versified texts when one more syllable was needed than provided by the Francien *mesme*. (Gossen 86.30; cf. 1794).

91   The countess' lament that the parents will be left alone without defense alludes to *Les Narbonnais*, where we encounter the same complaint; see 56.

100   *Salatré* is also a Saracen character in the *Prise d'Orange* (746), who reveals the disguised William's identity. His name was traditionally a Saracen name for both people and places in the William of Orange cycle. It is used for both Saracens and Christians in *Elye*, appearing as the name of one of Julien's men and also as the Saracen king who kills Elye's horse; see 468.

101   F mistakenly indicates a lacuna because he is closely comparing *Elye* with its later Norwegian translation which amplifies the original at this point. See Introduction.

109   Gossen discusses the evolution of initial "o" before a nasal into the Picard "a," the model of which is *domina > dame*, which he explained by the proclitic use of these words before proper names (Gossen 94.36). R emends the manuscript reading *viex* to *vieus* without noting it. Gossen states that the preferred Old Picard form was *vies*, with *vieus, viex* and *vix* rarely attested. (Gossen 79 n. 33).

127   The repetition of conjunctions in close succession (polysyndeton) is used for the stylistic effect of accumulation; the sophistication of the rhetorical development in *Elye* has been thoroughly documented by Melli.

135   The past participle of the Francien verb *descliquier* appears here in its Picard form in order to fit the assonance (Gossen 99.41.3b). F corrects to *desclice* and R to *des(c)lice(s)*.

141   *Sire* is sometimes scanned as one syllable and sometimes two; here there is a pause in the discourse, indicating that the mute "e" is silent at the caesura; cf. 118 and 148.

161   F unnecessarily emends *Que ne* to *U tu*; thereby attenuating the stunningly dramatic effect produced by the triple negative subjunctive.

161   The *paresis* was a coin minted in Paris, equivalent to the *denier* (cf. 78). "Not worth a *paresis*" is equivalent to "not worth a cent."

164   *Marberins* (Francien: *marbrins*) is a common Picardism with the insertion of the svarabhactic *e* which has been commented on by Gossen 103.44.

167   In keeping with the present tense of preceding verbs, F emended to the present tense, breaking the succession of dodecasyllabic lines with a single decasyllabic one (cf. 186). The use of tenses in Old French verse narrative does not correspond to modern French usage; Old French poets often switched tenses from past to present at points in the narrative where this would never occur in modern syntax. Fleischman has noted that

although the phenomenon of tense switching has received heightened critical attention and study as a philological or linguistic phenomenon, it is far from being understood. (Fleishman 21–23).

167   The names are both fictional and historical; *Gerardot le rous* (or *le roux*), for example, was a celebrated late twelfth-century troubadour in the service of a "Count Alphonso," either Alfonso of Toulouse, older brother of Raymond V, or Alfonse Jourdain (Finoli 1051, Boutière and Schutz 345). A knight named Gerardot, probably the same character, later saves Elye's life by identifying him to Malpriant when the latter is about to slay him (763). The same knight is referred to again by Elye later (1475). A similar situation occurs in BN fr 25516's version of *Beuves de Hanstone* in which the real-life *trouvère*, or troubador (court poet) Bertrand de Bar-sur-Aube appears in the poem as a minstrel who saves the hero's life (232–25 and 9682–86). The later case of the Chatelain de Coucy, both a *trouvère* and a literary character, also comes to mind. The other names in the short catalogue are drawn from the three epic cycles or *gestes* and refer to characters in the William of Orange cycle such as Aymer, Tibaut, as well as Thierri in the Charlemagne cycle and Sanghin in the Loherain cycle.

176   "The apostle whom pilgrims seek" is a stock epic formula. As well as Saint James of Compostella, patron saint of the Reconquest, it could perhaps allude to Saint Gilles who is referred to later in *Elye* (1339–40). Cf. 55 & 84.

184   Assuming that the scribe has mistakenly repeated *desous* from two verses above, F emends to *desor*, "over" or "near" the eyebrow, and R emends to *des(o)us*, also "over." But the brain could be coming out of the temple, as was the case in Roland's death (*Chanson de Roland* 1764), and thus under the brow, simply meaning "at eye-level."

188   F emends the masculine noun to *ueniemens* (although he notes the feminine form *vengance*, var. *venjance* at 943) on the analogy with *vengement* in *Aiol* 10213, apparently on the basis of the masculine past participle. Cf. 241.

201   *Loëys* is trisyllabic here, as it is generally throughout the poem; however it sometimes represents two syllables and will be noted as such when it occurs.

203   The messenger openly states that Louis was being crowned; in the complex nexus of allusions in *Elye*, the reference can be taken as a direct, overt reference to the *Couronnement de Louis*. Malicote, "Visual and Verbal Allusion."

210   The itinerary's fidelity to geography yields to the poetic necessity of preserving the assonance; the resulting apparent skewing of the logical sequence of toponyms was a prominent cause of the so-called distrust of verse and the preference for the more factually accurate prose form, which did not have to make such formal distortions and concessions.

212   F emends to *belement nous avint* ("all went well for us"), and in the *Varia lectio* he indicates the manuscript reading. R similarly emends to *belement nos avint*. We keep the manuscript reading *belement lor advint* ("all went well for them"), as it is evident here that the messenger is being ironic. For a similar use of irony, cf. 2290.

215   The common Picard form of the imperfect subjunctive, *fuissiemes*, is discussed by Gossen 136.79.

216   Both F and R emend to the *passé simple* form *revint*. The messenger's imminent demise forces an abbreviated telling of the suspenseful tale whose dramatic tone recounts

NOTES

the arrival of miraculous help in the midst of a see-saw battle. The same breathless paratactic effect is continued in 217, while F and R opt for emendation to the relative *que*.

241   See 188.

244   This episode of symbolical lay communion, centered on a blade of grass for the Viaticum (sometimes three blades), is found in more than a dozen epics and romances. These include two versions of the *Chanson de Roland*. The reference probably had its genesis in Geffrei Gaimar's early twelfth-century Anglo-Norman account in the *Estoire des Engleis* of the death of William Rufus in the New Forest. In Gaimar's story, a knight placed a bit of grass in the king's mouth upon the latter's request for communion. Gaimar specified that the king had received communion earlier that day, so that the act did not endanger his soul's journey (6330). It is noteworthy that Gaimar's episode includes his only use of Latin (*corpus Domini*) in the *Estoire*. The expression also occurs in Latin in *Raoul de Cambrai* 8442, and it is translated (*le cor dieu*) in *Garin le Loherain* 10,623. A similar episode takes place in *Aliscans*; William administers a consecrated host, which an archbishop had given to him, to the dying Vivien (826). The other poems mentioned specify that the grass is "in lieu of" or "for" the body of Christ. The *Elye* poet is even more circumspect, avoiding any direct reference to the body of Christ. The episode must have been well known by contemporaries, since it is parodied in the short Arrageois mock-epic poem *La Prise de Neuville*, or *Chanson XXIII* 112–15. It is also rewritten by the nearly contemporaneous poet Wolfram von Eschenbach in his *Willehalm*, a Middle-High German rewriting of *Aliscans*. Wolfram treats the rewrite of this episode in a characteristically concrete and explanatory manner, saying that William had obtained a consecrated host in Paris, from an abbot at Saint Germain where mass was celebrated, and that he had it in his pocket. (Berger 246; Wolfram von Eschenbach 55; see also 1053 & 1162). Bélanger has noted the strong Chartrian interest, during the period in which *Elye* was written, in the threefold nature of the body of Christ (the *trifarie corpus Domini*), in relation to the Eucharist (61–69). See also the articles of Ford, Hamilton, as well as Roach 359 and note.

246   Here we find the influence of the Chartrian concept of the soul returning to its end, or goal. Cf. the role of this philosophy in the conversion, without any recourse to divine revelation of the Saracen princess Rosamonde later in *Elye* 1370.

250   Elye is so distressed by his grief that he impulsively rushes away to avenge the messenger and leaves him unburied. A similar reaction is found in the *Chanson de Roland* when Charlemagne, in his grief at the death of his men, has to be reminded by Geoffroy of Anjou to bury the dead (2945 ff.). Elye, a newly-knighted youth traveling alone, has no one to offer him such advice; later the knights sent by Julien to follow his son find the dead body and bury it (680–83).

252   The *Elye* poet's creation is the result of a deft alteration of various details drawn from a wide variety of antecedent narrative material; in this case we can note the role reversal from Roland's rear guard to Macabré's advance guard; cf. the detail of the gold-embroidered glove sent by Baligant to Marsile in the *Chanson de Roland* 2677 and in *Elye* 1266.

253   This enumeration constitutes a brief little catalogue, characteristic of the epic genre, of ten kings. Jossué, a Biblical name, commonly appears as a Saracen king in the Old French epic canon; Aitropé, classical mythology's fate responsible for cutting the thread of life, appears only in *Elye*, as do Gambon (jambon) and Triacle (treacle). Unnamed in the catalogue, but participating in the battle which follows, is Salatré, mentioned above

187

(156), and Corsaut de Tabarie. His first name echoes that of the giant killed by William in the *Couronnement de Louis* 1136, and it also occurs in the *Chanson d'Antioche* 156; cf. Corsables de Barbarie in the *Chanson de Roland* 883. The Oxford version of the latter mentions two characters called Malprimes; the first is one of the twelve Saracen peers and the second is the son of Baligant. Macabré, Rodoant of Calabria, and Malprime are all Saracen characters in *La Chanson d'Aspremont*; Macabré appears also in the *Covenant Vivien*, but Macabré de Sorbrie is found only in *Elye*. Calabria is mentioned among Charlemagne's campaigns by Einhard, Charlemagne's famous early biographer, and also occurs in the *Chanson de Roland* 771; the character Rodoant appears in Raimbaut of Paris's *Ogier de Danemarche*. The following line in *Elye* (254) is alluded to in the William of Orange cycle's *Siège de Barbastre*; also taken from this cycle is the name Orable, William's wife, here used as the name of a masculine character, the only such usage in the Old French epic corpus. Although the poet states that Malpriant is the tenth knight, only nine knights are named in this passage; later, Brandone is given as one of the ten (562). This character appears in only one other poem, the later *Hugues Capet* 239. Macrobius's *Saturnalia* (Bk 5: 15), discusses the difference in construction between the epic catalogues, or lists of names, of Homer and those of Virgil and remarks that the latter omits mention of some names in his catalogue in the *Aeneid*, while later making reference to names not included. The *Elye* poet is imitating the Virgilian model of the catalogue structure, as opposed to the Homeric construction.

261   F, comparing *Elye* with its Old Norse translation, indicates a lacuna where there is none.

266   F emends to *el rivage*. The use of the oblique case may signal a genitive thus permitting *mer le rivage* to be understood as *le rivage de la mer*. The correct structure thus reads "the shores of the sea" and needs no emending.

276   The ironic humor of the Saracens who consistently calculate the monetary costs and the material value of people and objects alike is comparable to the later instances of the thieves' calculation of the costs of Elye's meal (1104 ff.) and the Saracen courtier's calculation of the cost of the theft of Lubïen's horse (2065).

284   This episode constitutes an imitation of the scene in *Aliscans* where Christian prisoners are harshly treated by their Saracen captors, and William is forced by Guibourc to prove his identity by rescuing them (1668 ff.). *Elye* includes multiple variations of the motif of the rescued prisoners; cf. William's rescue of the king during the attack at Angers (221 ff.) and the dramatic rescue of Elye by the combined forces of Christendom near the end of the poem (2516 ff.). Chrétien de Troyes' *Erec et Enide* similarly features an episode of the prisoner–knight abused at the hands of the captor–giants (4353 ff.).

305   It was in the captive knight's interest to identify himself fully in order to receive better treatment by captors who would wish to preserve their prisoner in good shape to be ransomed for a large sum. The lack of courtly treatment of the abused noble prisoners testifies to the ordinarily greedy Saracens' utter lack of humanity. Elye makes this point in the following scene through his self-identificaton hedges. He announces his wealthy background but adds that he is a middle-class provost's son merely out for a ride; he omits reference to his nobility, obviously to lull his attacker into a false sense of security. Only at the conclusion of the episode does Elye reveal his noble lineage (328). (Pastoureau 134).

332   In the apparently awkward absence of a definite article in the singular, F and R emend to the plural *diables...portaissent*. The poet subtly plays on the expressions *reclamer*

Notes

Deu (Dieu) and *reclamer sa culpe*, "to recite or make one's confession." In his death agony Rodoan does not request confession in the preceding line, but instead invokes the devil, *reclame diable*, rather than *Deu*, with *diable* being trisyllabic and synonymous perhaps with *Sathanas*. Rodoan's death is the antithesis (like the figure *diable/Dieu*) of the demise of the Christian messenger (244). For the omission of the definite article in fixed expressions in Old French, see Raynaud de Lage 32.

358 F and R emend *en deserre* to *en avale* in order to create an assonance in the Francien dialect. In the previous line, they also emend *elme* to *ialme* (and again at 417–18) for the same reason. Gossen discussed what others have called the Picard tendency to alternate "a" and "e" as a more generalized tendency in Old French, leading us to keep the manuscript reading despite the spelling. (Gossen 50–51.35; 62.12).

363 R's emendation of *le voient* to *l'i voient* is unnecessary and does not note the manuscript reading. Cf. the analogous instances at 528 and 564, where R keeps *le voient*.

376 This scene parodies and humorously amplifies the moment in *Erec et Enide* in which the custom of the day forbids three knights to fight against one because such conduct is uncourtly; cf. 1595. The *Chanson de Roland* dramatizes Roland's death by the battle of one against four hundred; cf. Baudry de Bourgueil, who states that such is the pagan ethic. (Jenkins 2115 ff. and note).

382 The reversal of syntactic elements (chiasm) in the second hemistich of 381 and 382 lends stylistic variety and elegance.

386 *Naie* is an adverb of negation constructed from *non-je*; cf. *oui* from *o-je*.

403 The Picard written texts or *scripta* used both *le* and *la* in the thirteenth-century charters and documents examined by Gosssen. It is noteworthy that the Francien form *la* was found in all of the texts he studied (Gossen 121–22.63). Therefore we do not follow the emendation of the *la* in the phrase *Tout la va* by F and R to the supposedly more correct Picard *le*.

433 The editorial problem of word division has become more complex since the appearance of Busby's *Codex and Context* and Parkes's, *Pause and Effect*. Both of these studies maintain that there was a reciprocal influence exercised by on the one hand word division and punctuation and on the other hand oral presentation. In this instance, F divides *sil a feru* and R, *si l'a feru*. We prefer the manuscript's word division and simply modernize the punctuation, *s'il a feru*.

441 The scribe punctuates with an exclamation mark following "Apolin," perhaps as a guide to oral presentation, as in numerous instances throughout the manuscript. F resolves the abbreviation "Jhe" as "Iesus" and R, as "Jesu." We emend as R, on the basis of the spelling used in the three other poems of BN fr 25516: *Aiol* 943, *Beuves* 2788 and *Robert* 5005.

442 F gives the manuscript reading *tiraie* but adds *je*, while R keeps *t'ira je*. R (xiv) points out that in the future tense, "a" and "ai" are used interchangeably with the first person by the scribe; cf. 1051, 1551, 1886, 2517 and 2703. Gossen (52.6) later concluded that for many Picard scribes "ai" and "a" were in fact interchangeable; he gave the commonly found forms *je dira, je croistera, je vaurra, je faurra* as typical examples.

446 The preposition is problematic; the context demands *soz* but the manuscript reads *sor*. This is a frequent misreading of the final letter not only by this scribe (cf. 475, for

example), but also by scribes copying other manuscripts. William Roach's textual note to l. 151 of his edition of Chrétien de Troyes' *Le Roman de Perceval* is perhaps most insightful on this issue. For him it was evident that when the meaning was absolutely clear, the scribes neglected to distinguish the final letter carefully: "Il est évident que, dans un passage tel que celui-ci, où le sens exige nettement 'sor', les copistes ne se donnaient pas le peine de distinguer soigneusement des lettres que le sens empêchait de confondre" (275). F regularizes to *sous* (*soz* < *subtus*).

448   The name presents a fascinating literary issue, characteristic of the epic genre. The Saracen Salatré (also the name of one of Julien's men at l. 100), was killed by Elye at 445, only to reappear at 468 and at 471. R's editorial confusion caused him to emend both instances to "Aitropé," another king named in the earlier catalogue (253); however, in his *Index des noms propres* he rescinded his original emendation and substituted "Malatré" at 405 and 448. Malatré appears as a character in the later Old Norse translation, from which R took the name, but never in *Elye*. R's change was influenced both by Gaston Paris's strong feeling that the scribe of BN fr 25516's *Elye* was negligent and careless and by his editorial conviction that both the Old Norse translation and *Elye* were being copied from a lost original Old French poem. There exists an insightful reflection on this phenomenon in Macrobius' *Saturnalia* where the later Latin writer imagines a discussion of precisely this sort of "careless inconsistency" in Virgil's references in the *Aeneid*, when characters ostensibly killed reappear later in the work. Macrobius's discussants also question the related matter of two characters with identical names; Macrobius's characters admire the explicitness with which Homer treated this situation, so that there is never a question about identity. Some of Macrobius's interlocutors attribute Virgil's errors to a failure to realize full emulation of his Homeric model; however, Rockwell's *Rewriting Ressemblances in Medieval French Romance* treats this issue in the more philosophical context of nominalism and discernment of the properties of an entity beyond the topos of appearances vs. reality. The *Elye* poet seems once again to be deliberately emulating the Virgilian model, to which he alludes by the apparent "careless inconsistency," both here and in dealing with the character Corsaut of Tabarie, killed in *Elye* 341 and reappearing later at 2428. In an excellent study of mocking irony in the late Latin epic, Kratz has documented that apparent carelessness of the poets is nearly always a clue to deeper meanings or allusions, and he cites examples from Chrétien de Troyes, G. Von Strassburg and Hartman von Aue, to stress the continuity of this narratological tradition. We retain, therefore, the manuscript reading. (G. Paris, *Deuxième article* 472–23; Macrobius, *Saturnalia* 5: 15.10–11, 5: 13.40; Rockwell 4–5, 38–42; Kratz 48, 140 ff.).

475   The manuscript reads *E. desor*. As in 446, we emend to "desoz," meaning "nearby," while F emends to "desous."

477   We adhere to the manuscript's Picardian reading, while R regularizes to *desloiés*.

480   R unnecessarily indicates a lacuna here and again at 498, as does F, based on their comparison with the later Norwegian translation, which amplifies the episode.

481   R emends to the singular *fiert*.

504   Gascony, a region in southwestern France, was famous for its war horses according to both epics and romances, such as *Ami et Amile* (Danon and Rosenberg n 138), and *Erec et Enide* (Chrétien de Troyes, ed. Roques 2659). Historians, however, have experienced some difficulty verifying the common literary references as factual. Thorough studies of the horse in medieval society have identified only one Anglo-Norman chronicle source

Notes

for the reference. This sole cartulary contains approximately one-third of its references for the priory of Saint-Mont mentioning gifts of Gascon horses to local nobles in return for their gifts and donations to the priory. The existence of a fair involving Gascon horses has been hypothesized but not proved. (Bautier and Bautier 36–37, and Bachrach).

511   F and R read *conuent*, but the manuscript reads *convent*, which we keep; it is an attested form occuring in *Aiol* 3351.

544   R uses the manuscript reading *eslice* and glosses the infinitive *eslicier* on the analogy of *delicier*, attested in Godefroy. F emends to *en sa eslice* without noting the manuscript reading, and for no clear reason. Godefroy's citation is not found in the *Dictionnaire de l'ancienne langue française*, but rather in the *Lexique de l'ancien français*. F glosses *esclicier*, meaning "to split"; for the form, see Gossen 99.41. We adhere to the manuscript reading.

562   In his Additions and Corrections for *Elye* (LIV–LV), F comments on the presence of Brandon (var. Brandone) and wonders whether *l'autre* of 361 refers to this character, or if Brandon might be identical to "Gaidonet" of 576.

571   This line has been cited by Melli for its skilful combination of the repetition of the same word at the head of each verse (anaphora) and antithesis (142).

576   R, convinced that the scribe errs more frequently than subsequent scholarship has shown that he does, erroneously glosses *samis* as a scribal error for *sains*, or "bonds." The manuscript shows four vertical strokes, and the "i" of *samis* is clearly denoted as such by the slanted stroke above it, by which the scribe dotted the "*i.*" The word refers to rich silken cloth, and F glosses it correctly as such, but adds a remark about the incongruity of using silken cloth for bonds: "Die Verwendung des *samit* zum Binden ist auffällig" (502). He adds the caveat that, in his opinion, there may be textual corruption. In the following verses, however, the Saracens' rich cloths and fabrics are offered as incentives to the peasant by the French knights asking for help. Perhaps the captors merely used materials they had at hand to bind their prisoners, or if one takes a less literal approach, the episode may metaphorically refer to the luxurious silken bonds of sins, *luxuria*, which hold the Christians captive.

580   The scribe punctuates with an exclamation mark following *Hé*, indicating either an unconscious habit, a guide to oral performance, or perhaps William's own deep disquiet.

582   *A iceste parole* simply means "at this point in the story."

586   William courteously addresses the *vilain*, or rustic laborer, in the same polite terms that he would use for a knight; no irony is intended, although such a form of polite direct address is very rare in any medieval narrative (cf. Freedman 133 ff.). William's use of such flattering terms may indicate his desperation to be free (cf. 580). The form of address also constitutes a verbal allusion to the famous episode of the beanfield in *Aliscans*, when Rainouart addresses the peasant in the identical noble terms, *sire vilain*, 7387b; (ed. Wienbeck, Hartnacke and Rasch). In *Aliscans*, the rustic character complains that he cannot feed his children because of the pillaging Saracens who ruin his crops. Rainouart then kills the Saracens and repays the peasant with their arms and especially their horses. *Elye*'s rewriting alters the incident by adding an element of realism: the laborer says that he can barely feed his own children, let alone a warhorse, accurately reflecting the fact that a rustic laborer could not afford the immensely costly upkeep of warhorses for even the period of a day. See Bachrach and Bautier and Bautier.

ELYE OF SAINT-GILLES

591   Although temporal references are often merely formulaic in the Old French epic, William accurately states here that he and his brothers have been captives for about two weeks. Raynaud relocated the poem's city of Saint-Gilles to the Angevin region, relying on 179, where Elye, having ridden for one day, encounters the dying messenger from Anjou. His change was in keeping with his thesis that *Elye* was a copy of a lost original, created by a hypothetical troubador in central France. Thus any references to the south were incidental copyist's interpolations. Delbouille's close study of *Elye* reassessed Raynaud's hypothesis and concluded that the poem's town of Saint-Gilles was indeed in the south, referred to in the Middle Ages as "Provence" or "Languedoc," as Raynaud himself had noted. See Delbouille's "Problèmes" and R, xvii n. 3. Two weeks' duration for the journey from Anjou to the famous pilgrimage city of Saint-Gilles is quite in keeping with studies of travel time under varying conditions in the Middle Ages. (Labarge 158, Boyer).

595   F and R correct the verbal form of the imperative to *vien*, probably on the model of *Aiol* 3614, but they keep both *prant* of 596 and *pren* of 607. Compare the latter with 1336 and with its doublet *pren* of 607. In the written texts, it is impossible to identify scribal error or inconsistency given the pervasive lack of rigidity of verbal forms, so we keep the manuscript reading.

602   The scribe mistakenly wrote *me delai* in the second hemistich, unconsciously repeating the structure of *me deserte* of the first hemistich; he expunctuated by placing a dot under each letter of *me*. This means of expunctuating letters was standard, starting with the fifth century. (Prou 267).

608   R & F correct the imperative to *ven*; cf. 595. The episode highlighting the plight of the worker is found in both epic and romance narratives, such as *Aliscans* 6838 ff. and Chrétien de Troyes' *Yvain* 5185 ff.

610   The messenger from Louis is the only Christian knight who has met his death.

614   *Liés* is monosyllabic(/ljes/); see R's introduction, xvi. Bisyllabic words with this form have the diaeresis in our edition (*liës*).

652   F mistakenly believes that a lacuna exists here, based on his comparison with the Norwegian translation. A "whoever would have seen" clause with the imperfect subjunctive is usually followed by a conditional, "that person would have concluded/thought/said...." Here the following line does fulfill this function, since Joshua of Alexandria provides his opinion after having observed Bernart in the middle of the fray.

671   We emend the hypometric line on the analogy of 677; its parallelistic echo effect is characteristic of both *Elye* and of the William of Orange cycle in general, as studied by Heinemann. See 672.

672   We follow the manuscript reading, as does F; R's emendation of *sentier antis* on the analogy of 696, is unnecessary and results in the loss of the subtle chiasm, or reversal of syntatic elements. The "ancient roads" of the Old French epics and romances generally referred to the old Roman roads still in use in the Middle Ages. Their survival is attested in the *Gesta Francorum* I.iii, when Robert, count of Flanders traveled during the First Crusade by the old Roman road. In *Elye*, the *sentier antis* may be a realistic reference to the Pont du Gard in view of Elye's later statement that he was taken prisoner near Arles. See Frappier 2: 188–91 for a discussion of these roads in the Old French epic.

Notes

675   The falsart was a double-edged slashing weapon with a long, pointed blade and two side appendages shaped like a sickle (Ascherl 273, Viollet-le-Duc 2: 316–18, with illustration). The scribe underlines the "c" of *faucars*; F noted that this form of punctuation had the same function as the modern cedilla.

677   The expression *chemin fer(r)é* was frequently used in both the epic and romance for the ancient Roman roads; they were paved with (iron) dross or slag (FEW) requiring that shoes be slipped over the horses' feet with straps, en route. In *Elye* such foot covering is described as worn by Lubien's horse in its cage (1925). The term was therefore originally meant to show what kind of footcovering a horse would need for a journey; it became metaphoric for "a hard road." See Ribard; Bachrach 173 and n 1; and Carnat 64–65.

687   For a useful discussion of the various kinds of falcons, see Wood and Fyfe, and for a simplified but beautifully illustrated cygenetic account, see Bise's brief presentation of Gaston Phoebus's hunting book.

688   Both F and R read *ataignant* as a present participle of the verb *ataindre*, "to reach" or "attain," referring to Elye's "reaching" or wounding a Saracen, rather than as a proper name. However at 1300, Ataignant de Sorbrie is named as the emir's son whom Elye killed in this episode, thereby earning Macabré's mortal hatred. In 689–90, this character is clearly identified as Macabré's son and the brother of Rosamonde. R later in his list of characters glosses correctly the character's name at 688. See 1300.

709   R emends to *ra*, while F justifies the manuscript reading of *re* as the equivalent of *rai*, 3rd person singular of *ravoir* (lat. *re-habere*), which we also keep.

726   The wooden hilt of the spear often had incised designs filled with *niel*, niello (black enamel). Viollet-le-Duc 2: 304.

761   Both F and R needlessly emend to *a Elye est venu*, but the manuscript's reading of *s'est* ("si est"), is a logical structure.

798   F regularizes the orthography to *primes;* (a misprint notes the change at 797).

801   The discourteous gatekeeper was an epic topos especially notable because of the significance of hospitality in the daily life of any medieval court. This example is particularly egregious, since it is Julien's own liege lord William whom he turns away.

803   The scene refers to the episode in *Aliscans* 1668, in which Guibourc fails to identify William because he is wearing a Saracen helmet, which prevents her from recognizing his distinctive nose.

806   R emends by changing *bouche*, "mouth," to *boche*, "bump," in accordance with the preposition *sor*. However, the textual reference to singing mass logically calls for the manuscript reading, and the scribe often misreads or writes terminal "z" for "r" (cf. 446 and 475).

818   The shield, as well as the spear noted at 726, was inlaid with black enamel.

832   The copyist wrote *plalefroi* but expunctuated the first "l" by placing a dot under the letter.

840   Both F and R emend the nominative *li kenu* to the oblique *le kenu* after *a tans e vous*, but the nominative is called for here.

841   The assonance "u" is noted as *brúis* from the manuscript reading of *.i. bruis* (like *fúi* 735, *lúi* 776 and *frúit* 747). F and R emend to *bruit,* creating a lone dramatic decasyllabic line in a very long succession of alexandrines. The most logical emendation would yield the expected dodecasyllabic line, with the expression *a une brúie,* meaning "all at once" or "at the same time."

846   F observes that the expression *mi frere* is technically inaccurate, since Bertrand is William's nephew, not his brother. The expression, however, results from metrical necessity (*nevos* = two syllables); it is to be taken by Julien in the general sense: William refers to the fraternity of comrades in arms.

849   The scribe erroneously punctuates with an exclamation mark after *ai,* indicating perhaps that an exclamation point would occur at the end of the line, which would interrupt the meaning and which is omitted here. The homophony of *ai* and *hé* may have caused the error. The punctuation might also serve as a guide for reading aloud (cf. 2688).

851   *L'aigue* is an anachronistic spelling; it should be read as the modern, monosyllabic (/o/); Gossen finds, for example, the written forms *aigue* and *aiwe* used interchangeably in both charters and literary texts (102.43).

851   Reading *l'aigue* as two syllables, F emends the manuscript's plural *l'avons geté* to the first person *l'ai geté* to avoid a hypermetric line; he suggests that a different and more logical structure would result from *geté l'avons en l'aigue.* We keep the manuscript reading.

863   The decasyllablic line starkly stands out in the succession of alexandrines; its stunning dramatic effect highlights the allusion to the *Couronnement de Louis, laisse* 50, in which William defeats Julien, who becomes his liegeman. It is this episode that concludes William's long pacification campaign on Louis's behalf and also provides the gap in the written narrative, or *faille,* from which *Elye* is textually generated. See the Introduction for the literary concept of the "texte générateur" or "faille." For the use of versification to achieve dramatic effect, see Melli.

865   *Guillame (Guillamè)* is trisyllabic here. For "ai" as a form of third person singular from *habere,* see 709.

876   Gossen notes the tendency of the Picard *scripta* or written documents and texts to insert the svarabhactic "e"; he notes, however, that the form *avera* is rather rare in the Picard written dialect, yielding more often *arai,* and he observes the presence of doublets, where both forms are used indiscriminately in the thirteenth century, northeastern scribe's *Aiol* (131.74). Baker observed that in the northeast in the thirteenth century, scribes used all three forms interchangeably (*averai, aura* or *avra*); in *Aiol,* however, he found 105 instances of "ar-" and 34 cases of "aur-," and in *Elye,* he found 6 spellings of "ar-» and 29 or "aur-," the *averai* clearly being a scribal abberation. (Baker 18).

880   F emends *nef* to *rive,* and R likewise, the latter without noting the manuscript reading. Both editors evidently feel that there should always be a feminine "e" at the caesura. The emendation is unnecessary, since the pagans logically return to the ship (*nef*) where the rest of the fleet (*navie,* attested with this meaning by Godefroy) also awaits. Whereas *nef* is generally used to indicate a ship in general, the term *barge* is more specific, referring to a flat-bottomed boat; the stylistic effect of gradation in terms is clearly discernable.

NOTES

881–82 The use of the same word at the assonance found here is repeated several times by the copyist; cf. 934–35, 976–77, 1267–68, 1272–73, 1274–75. R considers this phenomenon to be a tendency towards rhyme in the masculine assonances (xi).

885   F unnecessarily emends to *s'enpoignent*, glossing *enpoindre* (lat. *in-pingere*), as meaning "to oust, expel, drive out the enemy." The manuscript reading, however, derives from the lat. *pungere*, "to spur on" or "hasten away."

886   Although the geography of *Elye* sometimes results from a blend of the realistic and the fictional, this journey towards the East from Arles (and not, as Wolff erroneously read, "moving westward from the orient," 30), remains essentially realistic. "Baudas" is not always Bagdad in the Old French epic; in the *Prise d'Orange*, for example, it is in Aumarie or Almeria, in Spain. In this line, and in the context of *Elye*, Les Baux, the noted southern medieval city, slightly to the northeast of Arles, might be the most logical referent. The journey moves from Arles, through Les Baux, then past Hungary, following the coast, ending up by turning back westward and facing "Sorbrie." At this point, to the left would be the Latin Empire of Constantinople (Romaigne) and Philomelium ("Femenie" in Asia Minor), and to the right the city of Rousie, or Rusa on the Danube (in present-day Bulgaria). The identical route, which also includes the city of Rusa, is described in the account of the First Crusade in the *Gesta Francorum* (2: 5). Rusa is also referred to as *une cité que on appelle la Rousse* (var. *la Rosse*) by Geoffroy de Villehardouin in *La Conquête de Constantinople* (ccxi–ccxv). R could not make sense of the reference and concluded that the poet was referring to the country of Russia as a city; Wolff questioned this interpretation but could propose no solution. In the crusading context of *Elye* and *Aiol*, which refer to both the First and Fourth Crusades, the reference to Rusa makes the most sense. Bédier considered the reference to "Sorbrie" as purely fictional ("la ville fabuleuse de Sorbrie," *Légendes* 4: 47 n 1). According to Langlois, "Sorb(r)ie" is found only in *Elye* and in the later *Anseïs de Carthage* (*Table* 623); however "Sorbres," also referred to as "Sorz," is found in the *Chanson de Roland* 3226. Jenkins (225) noted its probable allusion to Einhard's account of Charlemagne's subjugation of this Slavonic people. Lubien's sword is later identified in *Elye* (2074) as belonging originally to "Murgale of Sor." In creating this itinerary the *Elye* poet deftly weaves references to diverse antecedent materials, both literary and chronicle, into a new and creative context. (Wolff, "Romania" 30 and n.).

887   The term "Romaigne" has attracted much critical interest. Langlois (*Table* 571) notes, following R, that in *Elye* the word refers to the Latin Empire of Constantinople. This usage concurs with the conclusion of Wolff's painstaking study that only after Count Baldwin of Flanders' Crusade in 1204, did the term "Romania" commonly refer to the Latin Empire, a deliberate usage reinforcing the concept that Emperor Baldwin was the legitimate successor of Constantine, Justinian and the Comnenoi. Wolff revised the study by Gaston Paris of the term "Romania," although he erroneously dated *Elye* as twelfth century and was therefore puzzled at this usage before 1204. (Wolff, "Romania" 29–30; 32–33; G. Paris, "Romani.")

890   These tall buildings are, according to F, mosques; he notes the metaphorical or figurative use of *baulient* (from the infinitive *baulioier*, "to flutter"); R glosses *baulier* as *s'élancer*, "to thrust upwards."

901   A line (or more) has been omitted, and the speaker obviously is once again Macabré. "Irlande" (var. Illande, Ilande, Islande), considered as a city in this passage, is difficult to

identify, although in the crusading context, this may constitute a reference to Illyria, which lay on the overland route to the Holy Land. Jenkins noted that the similar occurrence of Islande (var. Irlande) in the *Chanson de Roland* 2331, was found in epic and romance alike (cf. Chrétien de Troyes' *Lancelot* 5650), and he related the reference to Einhard's account of Charlemagne's diplomacy with the Scots and Irish. The reference may be purely fictional; on the other hand it must be noted in the context of text reception of *Elye* that interest in Ireland and its customs had been heightened during the second half of the twelfth century and early thirteenth century by the Anglo-Norman conquest of Ireland and by the writings of Gerald Cambrensis or Giraud de Barri. The latter wrote a mirror for princes for Prince Louis (Louis VIII) and supported Louis's campaign to become king of England. (Petit-Dutaillis 12).

903–4 The copyist accidentally reversed these lines, which he corrected and indicated in the left margin by the letters "b" and "a" preceding 903 and 904 respectively.

908 F's unnecessary regularization to *deriere* would yield a hypermetric line.

914 The *bronge trellie* is the hauberk (also called "byrnie" in English) and was made of chainmail sewn ("treslie") to leather.

919 F unnecessarily emends *toi* to *toin* but notes that he feels *tien* is better. Gossen observes examples of the open, free "e" usually yielding in Picard "ie" but occasionally and rarely giving "i" (57–58.10). The case of *baptestire* in both *Elye* and *Aiol* is cited as evidence, but it is important to remember that the word occurs at the assonance and may have been changed so as to assonate.

920 The manuscript reading causes a hypometric line in a series of dodecasyllabic lines. We emend to include the expression *chevaliers*, which is used later by Macabré to refer to Elye (1009). This seems preferable to R's solution, when he emends to *m. en ta vie*, an expression not used elsewhere in the poem. F's emendation of *u. tu* causes a decasyllabic line. Addressing Elye as a Christian and as a knight in successive lines sustains the standard epic linking of the two themes. The context as a whole recalls the "theological debate," a traditional epic topos, such as the one between Corsaut and William in the *Couronnement de Louis* (791–94 ff.) and the exchange between Feragut and Roland in the *Pseudo-Turpin* XX, 1–194.

926 *Une cose faillie* is reminiscent of the similar expression *ceste cose faillie* in *Aiol* 9715. The Saracen gods are merely hollow, inert objects, devoid of any generative or vivifying characteristics (cf. 1374).

941 Although indicating the question mark and interrogation, F surmises that this might well be an exclamation instead, despite the construction *ne vous en poist il mie* of 940.

952 F emends to *en l'ile*, but R keeps the manuscript reading of *el l'ile*. The scribe has inadvertently copied an extra "l" before "ile" after the enclisis "el" (*en + le*).

961 Here we follow the word division of the copyist, rather than reading *ne l'aie*, as R does. R's division indicates the phonetic reality: "nel" is really not an example of an enclitic "ne + el," since it's not in a blocked position. The scribe writes the enclisis, as in 952, perhaps from habit or as an indication of oral performance.

962 R divides *par milieu*, but we use the copyist's word division, as does F.

NOTES

968 While the usual Francien forms for "water" are: "eve, ieve, iave," the form "aigue" is found in Picard particularly in the charters of Tournai, Douai, Pontieu and Eu, and in *Aiol*, among other literary texts. The form is found alongside "aig(h)e," which is also found in *Elye* 1093. See 851.

970 F and R unnecessarily emend *a terre* to *en terre* without noting the manuscript reading.

981 R emends *narines* to *orilles* on the model of 1002, but the emendation sacrifices both the poet's rhetorical use of gradation (from the "nose" to the very "nostrils") and its humor. *Narine* (var. *naris*, vulgar lat. *naricem*) is attested from the twelfth century by Greimas.

982 With R and F, we emend "Malpriant" to "Macabrés" to suit the context. However R erroneously cites in his note at 965 that *l'abat mort* refers to Malpriant's being killed by Elye, when in fact Elye slays the unnamed pagan leading Malpriant's horse to his master (954). Malpriant will play a significant rôle in the latter part of *Elye*.

985 As in 962, we follow, as F does, the word division of the copyist. R alters it to *ne l'ataindrai*.

989 The carbuncle was a precious stone (perhaps a garnet) traditionally thought to be red and to give off a bright light, like the *carbunculum* or bright-burning small red coal from which it derives its name. It is associated in the Old French epic and romance with a knight's helmet ornamentation, as in the *Chanson de Roland* 1326, 1501, 1531 and 2633.

1002 Gossen notes the evolution of the Latin suffix, *icula*>Picard *–ille*; he gives *orille* as a prime example (89.34 n 40).

1003 A common epic topos, the gesture by which the right-hand glove is affixed in the hand or exchanged as a sign of trust and faith also occurs in the *Chanson de Roland* (331 ff). In *Elye* 1266, the glove is specifically described as being bordered or embroidered, an allusion to *Roland* 1005 where Baligant offers his gold-embroidered glove to Marsile. The allusion in *Elye* is reinforced when Macabré specifies that what he held in his hands, he threw to his feet, referring to Ganelon's dropping of the glove of trust. In *Elye* 1007, an overt allusion to *La Chanson de Roland* occurs when one of the soldiers Macabré summons is named "Baligant."

1005 Cf. the proverb: "Cil ki gete as piés la chose / Que il puet a ses mains tenir, / on ne devrait pas consentir / k'il abitast entr-autre gent." Le Roux de Lincy 2: 351.

1020 In this context, the geographical reference to "Sobrie" or "Sorbrie" (see 868) is likely to be yet another allusion of the *Elye* poet to the *Chanson de Roland*, as in 1003. By using the accumulation of allusions to the same work, the poet tends to confirm the identification with a direct and overt reference.

1022 R indicates a lacuna, but see the following note.

1023 *A iceste parole* is frequently found in the Old French epics without especially refering to a speech which has taken place; rather, it refers to the structure of the narrative itself (i.e., "At this point in the tale") and is akin to the conscious authorial intervention pointedly drawing attention to the construct of the narrative. F noted the similar meaning, "At this moment, or point in time."

1026 Both F and R correct to *trestous*, but the non-agreement of *tout* and *trestout* is much more frequent in this manuscript than their agreement. This dissonance corresponds to the thorough mixing of the cases in the poem. Note the agreement, for example, in 1030.

1038 This same Picard form of *desclouer* is also found in Chrétien de Troyes' *Erec et Enide* at 2153.

1045 Here is an interesting example of R's automatically correcting the manuscript reading, *jusques a le matin*, to *jusques al(e) matin [et]*, while F leaves it unchanged while observing that it is a remarkable example of non-contraction. F gives examples and remarks by Tobler to justify his refusal to emend. However, it is clear that the non-contraction exists for the scansion of the hemistich and for no other reason. These metrics provide an excellent example of the unusual degree of artistic sophistication in *Elye*'s versification that both Delbouille and Melli have noted.

1047 The copyist has expunctuated the word *issus* which follows *s'est* by putting a dot under each letter.

1053 The episode constitutes an allusion to the *Moniage Guillaume I & II*. Both versions I and II contain an episode involving thieves, ultimately alluding to the Gospel accounts of the Crucifixion and to repentant thief (Mt 27:38; Mk 15:27; L 23:32; Jn 23:35). *Moniage Guillaume II* amplifies the episode, which is used by the *Elye* poet to create a literary character who became the prototype for the epic characters Maugis (in *Renaut de Montauban*) and the famous Auberon (in *Huon de Bordeaux*) who eventually became Shakespeare's Oberon. The allusion to the repentant thief was used differently by Wolfram von Eschenbach when he rewrote Vivien's death scene, during which Vivien receives the Viaticum. The German poet refers to the repentant thief by the name "Dysmas," not found in Biblical accounts but made popular and famous from its appearance in the *Gospel of Nicodemus* ix–x. (See Passage 55–73 and 376, and Malicote, "Visual and Verbal Allusion.")

1079 The thieves do not greet their visitor in an acceptable courtly fashion; rather, their lack of greeting is a sure sign of their perfidity, their evil plotting having obviously been interrupted.

1085 This discourse creates a literary genealogy, since the work was "born" from the *faille* or gap at *laisse* 50 of the *Couronnement de Louis*. *Elye* constitutes an abbreviation of the entire William of Orange cycle, with allusions to the major episodes of *Aliscans*, the *Charroi de Nîmes*, the *Prise d'Orange*, the *Moniage Guillaume I and II* and the minor cycle of Aymeri within the greater William cycle. See Introduction.

1086 In this context, it is evident that *grans sire* designates the grandfather, both literary and fictional. Julien de Saint Gille was married to William's sister, an amplification that occurs in this poem when William is referred to as Elye's uncle. The word *grand-sire* generally designated the great-grandfather. The mid-thirteenth-century chronicler Albéric des Trois Fontaines constructed a genealogy for Elye and Aiol based on *Elye* and *Aiol* and on the chronicle of Baudouin d'Avesnes (R xxxiii). Heintze has contructed rather complete genealogies for these fictional families, which he refers to as the House of Bourgogne. See Bayot, "*Poème moral*" cxvi; Heintze, "Les techniques" 48; and Heintze, *König*, Appendix of

Notes

Genealogical Tables. For the similar concept of the historiographic use of the "intellectual genealogy," see Christiansen 209 n 315, and Jeaneau, "Heiric d'Auxerre."

1089 We prefer the manuscript's word division *lor suie*, as does F; note that R prefers *su je*.

1099 The Picard "w-" stems from the initial Germanic "w-," but Gossen (108–9) observed that although the spelling "w- + i" was rather exceptional in the literary texts that he studied, he did encounter it also in *Aiol*. The scribe has penned a definite "w," but R emends to *vuider* without noting the manuscript reading.

1103 Although F emended to *pa[r]*, R observed in his introductory notes on the language of *Elye* that there was a tendency not to pronounce the final "r." He cited the two infinitives that were written *encontré* 1818, for *encontrer*, and *soufri* 1738, for *soufrir*, and believed that the "r" was confused with the "l" in this expression *pa le* = *par la* (xiv). We simply keep the written evidence here, rather than hypothesizing about a conjectural pronunciation.

1105 Although the term was also used for silver, in this instance *cuit pessé* refers to a weight, or mark, of gold, which weighed roughly eight ounces. Elye will pay an exorbitant price for the meal; similar to the robbery of William in the *Moniage I & II*, these thieves will attempt to deprive Elye of all he owns. This produces the hero's ironic observation that this region is surely much more expensive than France and that in Paris, such a meal could be had more cheaply, but at a still-expensive price, making a humorous impression on an aristocratic Parisian audience (1111–15).

1112 The temporal expression, frequent in verse narrative, simply means "recently" or "not long ago," as in modern French.

1115 The great cost of the nobles' ceremonial robes was frowned upon by the clergy in Paris and in the north of France at the time of this poem. In response to such criticism, the court of Philip Augustus, for example, was noted for no longer bestowing expensive robes upon minstrels as a reward for their services. The money was donated to the poor instead. (Baldwin, *Aristocratic Life* 24–25; Rigord 71–72; Page, *The Owl* 16–17.)

1117 R evidently read the initial abbreviation as a "Q" and rendered *Que*, but the manuscript clearly uses the abbreviation for *con* here.

1119 The word *gones* (var. *gone, gonnelle, goule*) presents a problem; Godefroy defines *gone* as a long robe, and Greimas subsequently gives the example as meaning "long robes" in the mid-thirteenth-century romance epic *Eustace le moine* (ca. 1230), post-dating *Elye*. Apparently a capelike garment, it was worn by men and women, both nobles and peasants, and by clerics. Nobles' *gones* were brightly colored and lined with fur. They extended from the shoulders to calf length and were split into *pentes* or sections, front and back. For riding these *pentes* were bound at the waist by a belt. (See Viollet-le-Duc 2: 544–46, with illustrations.) The word *gonele*, attested in the late twelfth century, referred to these long tunics worn by the knight over the armor, the skirts referred to by Elye. There is little reason to suppose, as R did in his gloss, that the scribe intended to write *goles* or the border of fur trimming around the robe. F was perplexed by the word, because he defined it as a "monk's frock," based on its context in *Aiol* 6577, where the robber, disguised as a monk, is clothed in a *froc*, "frock," an *estamine*, an undergarment of wool and *une gone viés*, an old monk's robe with skirts. He glossed its use in *Elye* 1119 with a question mark.

1122 F, without emendation, noted that *nous* would be better than *vous*. To F, it seemed more logical that the leader of the band of robbers (who is speaking) wanted to include himself in the decision-making process and interpreted the line as "if *we* allow him to speak."

1126 This alludes to the *Moniage Guillaume I & II* and refers to the parodic procession, *conductus*, a popular part of the early thirteenth-century Feast of Fools which occurred on the Feast of the Circumcision, on Jan. 1. During this procession, a mock "boy–bishop" wore a stick or baton around his neck in lieu of carrying the crozier.

1152 *Pumier* is a good example of the Picard development of the closed "o," accented and nasal; the word is also found in *Aiol* 6803 (Gossen 84).

1155 The poet refers to one of the most famous epic passages, the episode in the *Couronnement de Louis* 130 ff., in which William slays the would-be usurprer Arneïs. It was often repeated, for example, in the *Moniage Guillaume I* 596 ff., and *Moniage Guillaume II* 1508 ff. See Henri Roussel for other examples from the *Prise d'Orange* and the *Charroi de Nîmes* and for an interesting analysis of the realistic physiological and medical aspects of the blow itself associated with the martial arts.

1162 The line alludes to the scriptural repentant thief of the Crucifixion, rewritten and amplified in the *Moniage Guillaume I* and especially *II*. A three-pronged study of 1) the etymology of the name "Galopin," 2) the relation of the genesis of the character's name in *Elye*, and 3) speculative grammar, combines to reveal the process of literary creation of a so-called secondary character such as Galopin. See Robert R. Edwards' discussion of *materia exsecuta* (matter that has been previously treated in verse) and *materia illibata* (material that the writer invents or adds to what he has inherited) in the process of aesthetic invention (75–87, especially 85–86).

1162 Although Picard lacks the intercalated consonant "d" in the groups "l'r," "n'r," and "m'l," *melior* occurs only with the intercalated consonant. Gossen gives the example *mi(e) udre(s)* found in the Tournai written documents, or *scripta*, and in literary works like *Aiol* (Gossen 64.14 and 117.61.a).

1169 F reads the manuscript as *li laidire* and emends to *li lai dires* on the basis of the structural analogy between the expression *li lai dires* and the fixed expression *li faires bien*.

1172 Although F and R emend, as we do, to the grammatically correct plural form, *poins*, the copyist has ended every noun in the line with an "s."

1173 No emendation of *cointous* is necessary, as in 642. The horses who appear in this part of the poem, especially Prinsaut, are indeed quick witted, clever and wise.

1176 Elye's discovery that Galopin is a Christian parallels Lubïen's later discovery that Elye is a Christian. It provides an opportunity to emphasize the contrary nature of the two characters' reactions. The fact that after Galopin identifies himself as a firm believer in Christianity and adds that there were four fairies present at his birth is neither irony nor naïveté on the poet's part. It represents instead a literary allusion (see 1184), and reflects the complex blend of pagan and Christian elements that characterized medieval faith.

1181 The most famous appearance of "Tieri d'Ardane" is probably in the *Chanson de Roland* 3843 ff., where Tieri champions the cause of Charlemagne. Both Keller and Benton have written about Tieri in relation to historical barons such as Count Thierry

Notes

of Flanders and have debated the connections with Flanders, the Plantagenets and the Oxford version of the *Chanson de Roland*. The connections of Tieri with Flanders would have been of great interest to the probable audience of *Elye* and certainly to the owners of the codex in which it appears. (See Introduction; see also Keller, "La *Chanson de Roland*" 234–35; Benton, "*Nostre Franceis*" 157 ff.; see also Bédier, *Légendes* 4: 281–83, and Lejeune, "L'Ardenne" 61–69).

1184 This reference to the four fairies recalls the most celebrated group of four fairies who appear in *Erec et Enide*, where they decorated Erec's coronation robes and represented the quadrivium. In *Elye*, fairies will later be described as having decorated Galopin's club or mace (1274–75), an image that can be viewed as a reference in some ways analogous to Erec's decorated scepter.

1189 Although F feels that an "i" must surely be missing in the Roman numeral, the substitution of .iiii. (*quatre*) would create a hypermetric verse. To be four feet six inches tall would be, in the Middle Ages, about average height and not *petit* as Galopin is continually described and shown in the pictures. Galopin's height is always referred to in *Elye* as three and a half feet tall.

1193 The reference is complex and represents a triple allusion to *Erec et Enide*, the *Couronnement de Louis* and *Aliscans*. First, a similar phrase occurs in *Erec et Enide*, referring to the evil dwarf who abuses the queen's maiden when she scorns him because of his size (*que lo nain ot an grant despit / por ce qu'ele li vit petit*, 177–78). These lines of Chrétien de Troyes refer to *Erec*'s three opening proverbial lines, *Que tel chose a l'an an despit / qui molt valt mialz que l'an ne cuide* (2–3). The dwarf in *Erec* is indeed to be scorned for his evil and uncourtly qualities rather than because of his size; his antithesis is Guivret, who has a small dwarf's body but a big, good heart. Secondly, at play is the allusion to the evil giant Corsaut's statement in the *Couronnement de Louis* that one must not scorn a small man (i.e., William) because of his size (*Molt par est fols qui petit ome blasme... / Molt pou preisai et lui et son barnage* 923…926). Thirdly, in *Aliscans*, King Louis explains that he cannot love the giant Rainouart because of his size: *Por ce k'est grans, ainc ne le poi amer* (3203). In the third case, the *Elye* poet skillfully includes elements of the character of the giant Rainouart in his creation of the dwarf Galopin. *Elye* later overtly refers to Rainouart; he is part of the king's army that rescues Elye and Galopin (see 2519). The topos of small size causing disrespect continues as a comic motif throughout *Elye*.

1209 This allusion, which ultimately derives from Lucan's *Pharsalia*, is often found in the Old French epics. It emphasizes the need for realism when facing enemy odds and the strategic necessity of fleeing or retreating for survival in order to "fight another day" (Crosland 97). The topos refers as well to *Aliscans* and to *La Chevalerie Vivien* where the eponymous hero vows (85–93) never to retreat from the enemy, despite his uncle's advice. Vivien's vow is paralleled by Aimer who swears never to sleep under a roof but to fight Saracens throughout his life (*Couronnement de Louis* 826–30). It will be Rosamonde who will teach Elye the lesson of moderation and reason in battle (1625–28).

1219 F comments that this instance of the indicative is infrequent; R emends to *k'eust* without noting the manuscript reading. F read as *k'eut*, one syllable; otherwise the line becomes hypermetric.

1230 F unnecessarily emends to *a .i.* noting that Elye was already riding a horse at 1228 and thus could not logically jump on a horse at this point (see 1231).

201

Elye of Saint-Gilles

1231 In keeping with his interpretation of 1230, F completely rewrites the second hemistich to read *le tendi Galopin*. He notes that *s'il tendi* would be even better, rendering the action prosaically and concretely, as it takes place, whereas the poet or scribe has preferred to repeat the formulaic hemistich for its echolike effect with 1229. In addition the poet uses the technique of abbreviation by implying (*intellectio*), rather than stating, the action. (See Faral, *Les Arts poétiques* 85.) F correctly notes that the action of offering the horse as a reward is what the poet intends to emphasize. For his editorial emendation of this entire episode, F relies on a comparison of *Elye* with its later Old Norse translation, in which Elye fights on foot and slays, among others, Hector, seizing the latter's horse, which he then offers to a reluctant Galopin. See R's translation *La Saga d'Elie* 133.

1236 With F, we prefer the scribal word division *nel ai*; R transcribes *ne l'ai*. It is unclear, however, why the scribe continues to use enclisis when not necessary; cf. 952 and 961. The explanation may simply result from scribal habit or preference, or it may indicate a guide to oral presentation.

1236 The episode amplifies a comic moment in *Aliscans* (6140 ff.), when Rainouart is riding horseback for the first time. This scene is later parodied in the short mock–epic poem, *La Prise de Neuville*, or "Chanson XXIII," written between 1218 and 1226 and found in the famous manuscript or *chansonnier*, BN fr 12615, commonly called *Chansons et dits artésiens du XIIIe siècle*. The connections between *Aiol, Elye* and this Arrageois mock–epic are explored by Malicote in "Cil novel jougleor" 391–97; a thorough study of the codex is found in Berger 239–49; cf. 244 above. The *Elye* poet rewrites the scene in the episode of the horse-theft by the dwarf Galopin 1961 ff.

1237 The verb form *Querroie* (which F glosses as *ke-ir*, var. *queoir*, *keoir*, Francien *chaoir*) represents either the future or the conditional tense. Here it should be interpreted as the future tense, as F notes.

1241 At this juncture, the poet foreshadows the moment when Galopin will steal the spirited Prinsaut and then must subdue the stallion's pride by beating it. The overspirited horse becomes emblematic of a topos that occurs throughout this poem and frequently in Old French epic narrative: youthful pride and uncontrolled passion or emotions must be mastered; see Brault 1: 264–65 and 449 n 41.

1248 This episode represents an abbreviated allusion to the moment in the *Prise d'Orange* 743 ff., when the pagan Salatre recognizes William. A similar scene occurs in the *Charroi de Nîmes* 1205 ff.

1250 The *caperon* or cloak could cover not only the body but also the face and the head; cf. Jenkins 70 n 829a.

1256 F senses that a lacuna might exist following this line, since a depiction of the pagans' deaths at the hand of the Frenchman is expected but not given. Once more, F anticipates a straightforward, factual and concrete narration, as he did in 1231 ff., whereas the poet is employing a more subtle and abstract mode of expression.

1258 Medieval lays, epics and romances often use a character's throwing aside a cloak as a gesture of defiance or self-assertion. The three most famous examples are the fairy in Marie de France's *Lanval* 604–5, Ganelon in the *Chanson de Roland* 281 and Lianor in Jean Renart's *Guillaume de Dole* 5094 ff. In *Elye*, the apocopation of this symbolic gesture combined with the rapidity of the action and ensuing commands to destroy Elye render the narration of Macabre's despair parodic and comic. See Brault 1: 137, 396 n 12 and 397 n 14.

NOTES

1265   F unnecessarily emends to *prenra*; he leaves *penras* unemended in 740, but glosses it as *prendre*. Jenkins glossed the occasional scribal confusion between the two verbs *prendre* and *pendre* (397); cf. Gossen's discussion of the examples *prenre, (a)penre, (ap)prendre* and the dissimulation of the "r" (113.56).

1267–68   A series of three interesting assonances begins here: *avés / avés*; 1272–73 *mené / amenés*; 1274–75 *loerés / loerés*. The poet seems to be drawing attention to the technique deliberately, perhaps as a form of parody or as an example of emulation of a model. The first case involving the same verb (*avés*), is akin to the technique of rhyming a word with itself. Roques discusses "identical rhyme," *rime du même au même*, which "was a technique of which Chrétien (de Troyes) was quite fond and which he exploited with considerable virtuosity" (Carroll 309 n 417). The second is a clever *rime riche* whose homophony is achieved by using the two verbs *amener* and *mener*. The third case of *loerés/ loerés* at 1274–75 may imitate the first, showing that the poet is aware of his versification skills. By interposing the second case between two instances of rhyming the same word with itself, the rhyme so skilllfully used by Chrétien, the poet of *Elye* demonstrates his own virtuosity. See also Delbouille's "La Signification des rimes répétées." The nineteenth century editors, considering the third case to be a scribal error, emended to a recognizable and contextually logical formula, *si con vous le volés*.

1289   F and R express puzzlement over *abresce*; R glosses it as *verger?*, and F likens it to *abarges*, used in a similar succession of places in 1640, meaning *herberges*, as used in 1858. Godefroy gives the meaning simply as *verger*.

1300   F notes this proper name, "Ataignant de Sorbrie" as being the copyist's misunderstanding of 688 (see above), an error he sees repeated in 1427, with "Ataignant d'Oliferne." But "Ataignant" (meaning "covetous") is merely another of the humorously appropriate names befitting the topos of the covetous Saracen mentality. They are used commonly in the epic genre for people and horses alike (Langlois, *Table*, 51). See 1427.

1306   There is no need to assume a lacuna here, as F and R do, since there is no abrupt change of subject or scene. Galopin's drawing near to Elye in preparation for combat is immediately followed by the description of the blows they strike. Once again, F's and R's reasoning is based on their comparison with the later Norwegian translation of the poem, in which Galopin's and Elye's conversation is interrupted by the description of the arrival of the enraged Saracens who erupt upon the scene, killing Elye's mount (an episode that occurs in *Elye* at 1313). See R's modern French translation of *La Saga d'Elie* XXXIV, pp. 134–35. The scene is an epic topos whose most famous example occurs in the *Chanson de Roland* 2160–61, when Veillantif, Roland's mount, is killed.

1307   F and R also emend this line because Galopin utters a similar statement as he does hommage when he becomes Elye's liege–man (1174). Here Galopin defends his lord with valor; the scene parallels the later episode in which Galopin vows that he will see that Elye safely reaches the castle (2403).

1310   Much discussion has ensued over the expression *entre...et...*, mostly in the context of the literary relationship of Gace Brûlé and Thibaut de Champagne as described in the *Grandes chroniques de France*. In a nutshell, some critics like P. Paris held that the expression does not imply an actual collaboration between two individuals, but simply means that the two poets separately composed beautiful lyrics. Others such as Fawtier believe that the expression implies an active collaboration between the two, and this scholar documents evidence that the poets were at Philip Augustus's court in 1212, at the time of *Aiol* and

Elye (see Introduction). This line in *Elye* clearly indicates that in this battle Galopin and Elye perform valiant deeds together.

1313 R glosses *Orcanie* as "Orcades" or the Orkneys; however this place of origin is unlikely since any horse from these islands north of Scotland would be the size of a Shetland pony. Langlois' *Table* gives "Orcanie" in general as a "Saracen country" (501); references to horses from this region are frequent in the epics. The Bautiers' article notes literary references to horses from the East: the Orient, Persia, Syria and Orcanie (Bautier and Bautier, "Contribution" 14).

1315 R indicates a lacuna based on his comparison with the later Norwegian translation. In the latter work's rewriting of this episode, immediately following the killing of Elye's mount (whose value is given as more than seven hundred *livres d'or*), Elye staves off the attack with skilful swordplay. Galopin assists by striking blows of his lance as best he can. The two of them manage to slay fifteen Saracens, and the rest flee. Immediately thereafter Galopin and Elye make their way to the garden; no reference is made to the number of Elye's wounds (*La Saga d'Elie* XXXIV, p. 135). However we cannot assume the existence of a lacuna, as the Old French text flows smoothly as is. The additional details more likely result from subsequent amplification in the Norwegian version.

1321 The manuscript reads *Et l*; the hypometric line is altered by the deletion of the initial *Et*; neither F nor R emend here.

1321 The word *anste* gives pause; both R and F emend it to *ante*. F no doubt correctly associates *ante* with *ente*, meaning "a newly grafted tree," attested in Godefroy. F glosses it as a "tree nursery," which would be in keeping with the concept of the "young orchard" (*li vergier fu jovenes*) of the first hemistich, meaning an orchard made up of newly grafted trees. Chrétien de Troyes uses the word *ante* to refer to the grafted trees in the orchard where Fénice and Cligés take refuge in *Cligés* (6312 ff.). The grafted tree sometimes appears as a metaphor representing a "newly converted Christian."

1322 *Dieu le veut* was the motto of the First Crusade to which *Elye* alludes. *Elye* creates a fictive narration of events of the First Crusade, which led to the founding of the kingdom of Jerusalem. Godefroy de Bouillon was its first king; and Fouques d'Anjou, the grandfather of Count Philip of Flanders, became king of Jerusalem in 1131; his heirs ruled at the time of Countess Jeanne of Constantinople's marriage in 1212, an event with which *Aiol* has been shown to be associated (see Introduction).

1326 Ms *s.li*; deletion of the pronoun (as F and R also delete), regularizes the hypermetric line.

1328 F worries that at this point Rosamonde seems already to know Elye's identity, whereas she later asks it of him (1411). In the Norwegian rewrite, she refers to Elye as "mon Franc" in R's translation and not by name, making no reference to his father.

1328 Rosamonde addresses this, the first of her prayers on Elye's behalf, to an as-yet undesignated "god" or *dieus*, while in the Old Norse rewrite, her prayer is directed to Mahomet (p. 136). In *Elye*, Rosamonde refers to "Mahom" rather than to the Christian God when she speaks in her official capacity as the emir's daughter and when she is in the presence of her own people. Her prayers promising to convert are stock epic prayers. The name "Rosamonde" sounds like an echo of "Bramimonde" in the *Chanson de Roland* as P. Paris noted (419). Her prayer addressed to *dieus* foreshadows her adoption

NOTES

of Christianity and is reminiscent of Bramimonde's long-prepared conversion. P. Paris remarked that "Rosemonde est chrétienne dans le cœur" (419). Langlois's *Table* indicates that *Elye* is the only epic in which the name "Rosamonde" occurs (574); Flutre gives "Rosamonde de Noble Vals" as a character in Gerbert de Montreuil's *La Continuation de Perceval*, a romance contemporaneous with *Aiol* and *Elye* (165). It remains unclear if the association of the name Rosamonde in *Elye* with Rosamonde Clifford is valid. She gave birth to Henry II's illegitimate son, Guillaume de Longue Epée, who was probably the dedicatee of Marie de France's *Fables*. He was a close advisor to King John and also a very strong ally of Count Ferrand of Flanders in 1212. (See Introduction.)

1337 F deems the position of the definite article curious, comparing it with 1943, *ains le jour esclairier*, but the two expressions are structurally different. *Demain* is a temporal adverb, and *jour*, a noun, the subject of the verb *esclairier*, so naturally the placement of the definite article will be different.

1338 Gossen refers to *deso(u)siel* (*desous ciel*), which he found in *Aiol* 1656, but which is also found here and again at 1343, as rare "Francien" spellings in Picard texts (92–93).

1339 Gossen discusses the dipthong "au" yielding "a" in the north, with the gradual loss of the second element of the dipthong, in words such as *pamier* in *Aiol* (1823); in *Elye* as well as *Aiol* (1554, 1565, 1590), the form *paumier* occurs. (Gossen 115.58.)

1357–58 These lines foreshadow the tenor of sacrifice and grief found later in *Elye* when Galopin, after experiencing the joy of his marriage to Rosamonde, must then give up both France and his beloved lord Elye in order to remain abroad. The conclusion of *Elye* is ultimately festive, taking place in Paris at Elye's marriage to King Louis's sister.

1366 The scene alludes to the similar lyric passage in the *Prise d'Orange* 81–91, where William listens to the birdsong and thinks of love; the lyric of the Provençal poet Jaufré Rudel is alluded to at the conclusion of *Elye* (see 2672). For relations between courtly literature and the *chansons de geste*, see James.

1370 This epic prayer makes it clear that Rosamonde has come to an apprehension of the Christian God and to her love for Him through the agency of her natural reason. This example of the natural knowability of the existence of the Creator through created things (*per visibilia creationis opera*) develops the strongly Chartrian philosophical context for *Elye* (cf. 246). Recent critics have explored the connections between the Chartrian philosophers (especially William of Conches and his narratological theories informed by the theology of the Incarnation) and the courts of the Plantagenets including their close relations to the House of Flanders in the late twelfth and early thirteenth centuries. See Dronke, *Fabula* 27–38, Wetherbee's "Philosophy, Cosmology" especially 28–33 and 36–41, and Malicote's "Visual and Verbal Allusion."

1373–75 F remarks that these words are strange, or curious, coming from the lips of a Muslim. He also wonders (at 1379–83) where the other Franks who were following Elye have gotten to during this battle, since he finds them in the Old Norse translation (*La Saga* XXXVI, p. 136).

1374 The degree of Chartrian philosophy shown in *Elye* is remarkable within the Old French romance epic corpus. Rosamonde's use of *presïous* (1370), a word considered by Gossen to be a learned term (93.38.26, cf. F's gloss <*pretiosum*) reinforces the theological context. The term is used in *Aiol* by Lusiane when she swears "by God, the Son of Saint

Mary" and all the "lois presieuses" of the martyrs and virgins (8048–49). Elye's argument at 926 resonates with this prayer given that he had insisted earlier to Macabre that pagan gods do not "vivify," that is to say, they have no creative or generative force and possess no word/Word. They are inanimate statues that literally are devoid of speech and thus are not associated with the Logos. Dronke has explored the importance of the Incarnation for the understanding of the rich possibilities of language and narratology and their relation to the new fiction of the late twelfth and early thirteenth centuries, such as Chrétien's (Dronke, *Fabula* 33–38).

1377 The *Chanson de Roland*'s Bramimonde, who had already shown the natural propensity to love, is taken by Charlemagne to France to be converted by love and not by force: *Ço voelt li reis par amor convertisset* (3674). These *laisses* recount the emperor's successful conversion of this queen by sermons and *exempla* (tales with moral applications): *En maison at une chaitive franche, / Tant at odit e sermons ed essamples / Creidre voelt Deu, chrestientet demandet* (39,978–80). (On Bramimonde's conversion, see Stranges 190–96, and see Kinoshita for the interpretation that in Bramimonde's conversion, alterity is articulated and overcome.) Rosamonde's somewhat different path to conversion comes about through her love of creation. Her love for Elye has not been solely inspired by her admiration for his prowess. She had heard of him and experienced the troubadours' "amor deloign." Her first glimpse of the hero occurs when he is in a less than heroic posture, unconscious and being carried off the battlefield by his dwarf–liegeman (1365–66), pictured graphically by the illumination (fol. 85v-b). Contrast the antithetical development of the poet in the Saracens' characterization as those who do not love (1379). In the person of Ataignant, defeated by Elye, they represent "attaining," self-interested gain, avarice and covetousness. (See 1300.) For the topos of the conversion of the Saracen princess, see Warren, Knudson, and DeWeever.

1384 The topos of the "terrifying noise" (*bruit* or *noise*) of the Saracens in battle has been commented upon from several perspectives. Jenkins notes it in the *Chanson de Roland* 1005, and details its affinities with the battle noise described in Virgil's *Aeneid*. He also evokes the Crusaders' real-life experiences with Arab battle cries as a possible influence in the Old French epic. The concept of the pagans' noise in the epics from the viewpoint of its representation of "chaos" has been examined by Nelly Andrieux-Reix in a fascinating study using Michel Serres's discussion of the book of *Genesis* and the concept of "beginnings." In this context, the relation of Bernard Sylvestris's *Cosmographia*, with its depiction of *sylva* and *hyle* as unformed matter with potentially evil undercurrents if not formed properly, is relevant to the Chartrian philosophical context of *Elye*. The cosmological perspective leads to an alternative view of the epic violence, which Haidu studied in a socio-anthropological context. Finally, this chaotic noise contrasts with the beautiful celestial harmony of the music of Rosamonde's bed (1669–76; see note). See the article by Andrieux-Reix and Haidu's study, especially the introduction and conclusion.

1390 The illumination at fol. 85v-b (Fig. 4), alludes pictorially to the Brindisi cathedral's famous Romanesque tympanum, which contains the celebrated mosaic in which Roland similarly carries his fallen companion Olivier; cf. also Triacle's threat of Elye's posture in defeat: *Les jambes vers le ciel et le cief contre terre* (397), a threat which Galopin will bring to reality when he slays Macabre (*Par les jambes le prent, si l'a amont levé*, 2632). In 1390, form reflects content: the decasyllabic line, which is humorously "too short," metrically corresponds to Galopin's size. Both word and image are put to dramatic use to reinforce

Notes

the abbreviated treatment in *Elye* of elements associated with the entire cycle of William of Orange; cf. Corsaut's dryly humorous comment that one should not scorn a little man, in the *Couronnement de Louis;* see 1193. For commentary on the Brindisi mosaic, see Jenkins 132 n 1737; Bédier 2: 267–68, and Brault 1: 239 and 436 n 30 and 31.

1393 The poet foreshadows Rosamonde's marriage to Galopin, who impresses her with his valor, a variation on the topos of the conversion of the Saracen princess by the Christian hero's prowess. Rosamonde will not wed an unworthy man, a nice additional bit of complexity provided by the poet. This line is a direct reference to the authorial intervention concerning Guivret the Small in *Erec et Enide*, when the narrator announces that Guivret was small of stature but courageous of heart: *De celui savrai ge bien dire / qu'il estoit molt de cors petiz, / mes de grant cuer estoit hardis* 3664–67. The *Elye* poet is in some ways rewriting and responding to *Erec et Enide* and to the genre of fictional Arthurian romance in relation to the traditional *chanson de geste*. In Galopin, the poet brilliantly creates an original character from a synthesis of antecedent models: first, the Biblical repentant thief of the Crucifixion story as rewritten in the *Moniage Guillaume I and II*; second, the character of Basin (from the now-lost epic of the same name); third, Guivret; and fourth, the giant Rainouart from *Aliscans*. The folkloric antecedents of the character of Galopin are vague but may be a part of the literary synthesis. Finally, the second hemistich ultimately implies the epic topos (early noted by Crosland) of the "small body and courageous great heart," which appeared in Virgil's description of "the small bees with mighty spirits" in the *Georgics* IV.83. This description is quoted by Jean Bodel, who uses the same topic in the *Jeu de Saint Nicolas: On a veü souvent grant cuer en cors petit* (409). For studies of the character Galopin and his epitomes, see Jonin; Delbouille, "Problèmes" 581; Lejeune 67–68 n 78; and Beardsmore.

1402 The striped silk from Biterne (here assumed to be in Egypt, cf. R's glossary), was celebrated for its high quality. Biterne is identified by Langlois as a Saracen city; the reference to Biterne silk occurs in *Elye* and *Floovant*, and in the later *Prise de Cordre*, with variants of Bisterne (Langlois 598) and Bitorne (Jenkins 2991).

1405 The postern was the rear gate of a fortifying wall, often hidden or concealed. The *guicet* or *guichet* (the original Germanic form was "wicket"), was a smaller door, window or gate.

1411 Rosamonde's asking Elye's identity, when she already knows it, represents a formulaic greeting traditional in diplomacy and in courtly behavior. It reflects neither inconsistency nor careless and inattentive composition (as F and G. Paris felt) since Rosamonde earlier referred both to Elye and to his father Julien by name, 1328–30. Rather, it demonstrates the poet's concern to depict the behavior appropriate to a courtier under any circumstances.

1419 We do not emend, since the verse makes sense as is; F emends to *v. Or requere*, and R emends to *v. soz requere*.

1422 These lines, as noted above, might seem to betray an inconsistency. However, as a character, Rosamonde resembles the fairy antecedents in the lay (*Graelent* and *Lanval*), as well as the romance figure of Melior in *Parthenopeus de Blois* (see Ewert 172–73, and Crapelet). Unlike those characters, who somehow know the knight's identity by magic, Rosamonde provides a realistic and logical explanation for her knowledge of his identity: she has heard everyone lamenting over the deaths of loved ones at the hands of Elye.

1425 In the Picard *scripta*, or written documents, the tendency in the affirmative imperative is for the pronoun to be postpositional, as with Francien, but it does not occur in its tonic form, as in *laissieme* + infinitive = *laissiés me*"; Gossen 144.81.

1427 "Oliferne" is referred to in the *Chanson de Roland* as well as in *Elye*; Langlois defines it as a Saracen city (*Table* 497). R tentatively suggests that it might refer to Alep, but Jenkins is unsure of its provenance (204 n 1924). It may simply be a name taken from the apocryphal story of Judith and Holofernes, which is used to reinforce the notion of treachery or malfeasance. See 688 and 1300.

1428 The expression "for all the gold in" various cities and countries is a commonplace in the epic and romance; it is frequently "in Russia," but the choice of the country is likely to be a function of the meter and assonance.

1429 Here is an example of the use of the Picard form *esparengiés*, as in *Aiol* (cf. 40, *esparenga*); however, the Picard form often yields a hypermetric verse (+1). Its use was one of many contributing factors to the double redaction theory of a Francien original poem copied by a Picard scribe. However, F's delineation of the orthographic difference between "ng," which he labels Picard, and "gn," which he labels Francien, was not found to be consistent by Gossen, who noted three simultaneously co-existing orthographies in the same examples in Picard literary texts: "gn," "ng" and "ngn" (119.62).

1433 F reads *Ar*.

1434 The line recalls Bramimonde's similar greeting to Ganelon in the *Chanson de Roland: Atant i vint reine Bramimonde, / 'Je vos aim molt, sire,' dist ele al conte* (635–36). Charlemagne uses a similar greeting to his army: *Seignors barons, jo vos aim* (3406). For Bramimonde's declaration as an example of the traditional diplomatic greeting, see Jenkins n 3406, and Stowell, "Personal Relationships" 390. For the formula and its role in the development of courtly behavior, see Jaeger's *Origins* 157–58.

1438 The scribe punctuates with an exclamation mark after "e."

1439 This line underscores Elye's youthful naïveté in relation to Rosamonde, who guides and educates him with respect to a certain form of wisdom inspired by the tradition of the consolatory role of Boethius's Lady Philosophy. As in the episode of the thieves above (1053 ff.), Elye is portrayed here as a *nice* or a naïve and foolish young knight, somewhat like Chrétien de Troyes' description of the character Perceval. The allusions in *Aiol* to *Perceval* have frequently been noted (Ménard, "Le thème comique"; LeRider; LeGros).

1441 R misreads the abbreviation *qui* as *que*. The episode refers to the palace named Gloriete in the *Prise d'Orange* (145), and ultimately to *la chambre de beautés* in the *Roman de Troie* II, 14631–958; Suard has noted the allusion of Gloriete to *la chambre de beautés* in his article "Les Héros" 199.

1443 The topos of the marvellous bed is frequent in the lay (Marie de France's *Guigemar* 172–74), and romance (Chrétien de Troyes' *Perceval* 7440 ff.), ultimately deriving from the Biblical tradition of the *Song of Songs* III.9–10, Vulgate. For a thoughtful study of the richly polyvalent meaning of the bed and its philosophical and literary implications, see Vauthier.

1445 Both spellings of the verb (*deferme, defreme*) coexist as metathesis (the reversal of two letters) in the Picard *scripta*. This episode begins with an allusion to *Yvain* and the episode

Notes

of the healing balm, which the *Elye* poet reshapes incorporating significant changes. In *Elye*, for example, it is the lady herself, rather than her attendants, who administers the medicine (a drinkable potion rather than a topical balm or ointment) in a skilful and prudent manner. The heightened realism of the poet is once again remarkable in the rewritten scene (cf. 587 and 1422). For a study of the scientific background of medicinal potions used in romances (including *Tristan*, *Cligés* and *Perceval*, as well as Marie de France's *Les deux amants*, see Lyons. For an analysis of the episode in relation to dialectical argumentation, see Vance, *From Topic to Tale* 48–49 and 80–83, and Malicote, "Visual and Verbal."

1447 R emends the manuscript reading of *pies, li glorieus chelestres* to *pies, le*, without noting the emendation; he alters the *cas sujet* or nominative case, accurately used by the scribe in apposition to *dieus* of the first hemistich, to the oblique case, or *cas régime*. Régnier has noted that Picard texts tended to be grammatically accurate in case usage, putting the attributive in the traditional *cas sujet*. Careful Picard scribes tended to follow traditional usage even up to the fourteenth century, in the time-honored use of cases. However, in the late twelfth and early thirteenth centuries, proper nouns in Picard tended to become invariable and the *cas sujet* was reserved for the subject, while the *cas régime* was used for the attributive. (Régnier, quoted in Gossen 122–23.63).

1451 This Picard form, *pisson*, came from the reduction of the "ei" before "s"; the form is also found in *Aiol*, alongside its doublet *pischon*. (Gossen 92.38.1.b). R emended to *en eve*, evidently on the premise that fish on land (*sor tere*) would be in bad shape. F keeps the manuscript reading and notes without approval P. Paris's suggestion *soz l'eve*. The sense is surely "all the fish in the world."

1452 R emends *.i. chevalier* to *au chevalier*, and F emends it to *le chevalier*; the second hemistich, an apposition, may be allowed to stand, and we do not emend.

1455 This line refers to the *Prise d'Orange* by a direct quote: *Dex, dist Guillelmes, paradis est ceans!* (376), and *Dex, dist Guillelmes, ceans est paradis!* (688). The *Elye* poet participates in the northern European literary discussion about fiction, literature and form. He rewrites the episode of the *Prise d'Orange* in order to avoid potentially heretical parodic overtones and to express his preference for the partly fictionalized point of view of the *chanson de geste* form based on historical fact. The poet does not treat lightly references to theology, historical antecedent or even possibly heretical parody, which he detects in both epic (*la Prise d'Orange*) and romance (Chrétien de Troyes' *Yvain*). See Ménard, "Le rire" 645; Lachet 31 ff., 80–81, 96–97, and 112; and Malicote, "Visual and Verbal Allusion." Finally, the allusion in both *La Prise d'Orange* and *Elye* ultimately goes back to Virgil's *Aeneid* 6: 751–54, to the moment when Aeneas asks his father if it is thinkable that souls would willingly trade the hereafter for earth.

1460 Here the poet adds a reference to *Yvain*'s episode of the ointment; Rosamonde's second preparation of the potion is greatly increased from two herbs to nine additional herbs, akin to the lavish overuse of Yvain's ointment. The *laisse* constitutes a striking adaptation of the epic narrative technique to rewrite the ointment cure in more orthodox and less comic terms, although the rewrite has its own subtle literary humor based on dialectical argumentation; cf. 1455. The subtle shift in the number of herbs used appeared to F simply as a copyist's forgetfulness, or inattention and haste.

1462 F reads *garris* here, and at 1454, he reads *garis*.

209

ELYE OF SAINT-GILLES

1465 F emends to *n'en a*, and R alters the scribal word division to *n'enn a*. We do not emend.

1469 See 1443.

1471 R emends to *q. el*, and F notes that *el* is better than *il*, since Rosamonde is not a Christian, but does not emend. However, "that he might not touch (that spot)" is logical without emendation.

1481 R misreads *fussiemes*.

1485 R indicates a lacuna; F does not, but says in a note that Rosamonde has just begun to speak. It may be the copyist's oversight, as the name of the speaker is usually given.

1490 The episode stresses the commonplace of an "old man's" desire to marry a "young woman." It is similarly used in Marie de France's *Guigemar*, and numerous examples of the topos are found throughout both epic and romance. The image of the "old man" further alludes to the Pauline conception (Rom 6: 6; Col 3: 9–10) familiar to medieval audiences, where it represents the believer's former self, which died with the acceptance of Christ. This theme occurs in *Aiol*, the companion poem to *Elye*, where the poet uses the model of the contemporaneous Byzantine epic *Digenis Akritas*, in which a serpent or dragon represents vice or evil. The serpent is artistically split by the *Aiol* poet into the character of the "old man," an incorrigible old thief or *lecheor* named Robaut, and a fearful serpent or dragon that swallows Aiol's leg while emitting a putrid odor of corruption and decay (see Bancourt for the discussion of this amplification and the Byzantine model). In the Saracen world, Rosamonde indicates that Lubien, an old man who wants to marry a young woman, is invested with the most power of all, but in *Elye* he will be soundly defeated by the youthful Christian hero.

1500 F and R do not observe the copyist's word order and write *aaisies* according to the model of 1554.

1508 In the Christian west in the early thirteenth century, war was not undertaken for the primary purpose of killing the enemy, but rather for doing damage, collecting ransom or otherwise impeding the daily life of the besieged in order to bring defeat and the realization of one's goal, mirrored here by the Saracen wars. Although the Church tried to discourage burning and laying waste to the land, the nobles continued to do so, and it represented a preferred technique during the reign of Philip Augustus (Strickland).

1520 F unnecessarily emends to *sus el palais*.

1523 Both F and R emend *peres* to *sire*; however, at 2120–21, it is made clear that in the world of the Saracens, messengers and emissaries are indeed the leaders' sons, nephews and very close blood relations. This situation differs from the Christian custom of *familiares* or members of the lord's entourage who were not necessariily blood related but belonged to the extended household.

1534 Both F and R read *dire*; they interpret the hemistich as "he [the messenger] heard the words spoken" (i.e., by Macabre in 1531–33). It could be interpreted, however, as written in the manuscript: "he [the messenger] had spoken the message well."

1541 Note the irony of *faillie*; this is the lack or "running out," the stoppage that marks the error of the Saracen ethos in the literary epic. In a forthright manner, Rosamonde will liken her brother's absence of courage to outright "failure" or exhaustion.

Notes

1549 F did not agree with R's interpretation of this line; R emended *por toi* and punctuated with a colon after *Lubïen*, meaning: "I've undertaken the combat against Lubïen for you. Why don't you want to do it?" F punctuates with a question mark: "Why did I undertake the combat against Lubïen? Why don't you want to do it?"

1564 R misreads the abbreviation *qui* as *que*, as he did in 1441.

1565 The proverb was well known; LeRoux de Lincy 2: 383; cf. *Li Respit del curteis et del vilein: Ki son nés traanche sa face deshonure* (strophe 22); and see LeRoux de Lincy 2: 294.

1583 The knight's wearing an item of his beloved's clothing into battle, is a feature usually found in the courtly adventure romances, rather than in the epics, as F noted. See James as well.

1593 R emends to *tourt*, rather than *court*.

1594–95 The copyist has encountered a preexisting hole in the parchment; he has neatly divided the lines after *estés* and *poestis*, to finish the lines after the hole. The same holds true for fol 87v-b, 1630–31 (see below).

1605 R alters the copyist's enclitic word divison to *se l'eüsse*; Chevalier and Gross, citing the studies of B. Cerquiglini, J. Cerquiglini, Marchello-Nizia and Perret-Minard, have observed that scribal preference for elided object pronouns and definite articles varied greatly and in some instances favored enclitic and in others proclitic (185–200).

1607 This line contains a reversal by the *Elye* poet of the scene in the *Prise d'Orange* 1463–77, where William and his men are overheard by Saracens who are in the room below.

1608 The emir's private chamberlain is his own son; cf. 2120.

1617 F has difficulty interpreting this line and emends to *m'encusses*, but tentatively suggests a more concrete alternative in a note: *Je cuic qu'espié estes* (oder *somes?*) *et vilment encusé*. F's preference for delineating the action as it unfolds blinds him to the poet's paratactic and elliptic skills. The Old Norse translation may have also influenced his interpretation; because he assumed that the Old French and Old Norse versions of *Elye* were being copied from a lost Old French original version, F assumed that the *Elye* copyist misread *nous* as *vous*.

1619 The scribe punctuates with an exclamation mark following *hé*; F places a comma after *hé* and adds in a note that a comma is needed after *las*; R puts the exclamation point after *hé* and a comma after *las*.

1623 *Veriés* is pronounced as two syllables /ve rjes/, rendering F's emended omission of *de* unnecessary, which he acknowledged later in a note.

1625 Rosamonde teaches the novice knight the quality of discretion, which will keep him from going into battle against overwhelming odds; cf. 1209.

1630–31 The copyist divides between *consel* and *aurés* at 1630 to write around a small hole in the parchment; in the following line, the copyist writes the first two letters of *plus* before the hole, and the last two, after it.

1633 Succumbing to the nineteenth century impulse to discover an Ur-text, F includes extensive commentary on the following descriptive episode in the mistaken belief that *Elye*, the Norwegian translation and all of their existing fragments stemmed from a lost Old French original; he therefore attempted to reconstruct the episode through a combination of all episodes and fragments. See Introduction and Gerritsen.

1636 F adds a quizzical note on the terminology, questioning the use of the terms *colombes* and *pilers*. He senses an allusion to the architecture of a tomb, and his literary instincts are, as usual, sound, as the Old French historical romance *Eneas*' brilliant ekphrasis of Camille's tomb comes obviously to mind. In *Elye* the allusion constitutes an important metaphor for understanding the nature of composition and the role that the *chanson de geste* was intended to have in courtly education. The columns of ivory that support the pillars are part of the description of a "two-story" edifice. Memory, as Carruthers has so elegantly demonstrated, was often envisioned as an edifice or house, the basis of which, in this text, is the supporting columns of ivory, or fiction. The literary antecedents reach as far back as Homer's *Odyssey* and Penelope's true-false dream with its ivory gates of fiction (XIX 535–53). When Aeneas emerges out of the underworld with the Sibyl (VI.941–46), Virgil reconceives the gates of ivory as, on the one hand, being the wrong way (i.e., not factually true), but at the same time being the right way (i.e., bearing a higher truth imparted by fiction). Combined with the importance Chartrian philosophy placed on fiction in conveying a higher, deeper meaning (i.e., the Aristotelean answer to Platonic objections concerning "poetic lies"), the allusion is a powerful one and compels meditation and interpretation. The early thirteenth-century literary debate centers on fables or lies (sometimes referring to Arthurian fictions) vs. the more serious literature of the *chanson de geste*. (See Carruthers 34–35, Minnis viii–ix, and Dronke, *Fabula* passim.) Elye is given guidance for remembering great deeds of the past (the historical kernel of the *chanson de geste*) by means of a carefully constructed fiction, that is, the ivory columns that hold up the edifice of memory.

1638 The emphasis is on the great width or breadth of the passage, about one-fifth the legal width of a roadway, or room for sixteen armed knights to ride abreast (Labarge 153).

1640 F does not understand why Elye would have to go into the garden. Thus he concludes that these lines must be out of order and that some lines must be missing. F's confusion is partly based on the fact that the Old Norse rewrite abbreviates this episode and omits reference to the paintings which Rosamonde describes. The construction of lines 1640–41 seems almost too literary for the traditional concept of the Old French *chanson de geste*. But upon reading further, we encounter an amazing blend of indoors and outdoors. By logical implication, the bowers, moats, gardens, birds, animals and later the four hundred knights and ladies are also part of the pictorial representations that Rosamonde had painted in her room. Here we encounter a tribute to the power of visual art that echoes Virgil's description of the paintings of the Trojan war on Dido's walls, which impelled Aeneas to tell his story. See also 1441. Cf. Carruthers 35 ff.

1641 The "turning palace" is an allusion, as F noted, to the *Voyage de Charlemagne* 334 ff.; further on (1645 ff.) the poet makes it clear that Rosamonde's discourse represents an ekphrasis, a verbal expression of the stories and tales painted on the walls of her room. These murals iconically recounted the capture of French knights who were imprisoned to die. Wace urged in the prologue to the *Roman de Rou* that narratives be saved for memory. This is what Rosamonde does in her paintings, but in a reversal of Wace's admonition to save narratives in words. Cf. Frappier's note that in the *Enfances Guillaume*, the verbal descriptions of the enchantments of Orable's *jeux d'Orange* and the entertainments by

NOTES

Saracen magicians during the wedding festivities that accompany the marriage of Orable to Thiebaut might be somehow related to the ornamentation of the animals and bas reliefs on the triumphal Arch of Orange (II 275–76 n 3).

1647 At first Rosamonde seems to declare that she has saved the lives of four hundred French knights; however, the story makes it clear that Elye, Galopin and Rosamonde are alone when they are beseiged in the tower (2510–11). F concluded that these lines must have been a later interpolation. But it can be assumed that Rosamonde's tale of rescue refers to the depiction of the valorous deeds of Elye's ancestors and the saving of their memory. This preserved memory of past deeds will come to Elye's aid when he most needs it and is fittingly described by Rosamonde as a treasure of which he has been hitherto unaware. The addition of the element of love comes naturally to Rosamonde who humorously includes her own implied hopeful amplification that she might become one day Elye's lady. The number four hundred exactly doubles the number of abused Christian prisoners encountered in *Aliscans* (1669 ff.). Rosamonde subsequently adds that she has saved the armor of slain knights (see 2608–10).

1655 F emends to *vielle*, and R, to *vieille*; neither spelling is used in the text.

1660 The allusion is probably to the curious *chiterne* in a scene in ms D of the *Prise d'Orange* (1572–1617), when Guibourc has two enchanters from "overseas" come out of a cistern (possibly used metaphorically) where she had been keeping them in order to divert and amuse the audience. F gives a more concrete interpretation to the cistern and questions its proximity to the bed. Rosamonde explains that the cisterns are paintings on the floor and not real objects.

1662 The line emphasizes the youthful inexperience and lack of judgment of Elye.

1664 F questions the referent to *autres* and does not see the reason for the verb *trespassés*. It is clear that Rosamonde, who is similar in many ways to both Boethius's Lady Philosophy and the sibyl in Virgil's *Aeneid*, urges Elye to "go beyond all the others," to look before his eyes and see into the very foundations of the edifice of memory. The foundations of the bed are built by enchantment or *ningromance*, such as that practiced by Melior in *Parthenopeus de Blois*, when at night she uses magic and causes scenes of battle to spring to life before her father's eyes. Melior uses the "magic" of fiction to recount epic narrative. Jaeger has observed the twelfth-century tendency to show "the poet as a wizard...exercising magical control over language" (161). The necromancy to which both *Elye* and *Parthenopeus* refer is not a black art, but rather the enchantment of that which is "made" or "constructed" from words, the *fictio*, or fictional literary tale. Note that this theme reemerges in *Elye* when Macabre states that his daughter has enchanted him and his court (2357). Cf. Alain of Lille's *fictio* and *pictio* in the *De Planctus Naturae (The Complaint of Nature)*, and his statement that poets construct and rearrange details from history in order to create a more meaningful and profound story. See Alain de Lille 8: 137.39; Jaeger *Origins*.

1667 The *paille galasien* (var. *galacien, galatien, galazin*) is a rich, vermillion silk traditionally identified in the Old French epic (*la Chanson de Roland, Ogier de Danemarche, Renaut de Montauban*) as coming from Galata, a "suburb of Constantinople where there was a famous factory of silken stuffs," according to Jenkins, who observes that this derivation is not altogether certain. F. Michel identified it as "of Galaza," a Sicilian town (Jenkins 207–8 n 2973). Langlois' *Table* (246–47) lacks this variant "galasien" in *Elye*; later in the poem a similar cloth covers the statue of Mahomet (1774).

Elye of Saint-Gilles

1669 The description of the bed accompanied by the ethereal music of the bells echoes the scene in Chrétien de Troyes' *Le Conte du Graal* or *Perceval* (cf. 1443). Just as Aeneas emerged from the underworld with the sibyl's guidance, the young knight Elye emerges from the underground room with the aid of Rosamonde's instructions, completely prepared to fight the great, definitive battle against the "old man" Lubien and all he represents. F's comments at this juncture in his edition reveal much about his nineteenth-century viewpoint. At the conclusion of this episode, vexed with what he deemed to be the errors of a careless scribe, a corrupted and incomplete manuscript tradition and veiled and confusing literary allusions, he launched into a long etymological and philological exposition of the concluding word of line 1674, *jougler*. What we view as complex richness and polyvalence, he decried as corruption.

1679 This narration concerning Galopin's having been *defors oublié* or "forgotten outside" by Elye and Rosamonde essentially rewrites the episode of Rainouart's having been forgotten by William in *Aliscans* (7507 ff.). Although Galopin finds himself in clear physical danger of being discovered by the enemy, his reaction is one of reinvigored service to his lord. The scene constitutes a doublet, ending in the antithesis of Rainouart's more dangerous threatened apostasy. In addition, the topos of the "faithful follower forgotten" is familiar from Marie de France's lay of *Lanval* 12–20, and forms the basis for Rutebeuf's later *Miracle de Théophile*.

1684 The scribe has expunctuated *sel re* following *reconnut* by placing a dot under each letter.

1685 By placing parallel lines after *la* and before *puchele* at the end of the line, the scribe indicates that he had omitted the word from the line. The letters "pa," copied by mistake after "la," are expunctuated by being marked through with a horizontal line. This verse and the preceding one indicate carefulness, rather than carelessness, on the scribe's part, as he reviews what he has written, detects and corrects his errors.

1695 F and R emend *estrains* to regularize the nasal vowel, which might have been pronounced in Picard. We choose not to emend on such a hypothetical basis.

1700 R glosses *cabetenc* as the name of the garment, taken from the word for the cloth from which it was made. R further surmised a connection between the Turkish word "caftan" and *cabetenc*, and the latter is similarly glossed by Greimas with an attestation of early twelfth century, and as a precious fabric by Godefroy. F discusses the problem of the terminal "-c." Cf. Gossen 132–33.75.

1704 Gossen discusses *igues* (<*aequalis*) as an example of the development of the word group ending in "-alis," yielding "-es" in Picard, but he indicates that it is by no means an exclusively Picard trait (51–52.5).

1715 F and R needlessly emend to *sa brace*, perhaps reflecting their longing for the older language; Greimas gives *brace* as attested in the *Chanson de Roland*.

1717 R unnecessarily emends *convenable* to *couveitable*, meaning " inspiring covetousness." However, Rosamonde is attired in a manner befitting (*convenable*) her station in life.

1725 F emends to *foudre*; the manuscript has two minims (vertical strokes) that could be either "u" or "n."

Notes

1736 When Rosamonde creates the analogy that likens an old man to an apple, she continues the theme she began at line 1490 of the young woman's rejection of the graybeard. The image she fashions serves to remind the audience of the Pauline concept of the "old man," the believer's former self which must be cast aside to make way for the "new man." Like Chrétien de Troyes' Erec before him, Elye serves as a type of "new man." See Wetherbee, *Platonism and Poetry* 224–41, and Mela.

1737 F emends to *desoz*, but the green skin of the apple is on the outside.

1738 F keeps *flairie* but notes that he prefers *flaistrie*. R similarly emends to *flatrie*. According to both Godefroy and Greimas, the verb *flerir* (var. *flairier*), means "to stink" or "give off a foul odor," either in reality or metaphorically. We do not emend, because Lubïen, whose name suggests *lubrïété* (*lubricité*) or "libidinousness" (echoing the name of the evil spouse, Lubie, of Ami in *Amis et Amile*), literally reeks of sin (see 1490 above). According to Langlois' *Table* (406), Lubïen and Lubie are the only two instances of the name in the Old French epics.

1739 The scribe wrote, but forgot to expunctuate, an "f" after *fuiroie*, a rare instance in which he does not correct his error (cf. 1734).

1743 The scribe started to write "cler" but wrote "fier" instead, expunctuating the "c" with a dot under the letter and altering the shape of the "l" into an "f."

1753 These paid soldiers in Northern France and the Anglo-Norman kingdoms came from the highest social ranks during the late twelfth and early thirteenth centuries.

1756 R needlessly emends to the future *venrés* and changes the verb of the second hemistich to its Francien form *charrés*, also emended to the future. F keeps *chees*, glossing *chaïr* as Francien *chaoir* (var. *cheoir*, Picard *caoir, caioir*). Greimas attests *cheoir, cheir, chair, chaier* from the tenth century *Vie de Saint Léger*; see 1237. See also Raynaud de Lage (93) for the Picard variants *keir* and *caïr* and the Francien form *cheoir*. The expression Rosamonde uses, while literally rendered "fall at my feet," is part of a juristic formula meaning "you will thank me"; similar expressions are used in the *Chanson de Roland* 3792 and in Chrétien de Troyes' *Yvain* 1862 and 2107.

1777 There is no lacuna here; the nineteenth century editors may have taken the *le* in *Rosamonde le voit* (1778) to mean «Rosamonde sees him" or Elye, which would have signaled a lacuna, as a person would have been identified before "le voit." We interpret it as "Rosamonde sees it" (*le* being *it* and not *him*), i.e., the oath-taking ceremony, to which she later refers at lines 2146–48.

1777 The reference to "good and evil" pagans and Saracens occurs but once in this text and is not typical of the Old French epic genre, which routinely casts Saracens as unequivocally "evil"; indeed, in *Elye*, they are characteristically portrayed as lacking humanity (305) or unchivalric (334). Norman Daniel has cited this unusual reference in *Elye de Saint-Gilles* as an exceptional example of a poem depicting Saracens who are preoccupied with standards of chivalry (43).

1778 The quality of the dialectical argumentation of this episode has been explored in Malicote, "Visual and Verbal Allusion."

1793 The reference to Solomon's wife is also found in Chrétien de Troyes' *Cligés* 5802–4; it is part of Elye's childlike reliance on proverbial wisdom; such proverbial or paremological knowledge must have been learned by all in early childhood, a phenomenon of "the nursery" to be set aside for a higher divine wisdom, as Conrad of Hirsau urged (525–33) and as William of Conches discussed in a somewhat different fashion (Dronke, *Fabula* 17–21). In order to arrive at genuine wisdom, Elye must move beyond the level of proverbial instruction and enter into dialectical argumentation as demonstrated by Rosamonde. F saw these lines as containing a "completely unmotivated" diatribe against women in the literary tradition of the Seven Sages. Gaston Paris studied this allusion, believing it to be of Eastern origin and arriving in the Old French and medieval Germanic epic through Byzantine sources ("La femme de Solomon" 436–38).

1794 *Meïsme* assonates in "-an"; F notes in the table of assonances that "an-e" and "en-e" are mixed and he observes the similarities of the assonances: *ame* 1794, and *feme* 1979. R emends to the Picard form *meesme;* however, Gossen found that in Picard texts, the form *meïsme* was much more frequent than *meesme* (86.30 n 39).

1798 F emends to *c'om*, but the emendation is not necessary.

1816 The reference to Spain does not appear to be merely formulaic; it alludes to the Reconquest (as does *Aiol*; see Introduction).

1817 The poet practices foreshadowing; Rosamonde's own brother Caïfas will make this type of wrongful statement, which hurts her (2162 ff.).

1818 R transcribes *encontré*, and F emends to the infinitive *encontrer*.

1839 Galopin's oath duplicates Elye's above (1815 ff.). Both knights do everything humanly possible, against all odds, to keep their oaths; this steadfastness contrasts dramatically with the mass oath-taking ceremony of the Saracens at 1777, an oath that is taken lightly and quickly broken by all. In addition, the poet will develop the subtle, dialectical argumentation or *disputatio* in the context of Boethian reasoning that in disobeying the commandment "Thou shalt not steal," Galopin hurts the enemy and helps his friend. (Cf. Vance, *From Topic to Tale* 35–37, and cf. 2070 below).

1847 F notes that *que il* (meaning "that it," *it* being "the horse") *neu (o. nel) jet a tere*, would be a better construction; *nel* would mean "that he wouldn't throw him off" and would be preferable to *n'en*, "thrown off of it."

1849 Galopin's theft of the horse alludes to the similar episode concerning Alexander the Great's legendary horse, Bucephalus in the *Roman d'Alexandre*, based on the Pseudo-Callisthenes romance. The intertextual resonance of this act adds to Galopin's luster as he performs a truly epic deed. Its significance is underscored by the poem's fifth miniature dramatically showing Galopin as he observes the caged and fiesty steed in the company of six guards. Miniatures of the caged Bucephalus were not uncommon in medieval illuminated manuscripts of the Pseudo-Callisthenes *Alexander Romance* (which at that time had already been translated into twenty-four languages). Weitzmann has studied prototypical illuminations of the caged Bucephalus and reproduces two illuminations, one from the Venice, Marciana, Cod. Gr 479.8v, and the second from the early thirteenth-century Greek codex, Oxford, Bodleian Library, cod. Barocci 17. The latter is reproduced as Plate XXXI, Figs. 109 and 111, to which *Elye*'s fifth miniature bears striking ressemblance. Crosland conjectured that the reference likening Marchegai (the horse in question in *Elye* under the name "Prinsaut") to "King Arthur's horse" in *Aiol* 936–37, was perhaps a mistranscribing (misheard or miscopied) of "Le roi Artu" for "Bucefalu," since

NOTES

the following line about its man killer behavior referred to Bucephalus' "propensity...for human flesh" (204).

1851   F says that he does not understand this line, since *aveste* does not have the meaning "to bind around" or "to fasten on." The latter inference, however, is clearly intended.

1858   F glosses *estres* (from middle Latin Provençal *estra*), meaning "houses" or "residences"; R glosses as "places" or "beings."

1864   The scribe used the abbreviation "P," but then proceeded to spell out the word; neither F nor R noted the abbreviation.

1867   Throughout this entire episode, the poet convincingly demonstrates his ability to establish fine psychological subtleties. The authorial intervention underscores Galopin's strategem, or *engin*, which is analogous to that of Rosamonde and her "enchantment."

1874   F takes "the lord of the land" to be Rosamonde's brother who ruled Alexandria.

1876   *Barges* presents a problem with the "e" assonance; Gossen emphasized the blurring of "-ar" and "-er" in Picard pronunciation; cf. 1794, 358 and 417. F thinks the alternate Francien form *berge* (<Lat. *barca*) must mean "home" or "house," but he later added the meaning "boat" for line 1882. Greimas attests "barge, berge" (found in the *Chanson de Roland*) as deriving from Vulgar lat. *barica*, derived from the Greek, meaning "bark" or "boat." Frappier noted its use in the *Couronnement de Louis* and said that the word meant "bâtiments de guerre et de transport" (2: 81 n 2).

1882   F emended to the plural *vos*, but *vo* was also an accepted plural form in Picard, so we do not emend (Gossen 127.68).

1884   The scribe punctuates with an exclamation mark after *ai*, perhaps accidentally because of its homophony with *hé* or as a guide to oral performance.

1894   The decasyllabic line describing the horse stands out dramatically in a long series of alexandrines; the description follows rhetorical conventions of portraiture for describing persons, i.e., starting with the head and descending to the feet. See for example Geoffrey de Vinsauf, *Poetria nova* and the rules for describing womanly beauty (567–617); see also Gallo, *Poetria nova* 44 and 46, and Colby.

1902   R emends to *encor(e)* and *c[e]ens*, apparently interpreting the line as "I still have such a one in here"; his emendations reflect a need to avoid a hypermetric verse resulting from his interpretation. F believes that a lacuna exists, based on his comparison with the later Norwegian translation in which Galopin discusses "horses," (in the plural) for "Jubien" (the name used in the Norwegian for Lubïen). When l. 1903 of the Old French text continues with a reference to "the horse" in the singular (*nel=ne le*), F thinks that some intervening action must be missing. Finally, it looks as though the scribe accidentally wrote *cent* and altered the "t" into the form of an "s" (cf. 1743, where he similarly alters a letter rather than expunctuating and rewriting it).

1907   F and R both emend; F does not follow the scribal word division *ne nert* and reads *nen ert*. R reads *nen iert*; cf. 1913.

1908   F emends to *veroi* and R to *verai*, but the manuscript reading of *veroie* is a normal Francien and Picard form; cf. the future form of "croire": *querrai* or *keroie*, as discussed by Gossen (113.56), and see also Raynaud de Lage 94.

ELYE OF SAINT-GILLES

1913 F and R both emend to *ies*, but *es* was an acceptable Francien form of the second person singular (Raynaud de Lage 96).

1916 The overturned chessboard during a game is a commonplace in medieval vernacular narrative. In the epic it serves a wide variety of purposes, including that of self-revelation and disclosure of one's destiny (Jonin, "La Partie d'échecs," 1: 496–97). Lubien's quick temper and his ultimate fate are revealed here by means of authorial intervention.

1917 F notes that an emendation could be made for the "c'a"; however, the subjunctive should follow; R emends *entendiest* accordingly, but F did not.

1920 F glosses *travail* (lat. *trabáculum*) meaning "framework" or "scaffolding," obviously the horse's iron cage. Godefroy gives only *poutre* or *catafaldque*; Greimas adds that the latter meaning is found in Froissart. The history of the etymology is of interest, since its original meaning was taken from lat. *trapáculum*; in northern Europe, the word *travail* originally referred to skein-winding reels used in the textile industry. The meaning of the term in *Elye* is, as Holmes noted in a review article, the "frame" or "cage" in which unruly horses were restrained by farriers in order to shoe, treat or groom them. In *Elye*, Holmes noted, the horse is confined for its own safe keeping; the cage consists of stakes, chains, leg bands or foot coverings (padded on the inside to keep the horse's leg from rubbing raw) and a "trelle" or "caging" and gratings, reinforced by steel bars (553–54). P. Paris noted that in his own era, both the term and the object were still in active use (HLF 22, 421).

1923 *Kaïnes* is trisyllabic. The reference to the horse's golden chains creates an allusion to Orable's gift horse in the *Enfances Guillaume* 426ff. Her steed was guarded by fourteen men and held by gold and silver chains. Bucephalus had similar gold chains in the Pseudo-Callisthenes romance (see 1849 above), and like Prinsaut, Bucephalus refused to let anyone touch him.

1927 F and R emend to *nef*; *nes* is the nominative form and the cases are so often mixed in this poem that we do not emend.

1934 F and R emend *ot* to *tost*, but the sense of the sentence is that, as a general rule, this is what would happen to a guard if he allowed the horse to be stolen.

1935 F and R emend the nominative case, *ses lignages*, to *son lignage*; the case should be the accusative, but the use of the nominative indicates again that the distinction between the two cases was fading away.

1936 The manuscript abbreviates *chier'es*. However, F concluded that it was not really an abbreviation; rather, he believed that the poet had written the letter "i" above the line: *cheiries*. This reading, however, would necessitate changing the number of candles or torches to add a syllable to the line, so he proposed changing *trois* to *quatre*. No such changes are needed; Goderoy glosses *chierere*, the usual resolution of the manuscript's abbreviation, as a feminine substantive meaning "candle" or "torch."

1947 F emends to *vantes*, but the infinitive makes sense with the modal auxiliary.

1949 F and R emend to *iert*; however *ert* was also a form of the future in Picard.

1954 F and R both read *nen ot*, but the scribal word division we follow is sensible.

Notes

1956 The differing treatment of *sear* by R and F provides a good illustration of the contentious atmosphere between *Elye*'s French and German editors (see Introduction). R stated that this word could not be the infinitive "seoir," which does not assonate in "-a"; the meaning demanded *seoir*, but R could not explain the form from a philogical perspective. F correctly noted that common sense was called for instead of a purely philological approach in editing: the word could only be *seoir* and the poetic need for the assonance simply overrode any phonological reality of everyday speech.

1961 Galopin's traditional epic prayer before undertaking the ordinarily dubiously heroic deed of horse theft strikes a humorous note. However, heroic horse theft was indeed a feature of the classical epic, such as Homer's *Iliad*; cf. the theft of the horses of Resos, noted by G. Paris (*Deuxième article* 476) and the theft of Bucephalus (Weitzmann 105).

1967 F and R emend to *s'esfree*; *esfreer* as glossed by Greimas and Godefroy has the identical meaning without the reflexive. Both forms are used by the scribe; cf. 1978.

1970 *Gaverlos* illustrates the development of the gutteral "g" shared by both the Picard and Norman dialects; Gossen discussed the example *gabalus > gaverlot*, found in both *Elye* and *Aiol* (100.42a).

1972 F observed that 1972 and 1974 seem to contradict each other. However, the poet's skillful narration of the psychological development makes the meaning clear: at 1972, Galopin fears the guards little, as he is hidden from them in the shadows. But in 1973, the guards, who are searching for the source of the noise that startled the skittish horse, pass so near to Galopin that each man brushes up against him without realizing it. Then (*adont*) the poet surmises formulaically that he would not be surprised if Galopin were afraid.

1980 The verse alludes to a now-lost epic, *Basin*, whose existence is attested in the inventory taken in 1405 of Marguerite of Flanders' library. In this inventory is also found BN fr 25516, which contains the unique copies of both *Elye* and *Aiol* (Deshaisnes 880–81; Hughes, Appendix II, Category VII, p. 182).

1985 The feminine noun *raille* is glossed as "bar" by Greimas.

1987 F prefers *mat* in his note, but does not emend.

1994 The humorous image of the unskilled novice knight who rides backwards is not uncommon in the Old French epic; the episode alludes to Rainouart's inexperience with riding in *Aliscans* (6157).

2008 F unnecessarily regularizes to *coi* and notes that the verb should be *ester*, as in 2036, but both orthographies are used by the scribe. The formula is altered by a chiasm or reversal of terms (*Tout le fait estre cois / Tout le fait coi ester*, 2036). The line makes it explicit that the horse's pride is being beaten down by Galopin.

2015 F emended to *destrier*, but the intended meaning of "stirrup" is clear. He later noted that the line should have read *estrier*.

2017 F noted that *flat* was possibly meant, rather than *fais*.

2020 The scribe expunctuated the "e" following *nel* by placing a dot under the letter. R divides the words differently from the scribe: *ne l'apprendra*.

Elye of Saint-Gilles

2022 F emends to *le maine* on the model of 2042, possibly assuming a more identically formulaic style than the poet generally practices (cf. 2008 and 2036).

2026 This lone, decasyllabic line provides a dramatic instance of the recurring motif of Galopin's being scorned by everyone, even a horse, because of his size.

2029 We keep the scribal word division; R divides *ne l'a*.

2030 In his notes, F determined that this verse belongs after 2033.

2032 F suggests *se le conseust bien* or *si bien le consiviest*; in his corrections and additions, he finally decided on: *se bien eust consivié* or *consieut*. R emended to *se bien le consuiest*, which he noted as the imperfect subjunctive. The line as written (*l'eüst consui*) makes sense, and the structure of the pluperfect subjunctive "if clause" followed by the imperfect subjunctive in the result clause, was used. (Johnston, "The French Conditional Contrary to Fact," 130). R glosses the infinitive "consuivre" ("attaindre," or "to attain, reach, get to"), while F glosses "consivre" (var. "consevre," "consivir"); with the later form "(con) su-ir." Godefroy attests "consievre" ("atteindre en frappant") while "consuivir" meant "to chase" or "pursue." Greimas cites the infinitive as "consievre, consivre, consuir."

2038 Tobler suggested to F a reading of *mestier* as more useful than *destrier*; since the latter term occurs at the assonance four times in the *laisse* of only 32 lines, the poet evidently uses repetition as a technique to drive home the significance of the taming of the unruly steed.

2039 This isolated decasyllabic line emphasizes the drama of the moment of battle between Galopin and the steed; cf. 2026.

2045 The poet economically adds Galopin's theft of the sword to that of the horse in a passage illustrating the rhetorical technique of abbreviation (*abbreviatio*) or brevity. Using the technique of ellipsis, he leaves out all but the most pertinent fact or action, without being vague. The passage is clarified later, when Elye slays Lubïen with the latter's own sword, which Galopin stole in this line.

2046 In their rendering of 2046–51 ff., both F and R are heavily influenced by their comparison of *Elye* with its later Norwegian translation. F explains his "logical" reordering of lines, according to the Norwegian version, and he indicates lacunae following 2048 and 2049. R thinks that 2047–48 and 2054–55 have mistakenly been copied twice and so omits the former and indicates a lacuna of two lines. However, the conclusion's lines describing the theft of the horse and sword exemplify the humor of brevity.

2047 This isolated decasyllabic line again dramatically signals that a stylistic effect is being deliberately created. Galopin's preparation for epic prayer ressembles its author; it is short (brief) and quick. When Elye repeats the identical gesture nearly word for word, the poet subtly adds two syllables.

2048 The scribe punctuates with an exclamation mark after "hai"; cf. 2055. It is likely that this punctuation was to be used for oral presentation or reading.

2049 The decasyllabic line's brevity emulates the rapidity of the action: Galopin's entire return trip is efficiently dispatched in just one ten-syllable line. (The journey to the Saracen camp, 1853–59, had taken place in six lines.)

Notes

2058 The word *geste* is used in the same sense as in Bertrand de Bar-sur-Aube's famous *trois gestes*, meaning "three lineages" or family lines (*Girart* 1–57; Van Emden, Introduction xxv ff.).

2065 As always, the Saracens calculate the monetary value of Lubïen's loss, an indication of their greed and materialistic world view; cf. 275. The implied author of the *geste de Saint Gille* (see Introduction) is resolutely opposed to the money-driven Christian merchant class's practice of usury. In the early thirteenth century in both Paris and in the north of France, the clergy systematically conducted a campaign against usury (see Introduction).

2066 F suggests *est*, but does not emend; the future *ert* of the manuscript reading is clearly intended.

2070 The verse is ironic: Lubïen, of course, is thinking of Galopin's "sin" of theft while being blind to his own shortcomings. The Saracen's lost horse becomes emblematic of his loss of control over his sexual desires and greed in his quest to obtain Rosamonde and his rival's lands.

2074 The allusion to "Murgale" is problematic. F reads *desor fu*, and Tobler suggested to him *des or fu* (meaning that the sword's name henceforth would be "Murgale"). In his corrections and additions, F noted that Nyr suggested a singular verb; LV). R probably correctly reads *de Sor fu*. He glosses the character as almost certainly identical to Murgale de Turnie (1056), whom the band of thieves had robbed earlier in the poem. The narrative's obvious irony is that Lubïen no longer possesses the two defining implements for any knight, the horse and the sword, and he must borrow them for this combat. "Murglais" is similar to "Murgale," the name of Ganelon's sword in the *Chanson de Roland* 346, 607.

2075 F punctuates with a comma after *amainent*, because "Bernaut" is hardly a horse's name; he reads it as a genitive. Comparing *Elye* with the Norwegian translation and fragments, F notes that the Old Norse translation inserted the name of another king, Jodoan de Valdune, who brought Lubïen a horse, thus making the verse singular. The most logical reading is that the sword is Murgale's, the horse, Bernaut's.

2080 Both F and R, ignoring the manuscript's abbreviation, which clearly reads *p'endre*, transcribe *pendre*. However, the notion of having the emir seized and taken prisoner in the castle is an appropriate one.

2083 F omits *Elies* and substitutes *honeste* for the assonance in "-e," while R changes the whole line to read: *Du bacheler Elie or vous dirons noveles*. It is conceivable that the name was given an alternate pronunciation /el jɛs/ for the assonance, much as Aiol's name was once deliberately altered to read "Aians" at the assonance (*Aiol* 2433).

2090–97 It is significant that Galopin's courtly, formal discourse is reinforced by the lengthy adverb *cortoisement* of 2090; cf. his formal and diplomatically correct greeting to King Louis at 2573–77. Galopin's covenant is the antithesis of Julien's original paternal curse (159 ff.).

2098–99 Rosamonde's prediction foreshadows Galopin's final reward of marriage to Rosamonde herself (2714–15).

2103 Castilian steel was famous in the late twelfth and early thirteenth centuries for its high quality and durability and is often referred to in epics and romances.

2105 After *larago-*, the scribe has expunctuated *larag* by placing a dot beneath each letter.

2110 Elye now has complete control over the horse, with all of the baptismal symbolism that its change of name represents. The name of the horse will be changed shortly from the "old name" to the "new name" (2566), reflecting the alteration from unbounded, uncontrolled youthful exuberance ("Prinsaut") to mature self-confidence and self-control ("Marchegai"). "Prinsaut" was a variant of "Clinevent," Gui d'Allemagne's horse in the *Couronnement de Louis* (1483). G. Paris felt that the name was substituted in a careless, bizarre fashion (*Deuxième article* 472–73). This name-change provided an additional reason for him to declare the final lengthy *laisse* a later interpolation, which he said need not be considered in his study of the poem (473).

2112 The line is a direct reference to Rainouart's nearly identical statement in *Aliscans* 6145.

2121 The poet clarifies what was formerly left unstated: the chamberlains are part of the royal family and make up the emir's courtly entourage.

2132 R emends to *traés* for the assonance. F thinks *tra és* better fits the assonance than does the manuscript's *traiés*, but does not emend. He adds that *en la* must mean "over there" and writes *en ariere*. However, *car* introduces the imperative. F also hypothesizes about the logistics of where the characters are standing, in order to make concrete what the poet leaves in the abstract. The horse is so spirited that Rosamonde must stand back for her own safety, as Elye himself cautions (yet another reference to the hero's newly won, mature control of his desires).

2141 F thought that this line did not make logical sense in relation to what follows. He described the pagans' and the king's reactions in the Norwegian version and tried to explain 2141–43 accordingly. F also failed to understand how the emir knew Elye's identity and suggested that at 2142 *cri* would be more logical than *ri*, but he did not emend. However, earlier in the poem, the emir expressed the wish that Elye were still with him because only Elye would be courageous enough to fight (1604–6).

2151 The altering of the name "Malpriant" to "Malpris" for the assonance is comparable to *sear* at 1956; see also 2083.

2155 The *esmeril* was a small falcon; the episode as a whole shows affinities with the Sparowhawk episode in *Erec et Enide*.

2165 The episode alludes to *Aliscans* when William furiously upbraids his sister, Queen Blancheflor, calling her a whore (2771 ff.).

2166 F reads *l'a tenu* ("she kept him"), rather than *l'a tenue* ("he kept her"), the manuscript reading. F again considers the situation in very concrete terms rather than in the abstract.

2173 R divides *fu je*; F writes *fuie=fui je*, comparable to the common forms *suie=sui je*, and *aie* (var. aiou)*=a je, jou*. Gossen notes that in Picard, enclisis of the subject pronoun in cases of inversion is a common phenomenon and cites *aie=ai je…suie-sui je*, etc.), corroborating F's reading (144.82).

2176 Like the pagan gods, Caïfas is a "lacking thing": he lacks courage because of his selfishness. The quality the Saracens generally lack most is love, and the vice that most governs them is its contrary: covetousness or selfishness.

Notes

2182   F and R emend to *feri*. We read the manuscript's *refiert* to mean that Caïfas strikes his sister more than once, and we maintain the present tense. This reading is reinforced by Galopin's recounting of this episode at 2340–43, where he reports that Caïfas struck and beat Rosamonde. At 2186, the poet further states that Galopin saw the act clearly.

2184   The scribe punctuates with an exclamation mark after *Hé*, perhaps as a guide to the reader's or minstrel's vocal presentation.

2188   R corrects to *li ber Elye* and F corrects to *li ber Elyes*, but we do not emend.

2197   F observes that the correct word is *boutellier*; however, the assonance forces the striking change in the word, perhaps to draw attention to it. In *Erec et Enide*, Chrétien de Troyes listed the wine steward and butler at King Arthur's court as being named "Lucan" (BN fr 794 (Guiot) 1509 and BN fr 1450, 6757). Chrétien was rewriting the traditional Old French *chanson de geste* form, epitomized by its classical antecedent Lucan's *Pharsalia*, echoes of which are found throughout the genre. Chrétien wrote in a new fictional form, thus relegating the traditional *chanson de geste* to an important, but secondary function at court, similar to the function of the butler. Through the Saracen's invitation to Elye to become the wine steward and butler at court, the *Elye* poet shows the untenability of such a servile role for the epic form. For the relation of *Erec et Enide* to the *chanson de geste*, see Zaddy's article and Hindman's *Sealed in Parchment*, Ch. 4, 129–61.

2198   If the number were read as "quatre mille Sarrasins," the line would be hypermetric, but if the number is read as "mil" it would not. Neither R nor F spell out the numeral.

2215   The scribe omitted the letters *pon* from the verb and indicated their insertion by parallel slashes before and above the "d" and before *pon*, which is written at the end of the line.

2219   The scribe expunctuated *des* before *destriers* by underlining the letters.

2222–23   It should be noted that Galopin's difficulties with the horse theft parallel Elye's problems in landing his blows accurately; both add an air of realism to the story. F notes that the Norwegian translation omits any reference to the knight's mistake.

2231   R and F noted that this line is contradicted by 2252, but it is not clear that Elye remounts Prinsaut after being unseated. It is Prinsaut that Elye gave back to Lubïen, rather than Balodru's horse, which the hero was riding. It is also obvious that Elye would remount Prinsaut the instant he killed Lubien (2317). This episode's drama, which stresses Elye's noble generosity, is heightened by the hero's magnanimous gesture, just as Lubïen's baseness is emphasized.

2234   F and R emend to *si l'abat*; R does not note the manuscript reading, which we keep.

2238   We keep the manuscript reading of the alexandrine, reading *avoëc* as trisyllabic. R emends the first hemistich to *autres (trois) avoec*, with *avoec* as two syllables. F emended to *autre avoec* to create a lone decasyllabic line, which dramatizes the Saracens' perfidy.

2255   The scribe characteristically punctuates with an exclamation mark after *hé*.

2257   F and R separate the words differently from the scribe; they prefer *de l'herbe*.

2266   The implication is that victory is associated with being astride the uniquely gifted steed. However, Elye already knows and then proves that he can defeat the old man without a special horse. His ultimate victory results not from his mount, but from his personal prowess.

2268 R indicates an emendation with *[i] monta*, but the manuscript clearly shows four vertical strokes; the scribe merely overlooked marking the first as an "i."

2272 Both F and R emend by omitting *droit* and adding "de" before "son." We do not emend.

2273 R emends the last word to *perles*, comparing the line with 400; see also 2284.

2275 F reads the abbreviation as *quins* (var. *coins*) meaning "corner of the shield," but *quirs* ("leather" or "hide") is the manuscript reading, which makes sense.

2283 F emends to *sor elme*, but does not note the emendation.

2290 R emends *li paien* to *li Français*; F does not emend, but adds a note that *li Français* would be better and remarks about the simplicity or naïveté of the scribe or poet. However, both R and F miss Rosamonde's trenchant irony conveyed by *le grans cos*. She calls upon her cowardly brother, who had so feared to encounter the mighty Lubïen in battle, to witness the ineffective blows the old pagan was really capable of striking, as witnessed by the fact that Lubïen is now lying powerless, dead on the field.

2294 F and R emend to *l'espee*, on the premise that things near the body also tend to have the definite article, but F corrects to *s'espee* in the notes. There is no need to change the contraction, since "with his sword" is the intended meaning.

2297 Although F and R emend to *essordent* ("come out of"), the manuscript reading of *essorbent* ("block," i.e., his way from the valley) is equally logical and possesses obvious metaphoric value. Elye's battle with the seven kings is reminiscent of Bernard Sylvestris's commentary on the *Aeneid* in which the seven bullocks (*iuvencos septem*), or bodily movements symbolizing earthbound matters, must be sacrificed in order to arrive at higher understanding (VI.38–39). The scene parallels the earlier episode in which the Saracens blocked Elye's progress, as well as the episode which follows, in which Caïfas becomes an obstacle in Elye's path. Having successfully overcome the "old man," Elye as a "new man" must continue to defeat vices or sins that obstruct his path.

2310 The short catalog of arch traitors is comic in tone; the comparison of Elye to "Satenas" (2309), or Satan, is amplified by references to the son of "Luchibus de la Roche Baudas" (a hybrid name evidently composed of "Lucifer" and "Begibus" and found only in *Elye*). "Begibus" is a variant of "Belgibus," or Beezelbub, often found in the *chansons de geste*, (Langlois, *Table* 83). The other traitors include "Pharaoh" (here a Saracen king of Spain, but obviously a reference to the Egyptian "pharaoh" of numerous epics such as the *Prise d'Orange*), "Judas" (also a Saracen king of Spain here, but clearly meant to refer to the biblical traitor–apostle); "Salatre" (cf. 100); and finally to "Constantin Macar" (an unidentifiable reference, found only in *Elye*; Langlois, *Table* 157).

2313 F & R emend to the expression *es canas* of 2316; however, *el arnas* makes sense if "arnas" is a variant at the assonance for "harnois, herneis, hernos." The Saracens will leave their tents, get into the saddle or into harness and ride to the sea, where they will enter their ships. F glosses "arnas, harnas" in *Aiol* (4731, 7070), used in the sense of "harness" or "equipment," but does not accept the same manuscript reading in *Elye*. R aand Normand similarly gloss *Aiol*'s use of *arnas* as "equipment." F later noted that since in the Norwegian

Notes

version there is no reference to the pagans' attempted escape in ships or even to water (all the deeds of this episode take place on land), his emendation, conjectured in 2316, was unnecessary.

2317 See 2331 and 2252.

2322 The line can be read as it is written, *de quatre milliers* (as F ultimately noted). It was emended by both F and R, who wrote *.iiii^m.* and added *homes* after the number to restore what they erroneously thought was a hypometric line.

2329 F emends the manuscript reading *hui ladouba* to *iehui*, and R emends it to *hui main* in order to correct the manuscript's hypometric line. This scene parallels an earlier one in the first part of the poem, where the emphasis was on the father knighting the son, who put on his own armor. In this doublet, Rosamonde helps in arming the young, but now fully educated knight. This new status is emphasized by the authorial intervention of 2330 that Elye has arrived at an understanding of how to wage war (literally and metaphorically).

2336 This episode echoes the scene in the first part of the poem, in which Elye questions the wounded messenger (*Amis, qui t'a chi fait?* 187) and then vows to do justice for the wrong committed against him.

2342 The second hemistich echoes Julien's parting words to his son at 160.

2349 We follow the scribal word division, as does F; R's division is *de l'elme*.

2353 R emends the verb to the plural: *l'ame en porte[nt] malfé*, and F emends the case of the noun: *l'ame en porte malfes*.

2356–57 F and R emend the word order *ne la* to *la ne* ("out there, we won't be able to last"). The meaning of the manuscript's word order is that they will not be able to survive (the battle, not referred to, but assumed), because Elye is an enchanter. We do not emend and assume that the poet is creating a chiasm (cf. 2420, 2434).

2360 The humor is notable here; virtually all of the Saracens and Slavs rush to take advantage of Macabre's offer of pardon, since all have been subject to his anger at one time or another. This is a society held together by fear of a despot, not through shared values and perhaps also metaphoric for the despotic nature of sin.

2363 F suggests an alternative reading, but without emendation, *por l'amor*. Such a reading, although technically correct, seems to run counter to the ongoing theme of the Saracen's basic lack of love, lusting only after personal gain. It is likely that we have here a clever pun, ("for the love of," / "because of the death of"), which would be evident to an audience listening to the verbal presentation.

2368 The scribe punctuates with an exclamation mark after *hé* and also in the following line after *ahi*. R follows scribal punctuation, as we do, but F uses a comma after both interjections, saving the exclamation point for the end. The punctuation apparently acted as a cue to oral presentation or reading.

2374 Galopin's *baton*, meaning "staff," "rod" or "stick," is reminiscent of Rainouart's *tinel* or club in *Aliscans*. The dwarf's rod is sculpted by four fairies, indicating the poet's variation and conflation of Chrétien de Troyes' description both of Erec's sculpted emerald scepter and of his coronation robes in *Erec et Enide*. The robes were also crafted by four fairies, commonly taken to embody the quadrivium. Cf. Galopin's description of the four fairies present at his birth, 1179 ff.

2377 The decasyllabic line (4/6) heightens the dramatic impact of the Saracen army's attack against two Christian knights, while being part of an ordinary epic formula. The first four monosyllables, coupled with the alliteration "t," reproduce the staccato sounds of the blows delivered and the rapidity of the fight. We leave the decasyllabic line, as does F. R emends to a dodecasyllabic line modeled on 2627, which also features the staccato alliteration, while adding *tant pié* following *puing*.

2381 The scribe places an exclamation mark after *hé*.

2383 *Reprovier* (var. *reprouvier*) was used in the twelfth and thirteenth centuries to mean "proverb," before the word *proverbe* gained dominance; earlier the word *respit* was more common. The allusion in the following verse to *la letre* is almost certainly to *Li Proverbe au vilain*, a compendium that had been commissioned by Count Philip of Flanders towards the end of the twelfth century, from which the proverb is quoted directly (Tobler, #121; LeRoux de Lincy 2: 355, 477, 495; Morawski #1003, p. 37 and 109). This particular proverb has been the subject of many etymological studies and interpretations, since P. Paris first indicated that it was not especially clear, despite its evident popularity (424). (See Schulze-Busacker, Stone and Smeets for varying interpretations.) The reference to Charles Martel is rare for the epic canon, despite the fact that he was a key figure in preventing the Islamic conquest of Christendom. The paucity of literary references is usually explained by the fact that the Church disapproved of Charles Martel's harsh treatment of church officials, churches and monasteries whose wealth he confiscated; he was therefore not considered as a model ruler for emulation in the "mirrors for princes" or in the *chansons de geste* (see Triaud 753 ff.). Nevertheless, Charles Martel does appear in poems of the Lorrain cycle, the *Chanson des Suisnes, Raoul de Cambrai*, and *Berte aux grans piés* (Langlois, *Table* 141).

2385 The line begins with a two-line capital, but without the change in assonance that such a capital usually indicates. The capital calls attention to the importance of the proverb just enunciated and probably signals a change in the reader's intonation, or *timbre d'intonation*. It also possibly attenuates the impression of the final *laisse*'s unusual length (see Hartman). The line is decasyllabic, emphasizing the drama and the gravity of the impossible odds faced by Galopin and Elye.

2389 *Solail* (rather than *soleil*) was a typical Picardism, according to Gossen (63.12c).

2390 The decasyllabic line within the epic prayer with its evocation of God's creation echoes Rosamonde's earlier prayer with Chartrian overtones (1370 ff.).

2393 F emends the abstrait *loi* (her people's religion or law) to the more concrete *gens* (her people themselves). However, Bouchard points out that *gens*, when used by a noble, frequently and more specifically referred to his or her entourage or *familiares*; thus Rosamonde is referring to the people of her land whom she will one day rule (2 ff.).

2394 The humor found in the prayer's last verse results from the psychological realism contained in the subtle acknowledgement of her personal wishes and human foibles; cf. Elye's sudden recognition of Galopin's innate goodness precisely when the latter offered him the thieves' treasure trove in the woods (1170–75).

Notes

2403 This situation parallels the first time that Galopin saved Elye by carrying him into Rosamonde's garden (1386 ff.).

2407 F emends to *destache les*, and R emends to *destache caines*; we do not emend because the verb form is correct and the line makes sense.

2410 F originally read: *Fierement a le bare et le pont sus leve*, but he later noted that he considered this line to be corrupt in the manuscript. He suggested that either *si a fermé* or *refermé a* would be more logical and in keeping with 2619. R also emended to describe the action: *Si a remis la bare*. By emending *fierment* to *ferment* and changing from *le pont sus levé* to *le pont ont levé*, we imitate 2619, with the addition of the chiasm of the subject and verb, characteristic of this poet's style.

2414 F notes (erroneously as 2419, rather than 2414) that he wonders where Elye's pangs of conscience are, since he now evidently permits the Saracen maiden to kiss his mouth, whereas at 1471, he turned away expressly to avoid touching her lips. However, due to Rosamonde's conversion this kiss may be interpreted as the Christian kiss of peace, which was given on the mouth. (Cf. Jaeger, *Origins* 104 ff; Camille, "Body, Soul and Surplus.")

2416 F and R do not follow the scribal word division that we follow, but divide *de l'avaine*.

2418 F notes that the noun is masculine here, although the gender of the word varied during the course of the Middle Ages. The scribe does not consistently observe the agreement of adjective endings.

2425 F reads *deffent*.

2428 The scribe places an exclamation mark after "hé," and we follow the scribal reading. F eliminates the punctuation, reading *he vous*, while R deletes the punctuation. The punctuation, however, does give the reader the cue to dramatize vocally the arrival of this well-known epic character. The episode and character allude to the *Couronnement de Louis* and the character Corsaut de Tabarie who cuts off the tip of William's nose (cf. 253).

2432 F observes that the noun *gent* is masculine here; its gender could be either masculine or feminine in the medieval period; cf. 2418.

2435 The scribe has written out *Elye* in the oblique case here and at 2446, since the nominative would have created a hypermetric line. F & R transcribe *Elye* in the oblique case, but they correct the case when they resolve the abbreviation for "Galopin." However, at 2446, F emends the oblique to the nominative since it does not affect the syllable count. We observe the scribal tendency in this part of the poem not to use the nominative with proper names.

2440 F's *Varia lectio* indicated that he read the abbreviation as *bras* and emended it to *brans*. However, the abbreviation reads *b'ns* = *brans*. The meaning of "steel blades" is clearly intended.

2450 Cf. 1435.

2453 F and R indicate a lacuna following this line, and a line may well have been omitted. However, the change in person and number of the verb is not unusual. Cf. 2456 and 2458, where the same shift from singular to plural naturally and logically occurs, and again at 2465–66, where Godefroi shifts from first person singular to first person plural. Fleischman has pointed out that a thorough philological survey of the spectrum of such idiosyncratic shifts and their significance is yet to be made (21–23).

2460 F remarks that *brestekes* is a variant alternative Picard spelling for *breteske* (Francien, *bretesche*), which he compared to *asmoine/asmoisne* at 2697.

2469 From this point of the poem through to the end, the second hemistiches are repeated for the echo effect. The repetition creates deliberate stylistic effects and does not reflect the laziness of a poet hurrying to finish the work. Heinemann closely studied the technique in the William of Orange cycle and especially in the *Prise d'Orange* (Heinemann, *L'Art* 37–41).

2493 F prefers *les* but does not emend.

2507 F emends *mi* to *me*; R emends the beginning of the line to read *P. moi*, and then emends *mi* to *lui devés*. We do not emend, since *mi*, from the dative late Latin *mihi*, is a Picard form used as well as *moi* and *me*. Cf. the example from Adam de la Halle given by Gossen: *par cele foi que tu dois mi*; in *Elye*, the formula, also found in charters, is altered for the assonance (Gossen 143.81b).

2519 F mentioned that Rainouart appears in *Aliscans*, but he did not comment on the allusion; cf. 2375.

2520 F emends to the tonic *iert*.

2532 F does not emend but would prefer that the *et* be dropped and that "Aïmers" be trisyllabic, rather than two syllables, "Aimers." R emended by omitting *et*; cf. 2594.

2536 *Riche* has a much broader meaning than that of material wealth, such as "strong, powerful"; cf. 2627, where *riche cop* refers to the powerful blows. It can also refer to the quality of nobility.

2537 All of Christendom's fighting on behalf of Elye parallels all of pagandom's combat in favor of Caïfas (2363).

2543 The polysyndeton, or repetition of conjunctions in close connection, expresses the immediacy and enormity of the massive effort to aid Elye (cf. 2537).

2549 Lead sheeting was used on the roofs of certain medieval edifices for protection against assault and fire.

2558 The scribe places an exclamation mark after *hai*.

2563 F misreads the abbreviation and resolves it as *qui*.

2566 F includes remarks about the abrupt and apparently careless change of the steed's name from "Prinsaut" to "Marchegai"; but see 2110.

2581 F emends *sui* to *fui*.

2584 At 2584, F's *Varia lectio* reads *fil*, probably an error for 2581.

2592 F thinks that there is a lacuna here indicating that the manuscript at this point is corrupt.

Notes

2594 F prefers to omit *et* and to pronounce "Aimer" as bisyllabic, as in 2532, but he does not emend; R omits *et*.

2598 The scribe writes out *Elye* in the oblique, rather than nominative, form; cf. 2435.

2609 Since all of the knights were already armed to begin with (2585 ff.), F questioned the order and logic of these lines in which Rosamonde provides these same knights with arms. The scene may emphasize the concept of Rosamonde's lavish generosity, duplicating her profligate application of the herbal potion of 1445 ff., or perhaps she is replenishing their supply with fresh or additional weapons. In either case, the scene is allusive to a strikingly similar episode in *la Prise d'Orange*, where Orable provides the Christians in Gloriete with fresh arms (936 ff.).

2613 F and R emend to omit *tout* and add *homes*.

2614 F and R emend by changing *joie* to *noise* on the model of 2625. But the pagans greet the battle with a joyful enthusiasm that will soon turn to the despair of utter defeat (cf. 1384). The topos of "joy turning to sorrow" is repeated throughout *Elye*.

2627 R emends to the Francien form *coper*.

2628 A parallelism appears here with 2377, a decasyllabic line that 2628 directly quotes and expands to an alexandrine. In it, a multitude of horses stumbled, fell and died. The *Elye* poet has consistently featured the topos of the horse of pride and here makes obvious the parallel with the arrogant, prideful Saracens.

2639–41 The reference to a prison full of serpents and poisonous toads is a common epic motif. It is especially allusive here to William's imprisonment in the *Moniage Guillaume II* (3204 ff.). A similar reference is found in BN fr 25516's version of *Beuves de Hanstone* (680 ff.).

2640 The form *culevres* is frequent in western Picard written texts and is also found in *Aiol* (Gossen 77.24 and n 33).

2645 F thought that a lacuna existed here; he believed that the whole story of the Christians' victory must have been omitted by the scribe who proceeds directly to tell the triumph's aftermath. F is correct about the omission, but probably incorrect about the lacuna: the poet is practicing abbreviation through ellipsis. Louis could not «populate» or send settlers to the region if the Christians had not emerged victorious.

2647 The reference to Louis's populating the city with Christians is a direct allusion to "Sancho le Poplador," or "Sancho the Populator," the king of Portugal, famous for his decisive role in the Reconquest in the early thirteenth century. Sancho received the name "the Populator" because he introduced settlers and rebuilt towns and castles in the north of Portugal, which had been devastated during the Reconquest. The reference to Sancho is to be expected in the poem, since he was the brother of the so-called "queen," Mathilda-Teresa, widow of Count Philip of Flanders. In addition, he was the father of her nephew Ferrand, count of Flanders and husband of Countess Jeanne. *Aiol* and *Elye* were associated with her wedding in Paris in January 1212. Mathilda's negotiations with Philip Augustus were decisive in arranging the marriage. See Introduction; see also Previté-Orton 2: 827–28.

2654 F sees the word *quant* either as part of an elliptical construction or as *con*. R emends the verb tense to *ert*. The ellipsis is part of the technique of abbreviation used frequently by the *Elye* poet and is appropriate here.

2656 We emend in keeping with the first part of the hemistich. This is the final passage in the poem using the fixed expression about Galopin's size, which has been a recurring motif and now becomes a final joke or "gab." The tense indicates that such scorn definitely belongs to the past. Here Galopin narrates the information that was not indicated earlier at 2642.

2668 The scribe punctuates with an exclamation mark after "hé."

2672 This episode rewrites the scene in the *Couronnement de Louis* in which William, at the advice of the pope, must abandon his intended bride at the altar in Rome in order to serve his king (1405 ff.). In the *Elye* poet's revision of this scene, the poet alludes to Jaufré Rudel's lyric "Lanquan li jorn son lonc en mai" and its reference to the cruel godfather who obstructs the beloved's happiness to provide a brilliant and artistically original nexus of *chanson de geste* and lyric motif. (See Pickens 268–69, and see also Switten 58–63). Rosamonde's apparently quick acceptance of Louis' offer to arrange a marriage with another of his barons is the antithesis of Aude's reaction to Charlemagne's offer in the *Chanson de Roland;* however, it represents a realistic and logical consequence of Rosamonde's long-developing esteem for Galopin, whose true worth she has recognized from the start (cf. 1393).

2675–76 The Church forbade marriage on grounds of consanguinity; in the early thirteenth century, this included relationships to the fourth degree, that is, a shared ancestor four generations back, and also any relationship involving the godfather or godmother. See Herlihy 97 and Lynch 219–57.

2688 The scribe places an exclamation mark after the "ai" of the second hemistich, perhaps to indicate vocal emphasis to the reader/lector.

2703 R reads *donna je*, and F divides *donraie*; cf. 2173.

2724 The topos of great sorrow at parting is common to the lyric, the *aube*, the *chanson de geste* and romance.

2732 The motif of the "wasteland" is generally taken in both romance and epic to refer to the non-Christianized lands, which remained the object of the Crusades throughout the late twelfth and early thirteenth centuries.

2745 There is a tear in the parchment at this line; the scribe writes the line up to, and including the word *dient*, then shifts to the following line to complete the verse and avoid the rip. F notes that "o" is preferable to *et*, but he does not emend.

2757 At this line and again at 2760, the poet is giving both the biological or human "genealogy" of Elye and Aiol and the literary genealogy of *Aiol*. The concept of literary genealogy is not to be confused with that of "literary genetics" (see, for example, Fleischman 25 n 22). From the text of *Elye* and its conclusion at 2758, the text of *Aiol* is generated. *Elye* comes to its end, and as one poem dies, a new one springs to life.

BIBLIOGRAPHY

Actes [du] VIe Congrès international [de la] Société Rencesvals, Aix-en-Provence, 29 août-4 septembre 1973. Aix-en-Provence: Université de Provence, 1974.

Actes du IXe Congrès international de la Société Rencesvals pour l'étude des épopées romanes, Padoue-Venise, 29 août-4 septembre 1982. 2 vols. Modena: Mucchi, 1984.

Ailes, Marianne, Philip E. Bennett, Karen Pratt, and Wolfgang van Emden. *Reading Around the Epic: A Festschrift in Honour of Professor Wolfgang Van Emden.* London: King's College London, Centre for Late Antique & Medieval Studies, 1998.

Alain de Lille. *The Complaint of Nature by Alain de Lille.* Translated by Douglas Maxwell Moffat. Yale Studies in English 36. New York: H. Holt and Company, 1908.

Albéric des Trois Fontaines. *Chronica, Monumenta Germaniae Historica Scriptores Series* 23. Hanover: Bibliopolii Hahniani,1874.

Amsler, Mark. *Etymology and Grammatical Discourse in Late Antiquity and the Early Middle Ages.* Amsterdam and Philadelphia: J. Benjamins Pub. Co., 1989.

Ascherl, Rosemary. "The Technology of Chivalry in Reality and Romance." In Chickering, *The Study of Chivalry*, 262–311.

Andrieux-Reix, Nelly. "Les Bruits et la rumeur: *Noïse* au Moyen âge." In Aubailly, *Et c'est la fin*, 1: 89–99.

Arnould, E.J., *et al.*, eds. *Studies in French Language and Mediaeval Literature Presented to Prof. Mildred K. Pope.* Manchester: Manchester University Press, 1939.

Aubailly, Jean-Claude, Jean Dufournet, *et al.*, ed. *Et c'est la fin pour quoy sommes ensemble: Homage à Jean Dufournet.* 3 vols. Paris: H. Champion, 1993.

Bachrach, Bernard S. "*Caballus* and *Caballarius* in Medieval Warfare." In Chickering, *The Study of Chivalry*, 173–211.

Baker, A.T. "Le Futur des verbes *avoir* et *savoir*." *Romania* 63 (1937): 1–30.

Baldwin, J.W. *Aristocratic Life in Medieval France: The Romances of Jean Renart and Gerbert de Montreuil, 1190–1230.* Baltimore: Johns Hopkins University Press, 2000.

Bancourt, Paul. "Etude de quelques motifs communs à l'épopée Byzantine de *Digénis Akritas* et à la chanson d'*Aiol*." *Romania* 95 (1974): 508–32.

Baumgartner, Emmanuèle, ed. *La Chanson de geste et le mythe carolingien: Mélanges René Louis*. 2 vols. Saint-Père-sous-Vézelay: Musée archéologique régional, 1982.
Bautier, Anne-Marie. "Contribution à l'histoire du cheval au moyen âge." *Bulletin philologique et historique (jusqu'à 1610) 1976* (1978): 209–49.
Bautier, Robert-Henri, and A-M Bautier. "Contribution à l'histoire du cheval au moyen âge: l'élevage du cheval." *Bulletin philologique et historique (jusqu'à 1610) 1978* (1980): 9–75.
Bayot, A. "La chronique dite de Baudouin de Flandres." *Revue des Bibliothèques et Archives de Belgique* 2 (1904): 419–32.
—, ed. *Le Poème moral*. Paris: Palais des Académies, 1929.
Beardsmore, Barry. "Auberon and Galopin." *Romania* 101 (1980): 98–106.
Bédier, Joseph. *Les Légendes épiques: Recherches sur la formation des chansons de geste*. 4 vols. 3rd ed. Paris: Champion, 1926.
Bélanger, J.C. Roland. "Au commencement était l'école (de théologie)." In Keller, *Romance Epic*, 57–72.
Benton, John F. "'Nostre Franceis n'unt talent de fuir': The *Song of Roland* and the Enculturation of a Warrior Class." *Olifant* 6 (1979): 237–58; rpt. in Benton and Bisson, *Culture, Power*, 147–66.
—, and Thomas Noël Bisson, eds. *Culture, Power, and Personality in Medieval France*. London/Rio Grande, OH: Hambledon Press, 1991.
Berger, Roger. "Littérature et société arrageoises au XIIIe siècle: Les chansons et dits artésiens." Diss.: Arras: Commission départementale des monuments historiques du Pas-de-Calais, 1981.
Bernard Silvestris. *The Cosmographia of Bernardus Silvestris*. Translated by Winthrop Wetherbee. Records of civilization, sources and studies, no. 89. New York: Columbia University Press, 1973.
Bertrand de Bar-sur-Aube. *Girart de Vienne*. Edited by Wolfgang van Emden. Paris: Société des Anciens Textes Français, 1977.
Besamusca, Bart. *Cyclification: The Development of Narrative Cycles in the Chansons de Geste and the Arthurian Romances*. Amsterdam: North-Holland, 1994.
Bianciotto, Gabriel, et. al, eds. *Études de langue et de littérature du Moyen Age offertes à Félix Lecoy par ses collègues*. Paris: H. Champion, 1973.
Bise, G. *Medieval Hunting Scenes (The Hunting Book by Gaston Phoebus)*. Translated by J.P. Tallen. Barcelona: Regent Books, Hughtext Ltd., 1978.

Bibliography

Bodel, Jean. *La Chanson des Saxons*. Edited by Francisque Michel. Paris: J. Téchener, 1839.

—. *Le Jeu de Saint Nicolas*. Edited by A. Henry. 3rd rev. ed. Brussels: Palais des Académies, 1981.

Bouchard, Constance. *"Those of My Blood": Constructing Noble Families in the Middle Ages*. Philadelphia: University of Pennsylvania Press, 2001.

Boutière, Jean, and A.H Schutz. *Biographies des troubadours: Textes provençaux des XIIIe et XIVe siècles*. Paris: A.-G. Nizet, 1964.

Boyer, Marjory Nice. "A Day's Journey in Medieval France." *Speculum* 26 (1951): 597–608.

Brandin, Louis, ed. *La Chanson d'Aspremont*. Paris: Boivin, 1925.

Brault, Gerard J. *The Song of Roland: An Analytical Edition*. 2 vols. University Park, PA: Pennsylvania State University Press, 1978.

Bréhier, Louis, ed. and tr. *Histoire anonyme de la première croisade*. Paris: Champion, 1964.

Busby, Keith. *Codex and Context: Reading Old French Narrative Verse in Manuscript*. 2 vols. Amsterdam: Rodopi, 2002.

Buschinger, Danielle, and Wolfgang Spiewok, eds. *L'Image au moyen âge: Actes du colloque, Amiens, 19–23 mars 1986*. Amiens: Centre d'études médiévales de l'Université de Picardie, 1992.

Camille, Michael. "Body, Soul and Surplus: The Kiss in Medieval Art." In *Yale French Studies Special Edition: Contexts, Style and Values in Medieval Art and Literature*. Edited by Daniel Poirion and Nancy Freeman Regalado (1991): 151–70.

Carnat, Germain. *Le fer à cheval à travers l'histoire et archéologie*. Paris: Vigot Frères, 1951.

Carruthers, Mary. *The Book of Memory: A Study of Memory in Medieval Culture*. Cambridge: Cambridge University Press, 1990.

Chailley, Jacques. "Du *Tu Autem* de *Horn* à la musique des chansons de geste." In Baumgartner, *Mélanges René Louis*, 1: 21–32.

Chevalier, Jean-Claude, and Maurice Gross. *Méthodes en grammaire française*. Paris: Klincksieck, 1976.

Chickering, Howell, and Thomas H. Seiler, eds. *The Study of Chivalry: Resources and Approaches*. Kalamazoo: Medieval Institute Publications, Western Michigan University, 1988.

Chrétien de Troyes. *Guillaume d'Angleterre: Roman de XIIe siècle*. Edited by Maurice Wilmotte. Les Classiques français du moyen âge 55. Paris: H. Champion, 1927.

———. *Les romans de Chrétien de Troyes: Édités d'après la copie de Guiot. IV, Le chevalier au lion, Yvain.* Edited by Mario Roques. Paris: H. Champion, 1960.
———. *Erec et Enide.* Edited by Mario Roques. Paris: H. Champion, 1968.
———. *Cligés.* Edited by Alexandre Micha. Paris: H. Champion, 1970.
———. *Chrétien de Troyes, Erec et Enide.* Edited and translated by and C.W. Carroll. New York: Garland, 1987.
Cloetta, Wilhelm, ed. *Les Deux rédactions en vers du Moniage Guillaume.* 2 vols. Paris: Firmin Didot, 1906–10.
Colby, Alice M. *The Portrait in Twelfth-Century French Literature: An Example of the Stylistic Originality of Chrétien de Troyes.* Geneva: Droz, 1965.
Cooper, A.J., ed. *Le Pèlerinage de Charlemagne.* Paris: A. Lahure, 1925.
Crapelet, Georges, ed. *Parthonopeus de Blois.* 2 vols. Paris: Crapelet, 1834.
Crosland, Jessie. *The Old French Epic.* Oxford: Basil Blackwell, 1951.
Daniel, Norman. *Heroes and Saracens: An Interpretation of the Chansons de Geste.* Edinburgh: Edinburgh University Press, 1984.
Danon, Samuel, and Samuel N. Rosenberg, trans. *Ami and Amile.* York, SC: French Literature Publications Company, 1981.
De la Grange, Adélaide Edouard, ed. *Hugues Capet, chanson de geste.* Paris: A. Franck, 1864.
Delbouille, Maurice. "Problèmes d'attribution et de composition II: La Chanson d'*Elie* et la geste de Saint-Gilles." *Revue belge de philologie et d'histoire* 11 (1932): 577–97.
———. "A Propos des rimes familières à Chrétien de Troyes et à Gautier d'Arras," In Bianciotto, *Etudes Lecoy,* 55–65.
Deshaisnes, C.C.A. *Documents et extraits divers concernant l'histoire de l'art dans la Flandre, l'Artois, et le Hainaut avant 1500.* Lille: L. Danel, 1886.
De Weever, Jacqueline. *Sheba's Daughters: Whitening and Demonizing the Saracen Woman in Medieval French Epic.* New York: Garland, 1998.
Dijk, Hans van, and Willem Noomen, eds. *Aspects de l'épopée romane: Mentalités, idéologies, intertextualités.* Groningen: E. Forsten, 1995.
Dronke, Peter. *Fabula: Explorations into the Uses of Myth in Medieval Platonism.* Leiden: E.J. Brill, 1974.
———. *A History of Twelfth-Century Philosophy.* Cambridge: Cambridge University Press, 1988.
Dudo of Saint Quentin. *History of the Normans.* Translated by Eric Christiansen. Woodbridge, Suffolk, UK and Rochester, NY: Boydell Press, 1998.

Bibliography

DuMéril, E., ed. *La Mort de Garin le Loherain*. Paris: Franck, 1841.
Duparc-Quioc, S., ed. *La Chanson d'Antioche*. Paris: Geuthner, 1976.
Edwards, Robert R. *Ratio and Invention: A Study of Medieval Lyric and Narrative*. Nashville, TN: Vanderbilt University Press, 1989.
Einhart. *The Life of Charlemagne*. Translated by Sidney Painter. Ann Arbor: University of Michigan Press, 1960; rpt. 1967.
Faral, Edmond. *Les Arts poétiques du XIIe et du XIIIe siècles*. Paris: H. Champion, 1924).
Fawtier, Robert "Thibaut de Champagne et Gace Brûlé." *Romania* 59 (1933): 83–92.
—. "Notes pour le commentaire des vers 1877–1881 et 485–487 de la *chanson de Roland*." In Arnould, *Studies in French Language*, 99–102.
Finoli, A.M. "Le poesie di Guiraudo lo Ros." *Studi Medievali* 15 (1974): 1–57.
Fleischman, Suzanne. "Philology, Linguistics, and the Discourse of the Medieval Text." *Speculum* 65 (1990): 19–37.
Foerster, Wendelin, ed. *Aiol et Mirabel und Elie de Saint Gille*. Heilbronn: Henninger, 1876–82.
Ford, J.D.M. "'To Bite the Dust' and Symbolical Lay Communion." *PMLA* 20 (1905): 197–230.
Frappier, Jean, ed. *Les Chansons de geste du cycle de Guillaume d'Orange*. 2 vols. Paris: Soc. d'Ed. d'Enseignement Supérieur, 1965.
Freedman, Paul. *Images of the Medieval Peasant*. Stanford: Stanford University Press, 1999.
Gaier, Claude. *Armes et combats dans l'univers medieval*. Bruxelles: De Boeck Université, 1995.
Gaimar, Geoffrei. *L'Estoire des Engleis*. Edited by Alexander Bell. Oxford: Basil Blackwell, 1960; New York: Johnson Reprint Corp, 1971.
Gallo, Ernest. *The Poetria Nova and Its Sources in Early Rhetorical Doctrine*. The Hague: Mouton, 1971.
Gautier de Châtillon. *The Alexandreis*. Translated by R. Telfryn Pritchard. Toronto: Pontifical Institute of Mediaeval Studies, 1986.
Geoffrey de Vinsauf. *Poetria Nova*. Translated by M.J. Nims. Toronto: Pontifical Institute of Mediaeval Studies, 1967.
Geoffrey de Villehardouin. *La Conquête de Constantinople*. Edited by Natalis de Wailly. 2 vols. Paris: Firmin Didot, 1882.
Gerritsen, W.P. "Les Relations littéraires entre la France et les Pays-Bas au Moyen Age." In *Actes du septième congrès national de la Société*

Française de Littérature Comparée, Poitiers 17–19 Mai 1965. Paris: Didier, 1967, 28–46.
Godefroy, Frédéric. *Dictionnaire de l'ancien français et de tous ses dialects du IXe au Xve siècles*. 10 vols. Paris: Wieweg et Bouillon, 1881–1902; rpt. New York: Kraus Reprint Corp., 1961.
—. *Lexique de l'ancien français*. Paris: H. Welter, 1901; rpt. Paris: H. Champion, 1994.
Gossen, C.T. *Grammaire de l'ancien Picard*. Paris: Klincksieck, 1970.
Greimas, A.J. *Dictionnaire de l'ancien français jusqu'au milieu du XIVe siècle*. Paris: Larousse, 1968.
Guessard, F., and A. de Montaiglon, eds., *Aliscans*. Paris: A. Franck, 1870.
Haidu, Peter. *The Subject of Violence: The Song of Roland and the Birth of the State*. Bloomington: Indiana University Press, 1993.
Hamilton, George L. "The Sources of Symbolical Lay Communion," *Romanic Review* 4 (1913): 220–40.
Hartman, A. Richard. "Initials and *Laisse* Division in Two Later Epics: *Aiol* and *Parise la Duchesse*," *Olifant* 12 (1987): 5–27.
Heinemann, Edward A. *L'Art métrique de la chanson de geste: Essai sur la musicalité du récit*. Geneva: Droz, 1993.
—. "Patterns of Narrative and Poetic Organisation in the Kernel William Cycle." In Ailes, *Reading*, 249–68.
Heintze, Michael. *König, Held und Sippe: Untersuchungen zur chanson de geste des 13. und 14. Jahrhunderts und ihrer Zyklenbildung*. Heidelberg: C. Winter, 1991.
—. "Les techniques de la formation de cycles dans les chansons de geste." In Besamusca, *Cyclification*, 21–58.
Henry, Patrice, ed. *Les Enfances Guillaume*. Paris: Société des anciens textes français, 1935.
Herlihy, David, ed. *Women, Family, and Society in Medieval Europe: Historical Essays 1971–91*. Providence, RI: Berghahn Books, 1995.
Hill, Rosalind, tr. *Gesta Francorum*. London: T. Nelson, 1962.
Hindman, Sandra. *Sealed in Parchment: Rereadings of Knighthood in the Illuminated Manuscripts of Chrétien de Troyes*. Chicago: University of Chicago Press, 1994.
Holmes, Urban T. Review of Charles H. Livingston's *Skein-Winding Reels: Studies in Word History and Etymology*. *Speculum* 33 (1958): 553–54.
Homer. *Homer's Odyssey, Books XIII-XXIV*. Edited by D.B. Monro. Oxford: Clarendon Press, 1901.

Bibliography

Hughes, M.J. "The Library of Philip the Bold and Marguerite of Flanders, First Valois Duke and Duchess of Burgundy." *Journal of Medieval History* 4 (1978): 145–88.

Huygens, R.B.C., Conradus Hirsaugiensis, and Bernardus. *Accessus ad auctores, Bernard d'Utrecht, Conrad Hirsau: Dialogus super auctores édition critique.* Leiden: E.J. Brill, 1970.

Jaeger, C. Stephen. *The Origins of Courtliness: Civilizing Trends and the Formation of Courtly Ideals, 939–1210.* Philadelphia: University of Pennsylvania Press, 1985.

—. *The Envy of Angels: Cathedral Schools and Social Ideals in Medieval Europe, 950–1200.* Philadelphia: University of Pennsylvania Press, 1994.

James, Sara I. "'Pseudo'-Courtly Elements in a Canonical Epic." In Mullally, *The Court and Cultural Diversity*, 367–74.

Jaufré Rudel. *The Songs of Jaufré Rudel.* Edited by Rupert T. Pickens. Toronto: Pontifical Institute of Mediaeval Studies, 1978.

Jeaneau, Edouard. "Heiric d'Auxerre, disciple de Jean Scot." *Auxerre* (1989): 353–70.

Jenkins, T.A., ed. *La Chanson de Roland.* Boston: D.C. Heath, 1924.

Johnston, Oliver. "The French Condition Contrary to Fact." *Modern Language Notes* 16 (1901): 129–37.

Jonckbloet W.J.A., ed. *Guillaume d'Orange: Chanson de geste des XIe et XIIe siècles.* Vol. 1. *Li Convenaus Vivien.* La Haye: Martin Nyhoff, 1854.

Jonin, Pierre. "La Partie d'Echecs dans l'épopée médiévale." In *Mélanges...Frappier*, 483–97.

—. "Les Galopin épiques." In VIe Congrès international de la Société Rencesvals, *Actes*, 731–45.

Keller, Hans-Erich. "La *Chanson de Roland*: Poème de propagande pour le royaume capétien du milieu du XIIe siècle." *Travaux de linguistique et de literature* 14 (1976): 229–41.

—, ed. *Romance Epic: Essays on a Medieval Literary Genre.* Kalamazoo: Medieval Institute Publications, Western Michigan University, 1987.

Kelly, Douglas. *The Art of Medieval French Romance.* Madison: University of Wisconsin Press, 1992.

Kinoshita, Sharon. "'Pagans Are Wrong and Christians Are Right': Alterity, Gender, and Nation in the *Chanson de Roland*." *Journal of Medieval and Early Modern Studies* 31 (2001): 79-111.

Knudson, Charles A. "Le thème de la princesse sarrasine dans *la Prise d'Orange*." *Romance Philology* 22 (1969): 449–62.

Kratz, Dennis M. *Mocking Epic: Waltharius, Alexandreis, and the Problem of Christian Heroism.* Madrid: J.P. Turanzas, 1980.

Labarge, Margaret Wade. *A Baronial Household of the Thirteenth Century.* New York: Barnes & Noble 1965.

Lachet, Claude. *La 'Prise d'Orange', ou la parodie courtoise d'une épopée.* Paris: H. Champion, 1986.

Langlois, Ernest, ed. *Le Couronnement de Louis: Chanson De Geste.* Paris: Librairie de Firmin Didot, 1888.

——. *Table des noms propres de toute nature compris dans les chansons de geste.* Paris: É. Bouillon, 1904.

Lecoy, Félix, ed. *Le Conte du Graal.* Paris: H. Champion, 1981.

LeGros, H. "De *Vivien* à *Aiol*, ou, d'une sainteté archaïque à la sainteté moderne." In *Actes du IXe Congrès: Essor*, 2: 931–48.

Lejeune, Rita. "L'Ardenne dans la littérature médiévale." *Anciens pays et assemblées d'états* 28 (1963): 44–78.

LeRider, Paule. *Le Chevalier dans Le Conte du Graal de Chrétien de Troyes.* Paris: Société d'édition d'enseignement supérieur, 1978.

——. "Le Rire dans *Aiol*." *Pris-ma: Bulletin de liaison de l'équipe de recherché sur la littérature d'imagination du moyen âge* 12 (1996): 57–71.

LeRoux de Lincy. *Le Livre des proverbs français.* 2 vols. Paris: Paulin, 1842.

Lynch, J.H. *Godparents and Kinship in Early Medieval Europe.* Princeton: Princeton University Press, 1988.

Lyons, Faith. "'Vin herbé' et 'gingembras' dans le roman Breton." In *Mélanges…Frappier*, 2: 689–96.

Macrobius, Ambrosius Theodosius. *The Saturnalia.* Edited by P.V. Davies. New York: Columbia University Press, 1969.

Malicote, Sandra C.O. "Visual and Verbal Allusion: *Disputatio* and the Poetics of *Elie de Saint Gille* and *Aiol.*" *Romania* 124 (2006): 77–111.

——. "'Cil novel jougleor': Parody, Illumination and Genre Renewal in *Aiol.*" *Romania* 120 (2002): 353–405.

Marie de France. *Lais.* Edited by Alfred Ewert. Oxford: Blackwell, 1947; rpt. 1960.

Martin, Jean-Pierre. *Les Motifs dans la chanson de geste: Définition et utilisation.* Lille: Centre d'études médiévales et dialectales, Université de Lille III, 1992.

Mela, Charles. "'Poetria Nova' et 'Homo novus'." *Littérature* 74 (1989): 4–26.

Mélanges de langue et de littérature du Moyen Age et de la Renaissance offerts à Jean Frappier, professeur à la Sorbonne. Publications romanes et françaises 112. Geneva: Droz, 1970.

Bibliography

Melli, Elio. "Nouvelles recherches sur la composition et la rédaction d'*Aiol* et d'*Elie de Saint Gille*." In *Actes du IXe Congrès: Essor*, 1: 131–49.

Ménard, Philippe. "Le Thème comique du 'nice' dans la chanson de geste et le roman arthurien." *Boletín de la Real Academia de buenas Letras de Barcelona* 21 (1965–66): 177–93.

—. *Le Rire et le sourire dans le roman courtois*. Genève: Droz, 1969.

Meyer, Paul, and A. Longnon, eds. *Raoul de Cambrai: Chanson de Geste*. Paris: Firmin Didot, 1864.

Minnis, A. J. and A.B. Scott, eds. *Medieval Literary Theory and Criticism c.1100–1375: The Commentary Tradition*. Oxford: Clarendon Press; New York: Oxford University Press, 1988.

Morawski, Jozef. *Proverbes français antérieurs au XVe siècle*. Paris: Champion, 1925.

Mullally, Evelyn, and John Thompson. *The Court and Cultural Diversity: Selected Papers from the Eight Triennial Congress of the International Courtly Literature Society, The Queen's University of Belfast, 26 July–1 August 1995*. Cambridge: D. S. Brewer, 1997.

Newth, Michael A.H., ed and trans. *Aymeri of Narbonne*. New York: Italica Press, 2005.

—. *Fierabras and Floripas*. New York: Italica Press, 2010.

Norman, Jacques Clary Jean, and Gaston Raynaud, eds. *Aiol: Chanson de geste*. Paris: Firmin Didot, 1877.

Page, Christopher. *The Owl and the Nightingale: Musical Life and Ideas in France, 1100–1300*. Berkeley: University of California Press, 1990.

Paris, Gaston. "Romani, Romania, Lingua Romana, Romancium" *Romania* 1 (1872): 1 ff.

—. "Note sur La Femme de Salomon." *Romania* 9 (1880): 436–38.

—. Review of Publications de la Société des Anciens Textes Français (1872–86). "Deuxième Article." *Le Journal des Savants* (août 1886): 469–80.

Paris, Paulin. *Histoire Littéraire de la France*. 22 vols. Paris: V. Palmé, 1842–52), 22: 416–25.

Parkes, M.B. *Pause and Effect: An Introduction to the History of Punctuation in the West*. Aldershot: Scolar, 1992.

Pastoureau, Michel. *La Vie quotidienne en France et en Angleterre au temps des chevaliers de la Table Ronde: XIIe-XIIIe siècles*. Paris: Hachette, 1976.

Perrier, J.L., ed. *Le charroi de Nîmes: Chanson de geste du XIIe siècle*. París: Librairie Honoré Champion, 1972.

—, ed. *Le siège de Barbastre: Chanson de geste du XIIe siècle.* Les Classiques français du Moyen Age 54. Paris: H. Champion, 1926.

Petit-Dutaillis, Charles. *Etude sur la vie et le règne de Louis VIII (1187–1226).* Paris: É. Bouillon, 1894.

Picherit, Jean-Louis G. *The Journey of Charlemagne.* Birmingham, AL: Summa Publications, 1984.

Prévité-Orton, C.W. *The Shorter Cambridge Medieval History.* 2 vols. Cambridge: Cambridge University Press, 1971.

Prou, Maurice. *Manuel de Paléographie latine et française.* Paris: Picard, 1924.

Raimbert de Paris. *La Chevalerie Ogier de Danemarche.* Edited by Joseph Barrois. Paris: Techener, 1842.

Raynaud, Gaston, ed. *Elie de Saint Gille.* Paris: Didot, 1879.

Raynaud de Lage, Guy. *Introduction à l'ancien français.* Paris: Société d'édition d'enseignement supérieur, 1970.

Régnier, Claude, ed. *La prise d'Orange: Chanson de geste de la fin du XIIe siècle.* Paris: C. Klincksieck, 1967.

Renart, Jean. *Le Roman de la Rose ou de Guillaume de Dole.* Edited by Félix Lecoy. París: Librairie Honoré Champion, 1969.

Ribard, Jacques. "'Chausée' et 'chemin ferré'." *Romania* 92 (1971): 262–66.

Rigord. *Oeuvres de Rigord et de Guillaume le Breton.* Edited by Henri-François Delaborde. Paris: Renouard, 1882.

Roach, William, ed. *The Continuations of the Old French Perceval of Chrétien de Troyes: The Third Continuation by Manessier.* Philadelphia: American Philosophical Society, 1983.

Rockwell, Paul Vincent. *Rewriting Resemblance in Medieval French Romance: Ceci n'est pas un graal.* New York: Garland, 1995.

Roussel, Henri. "'L'os de la golé': Réflexions sur le coup de poing meurtrier de Guillaume (*Couronnement de Louis*, vers 129–138)." In Baumgartner, *Mélanges René Louis,* 2: 591–606.

Russo, Joseph, Manual Fernández-Galiano and Alfred Heubeck. *A Commentary on Homer's Odyssey.* Oxford: Clarendon Press, 1992.

Rutebeuf. *Le Miracle de Théophile.* Edited by Grace Frank. Paris: H. Champion, 1967.

Schultze-Busacher, Elizabeth. "Les 'Proverbes au vilain'." *Proverbium* 6 (1989): 113–27.

Serres, Michel, *Genèse.* Paris: B. Grasset, 1982.

Bibliography

Simpson, James. *Sciences and the Self in Medieval Poetry: Alan of Lille's Anticlaudianus and John Gower's Confessio Amantis*. Cambridge: Cambridge University Press, 1995.

Smeets, J. R. "'*La Force paist le pré*': Un vieux problème—une nouvelle solution?" *Rapports: Het Franse Boek* 39 (1969): 53–56.

—. "Les Cornes de Moïse." *Romania* 114 (1996): 235–46.

Stone, Louise W. "Un proverbe du Moyen âge: *Force paist le pré.*" *Zeitschrift für romanische philologie* 73 (1957): 145–59.

Stowell, William A. *Old French Titles of Respect in Direct Address*. Baltimore: J. E. Furst Co., 1908.

—. "Personal Relationships in Medieval France." *PMLA* 28 (1913): 388–416.

Stranges, John. "The Significance of Bramimonde's Conversion in 'The Song of Roland'." *Romance Notes* 16 (1974): 190–96.

Strickland, M. *War and Chivalry: The Conduct and Perception of War in England and Normandy, 1066–1217*. Cambridge: Cambridge University Press, 1996.

Suard, François. "Les Héros Chrétiens face au monde Sarrasin." In Van Dijk, *Aspects*, 187–208.

Suchier, Hermann, ed. *Les Narbonnais: Chanson de geste*. 2 vols. Paris: Firmin Didot, 1898.

Switten, Margaret Louise, et al., eds. *The Medieval Lyric*. 2 vols. South Hadley, MA: Mount Holyoke College, 1988.

Terracher, Louis Adolphe, ed. *La Chevalerie Vivien: Chanson de geste*. Paris: H. Champion, 1909.

Tobler, Adolf, ed. *Li Proverbe au villain*. Leipzig: S. Hirzel, 1895.

Walter of Chatillon. *The "Alexandreis" of: Walter of Chatillon: A Twelfth-Century Epic*. Translated by David Townsend. Philadelphia: University of Pennsylvania Press, 1991.

Triaud, Annie. "A Propos du Boniment du Jongleur en tête du ms d'Oxford de *Girart De Roussillon*." In Baumgartner, *La Chanson de geste*, 737–66.

Vance, Eugene. *From Topic to Tale: Logic and Narrativity in the Middle Ages*. Minneapolis: University of Minnesota Press, 1987.

Vauthier, Michèle. "Le lit de la merveille dans *le conte du Graal* de Chrétien de Troyes: Le jeu des images." In Buschinger, *L'Image*, 303–27.

Viollet-le-Duc, Eugène. *Encyclopédie médiévale*. 2 vols. Tours: Inter-Livres, 1996.

Walpole, Ronald N., ed. *Le Turpin français, dit le Turpin I*. Toronto: University of Toronto Press, 1985.
Walters, Lori, "Jeanne and Marguerite de Flandre as Female Patrons." *Dalhousie French Studies* 28 (1994): 15–27.
Warlop, E. *The Flemish Nobility before 1300*. 2 vols. Kortrijk: G. Desmet-Huysman, 1975.
Warren, F.M. "The Enamoured Saracen Princess in Orderic Vitalis and the French Epics." *Publications of the Modern Language Association* 29 (1914): 341–58.
Wartburg, W.V. *Französisches etymologisches Wörterbuch*. Basel: R.G. Zbinden, 1922–.
Weitzmann, Kurt. *Greek Mythology in Byzantine Art*. Princeton: Princeton University Press, 1984.
Wetherbee, Winthrop. *Platonism and Poetry in the Twelfth Century: The Literary Influence of the School of Chartres*. Princeton: Princeton University Press, 1972.
—. "Philosophy, Cosmology, and the Twelfth-Century Renaissance." In Dronke, *History*, 21–53.
Wienbeck, Erich, Wilhelm Hartnacke, and Paul Rasch, eds. *Aliscans*. Hall: Niemeyer, 1903.
Wolff, Robert Lee. "Romania: The Latin Empire of Constantinople." *Speculum* 23 (1948), 1–34.
—. "Baldwin of Flanders and Hainaut, First Latin Emperor of Constantinople." *Speculum* 27 (1952): 281–322.
Wolfram of Eschenbach. *The Middle High German Poem of Willehalm*. Translated by Charles E. Passage. New York: F. Ungar Pub. Co, 1977.
Wood, Casey Albert, and F. Marjorie Fyfe. *The Art of Falconry: Being the De Arte Venandi Cum Avibus of Frederick II*. Stanford: Stanford University Press, 1943.
Zaddy, Z.P. "Chrétien de Troyes and the Epic Tradition." *Cultura Neolatina* 21 (1961): 71–82.

INDEX OF PROPER NAMES

Reference is made to the first line in which the name appears in the Old Franch; variants are given.

A

Abilande (Miron d') 1489; Abilant (Clamador d') 1488
Aïmers 66, (li caitis) 2532; Aimer 2496; Aymer 167; Aimart (assonance; le conte) 1476
Aitropé (roi de Barbastre) 255
Alixandre 1295 (see Jossé d')
Amauri (le conte) 197
Angers 229
Anseïs de Cartage 67
Anseunne (see Garin d')
Apolin 441
Arabi 195; Arabe (destrier d') 276; Arabe (or d') 1668; l'Arrabi 2346
Aragon 1826
Ardane 1181, Ardenois 2551
Arle 2205
Artus (de Bretaigne) 654
Ataignant 688; (de Sorbrie) 1300; (d'Oliferne) 1427
Aumarie 923
Auvergne 210
Avisse 2703; Avise 2748
Aymeri de Nerbone 848
Ayoul 2760; Ayous 2757

B

Baligant 1007
Barbastre 255
Basin 1980
Baudas (Trüant de) 667; (Lubïens de) 1490 (Luchibus de la Roche Baudas) 2309
Begibus 2357
Behorges 2705
Beraut de Valodru 2075
Bernart de Brubant 224; Bernars 702
Berrars (Galopin's brother) 1182
Berri 210
Bertran (nephew of William of Orange) 223; Bertram 318

Beruier 2623
Bevon de Conmarchis 2497; Beves de Conmarchis 2514; Beuves de Conmarchis 2531
Biaulande 18
Biterne 1402
Blaives (le chité de) 424
Borgengon 2622
Brandis (Brindisi) 2487
Brandone 562
Brehaigne (.i. rois de) 1489
Bretaigne 211
Brubant (see Bernart de)

C

Caïfas (le proisiet) 1512
Calabre (see Rodoan)
Cartage (Anseïs de) 67
Castele (fer de) 2103
Charle 50 (see Karles)
Chartes 48; Chartres 61
Clamador d'Abilant 1488
Codroés (le rois) 1026
Conmarchis (see Bevon)
Constantin Macars 2311
Corsus de Tabarie 330; Corsaut de Tabarie 343; Corsaut (rois de Tabarie 2428)

D

Dameldé 39; Dameldex 577; Dameldieu 174
Dé 90
Dieus 1; (li cors) 439; (de Paradis) 216

E

Ector 1206; Hector 1211
Elye 22
Engleterre 1428
Esclabonie (Lubïen's daughter) 2200
Escler 1040
Espaigne 49; (li vaires d') 1622

243

F

Femenie 887
Feraon 2310
Flamenc 2623
Franche 490; (la flor de la) 640; (douche) 1084
Franc 669
François 261
Frans (la terre des) 521

G

Galopin 1162
Ganbons 256
Garin 1980; Garin d'Anseune 2496; Garin de Piereplate 41
Garlans 2237
Garnimas (les puis de) 1979
Gautier 1207 (see Gontier); Gautier (Christian knight of Julien) 1475
Gavain (nephew of King Arthur) 654
Gaydonet 350
Gerardot le rous 168
Gerart 763; Gerart (Christian knight) 1475
Glorïeus del ciel 1146
Godefroi 2452
Gontable d'Orlie 2237
Gontier 1007 (see Gautier)
Gosses d'Alexandre (=Josse) 1207; see Jossés
Guichart (companion to Hugon de Paris) 1477
Guillaume d'Orenge 222; Guillaume 577; Guillame 586
Guimer (l'amoreus) (Christian knight) 1476

H

Hector (see Ector)
Hernaus 624; Hernaut (li floris) 224; (à la barbe) 265; (li menbrés) 319; (l'aïrous) 647; (li kenu) 737; (le chenus) 785
Hugon de Paris (Christian knight) 1477

I

Irlande 894

J

Jhesu 441
Jonacles 2306
Josïas (king of Ireland) 894
Jossés 253, (d'Alexandre) 371; Josüé 1248
Jossïens (uncle of King Salatré) 448
Josué (li viex) 257
Judas 2310
Juliens 10; Julien 431

K

Karles 1982 (see Charles)
Karles Marteus (Charles Martel) 2383

L

Leün 798
Loëys (King of France) 50
Loire 220
Lubïens (de Baudas) 1490
Luchibus (de la Roche Baudas) 2309
Luiserne 1868

M

Macabrés 253; Macabré 891
Macars (Constantin) 2311
Mahomet 260; Mahom 441; Mahon 748
Maine 210
Malpriant 258; Malpris 2151; (See Priant)
Malvergiés (li rois) 2307
Marchegai (2566) (See Prinsaut)
Menalis 667
Monmartre 202
Mordrant (l'airous) 655
Morin d'Abilande (Saracen knight) 1489
Murgale de Turnie 1056; Murgale de Sor 2074

N

Navaire (roi de) 49; (escus de) 71
Noë (l'arce de) 1644
Noel 47
Noiron pré 84; Norron pré 1098

Index of Proper Names

O
Oliferne (See Ataignant d')
Olive (Elye's sister) 30
Ongrie 886
Orables (knight) 256
Orcanie (destrier d') 1313
Orenge, Orange (see Guillaume d')
Oriande 1826
Orlie (Gontable d') 2237
Orliens 2705

P
Palerne (l'or de)1871
Paris 59
Pasques 47; Paske 1723
Pavie 915
Peitiers 198
Pentecouste 1803
Pere de gloire 2048
Perse (admirals de) 2280
Piereplate (see Garin de)
Pilate (d'enfer) 655
Priant (li rois) 469 (See Malpriant)
Prinsaus (l'Aragon) 1826
Provenche 287; Provence 387

R
Rainewart 2519, (au tinel) 2535
Reims 865; (Rains, l'archevesque de) 2498
Roche de Clin 220
Rodoan de Calabre 342; Rodoé de Calabre 254; Rodoant 290; Rodoan 316
Romaigne 886
Rome (Saint Piere de) 97
Rosamonde 690
Rousie 888

S
Saint Denis de Franche 1356; Saint Denise de Franche 264
Saint Gille 4; (de Provence) 387; (el mostier) 932
Saint Jonas 1962
Saint Piere de Rome 97
Sainte Marie 2; (le fiex) 534; Dame 959
Sainte Viergene 1374
Salatré (Julien's man) 100; Salatrés (li rois) 405; (li viel) 2311
Salatrin 666
Salemon 1793
Sanghin 168
Sarrasine gent 7; Sarrasin 211; Sarrasins 249
Satenas 2308
Signor (biaus) Lord God 1076
Sobrie 1020; Sorbrie 1247; Sor 2074
Surie 908

T
Tabarie (see Corsaut de)
Tervagant 1261
Thieri (Christian knight) 166
Tibaut 168
Tieri (comte d'Ardane; Galopin's father) 1181
Tornebrans 2236
Trapes 65
Triacre 257; Triacles (li rois) 364; Triacle 394
Trüant de Baudas 667
Turc 1578; Turs (les) 2320
Turfier (Saracen knight) 1489
Turnie (see Murgale de)

U–Z
Valence 2464
Valodru (see Beraut de)
Vierge puchele 1457

*This Work Was Completed on December 1, 2010
at Italica Press, New York, New York.
It Was Set in Charlemagne and
Garamond and Printed on
55-lb. Natural Paper
in the U. S. A.
and E. U.*
❀

www.ingramcontent.com/pod-product-compliance
Lightning Source LLC
Chambersburg PA
CBHW022054160426
43198CB00008B/234